Utopian Imaginings

SUNY series, Humanities to the Rescue

David R. Castillo, editor

Utopian Imaginings

Saving the Future in the Present

Edited by

VICTORIA W. WOLCOTT

Cover design by Julian Montague

Published by State University of New York Press, Albany

© 2024 State University of New York

All rights reserved

Printed in the United States of America

No part of this book may be used or reproduced in any manner whatsoever without written permission. No part of this book may be stored in a retrieval system or transmitted in any form or by any means including electronic, electrostatic, magnetic tape, mechanical, photocopying, recording, or otherwise without the prior permission in writing of the publisher.

For information, contact State University of New York Press, Albany, NY
www.sunypress.edu

Library of Congress Cataloging-in-Publication Data

Name: Wolcott, Victoria W., author.
Title: Utopian imaginings : saving the future in the present / edited by Victoria W. Wolcott.
Description: Albany : State University of New York Press, [2024] | Series: SUNY series, humanities to the rescue | Includes bibliographical references and index.
Identifiers: LCCN 2023039270 | ISBN 9781438497518 (hardcover : alk. paper) | ISBN 9781438497495 (pbk. : alk. paper) | ISBN 9781438497501 (ebook)
Subjects: LCSH: Utopias. | Future, The.
Classification: LCC HX806 .U775156 2024 | DDC 321/.07—dc23/eng/20230824
LC record available at https://lccn.loc.gov/2023039270

10 9 8 7 6 5 4 3 2 1

For all the utopian dreamers, past and future

Contents

List of Illustrations   xi

Acknowledgments   xiii

Introduction   1
   Victoria W. Wolcott

Part 1: Toward a Utopian History

Chapter 1
From "Surcharged Sympathy" to a "Cold Current of Neglect": The Rev. Thomas James, Abolitionism, and Black Expectations for a Racial Utopia in Reconstruction America   15
   Francis J. Butler and Jennifer Hull Dorsey

Chapter 2
Black Cooperators: Owenism and Utopia in Black America   37
   Victoria W. Wolcott

Chapter 3
"The Women Activists Found Little Peace at Bucolic School": Utopian Dreams, Radical Feminist Nightmares, and the Pedagogical Potential of Sagaris   67
   Katelyn M. Campbell

Part 2: Toward a Utopian Method

Chapter 4
Utopian Imaginings: Migration as the Pursuit of the Utopian Society 89
 Secil E. Ertorer

Chapter 5
Public Ritual and Utopia: How Torn Space Theater's Creative Placemaking Strategies Activate the Public Realm 99
 Dan Shanahan

Part 3: Toward a Troubled Utopia

Chapter 6
Repossessing Utopia from Below: Black/Feminist/Queer Utopianism in American Political Thought 121
 Alix Olson and Alex Zamalin

Chapter 7
"If you don't love children, you don't understand socialism": The Children of Peoples Temple 143
 Alexandra Leah Prince

Chapter 8
Kabbalah, Sex Magic, and the Trans-Utopia: Powerful Genderings and Sexualities in the *Zohar* and Moshe Cordovero's Writings 175
 Marla Segol

Part 4: Toward a Utopian Pedagogy

Chapter 9
Migrantopias: Teaching the Dystopian/Utopian Narratives of Migration through a Pedagogy of Hope 201
 Richard Reitsma

Chapter 10
The Classroom as a Community of Learning: Confronting Utopia by Teaching Dystopia 215
 Anita C. Butera

Chapter 11
The Impossible Project: A Utopian Pedagogy for a
Dystopian Moment   231
   Dalia Antonia Caraballo Muller

Contributors   251

Index   257

Illustrations

Figure 1.1	The Fifteenth Amendment (1870).	26
Figure 4.1	The Sword of Damocles (1812).	91
Figure 5.1	"They Kill Things," Torn Space Theater, Silo City, 2015.	104
Figure 5.2	"FEAST," Torn Space Theater, Silo City, 2019.	109
Figure 5.3	*FEAST*, Torn Space Theater, Silo City, 2019.	112
Figure 5.4	"The Gathering," Torn Space Theater, Silo City, 2017.	113
Figure 5.5	"Storehouse," Torn Space Theater, Silo City, 2015.	114
Figure 7.1	From *The Indianapolis Recorder*, April 1, 1961.	148
Figure 7.2	From the 1976 Pamphlet "Peoples Temple Christian Church, Jim Jones, Pastor."	150
Figure 7.3	A 1972 photograph of Pastor Jim Jones and children used in promotional material to demonstrate Peoples Temple's commitment to racial diversity.	152
Figure 7.4	Temple member Mark Cordell, age twelve, raises a flag.	153
Figure 7.5	Don Beck (far right) poses with Peoples Temple children in his kindergarten class at Yokayo School in Ukiah, California. Second row: (fourth student) Stephanie Swaney; (last on left) Jimmy Moore. Back row: (eighth student from left): Chris Buckley.	155

xii | Illustrations

Figure 7.6   From a Peoples Temple pamphlet entitled "Peoples Temple Christian Church, Jim Jones, Pastor," published in 1976.   156

Figure 7.7   Temple youth at a demonstration in Fresno, California in 1976 in support of the "Fresno Four," a group of reporters who refused to reveal their sources. Among those pictured are Emmett Griffith, Tommy Beikman, Lew Jones, David Solomon, and Jocelyn Brown.   162

Figure 7.8   A drawing included in a flyer distributed by the Concerned Relatives showing a child in the "Jonestown concentration camp."   165

Figure 7.9   A photograph taken in Jonestown dated 1978 showing Pop Jackson, Lisa Rodriguez, and other children.   168

Figure 9.1   Immigration papers of my great-grandparents.   203

Acknowledgments

It is ironic that a volume about utopia came about during very dark times. In the spring of 2020, I was a faculty fellow at the University at Buffalo's Humanities Institute. At the time I was completing my book manuscript, *Living in the Future: Utopianism and the Long Civil Rights Movement*. I was thrilled to learn that the Institute's theme for their Humanities Festival in Fall 2020 was to be utopia and immediately signed on to help organize the event. I also agreed to edit the third volume in SUNY Press's "Humanities to the Rescue" series, with a focus on utopia. It was a challenge I was happy to take on. Then the world shut down.

In lieu of an in-person festival, the Institute's visionary director, David Castillo, asked me to organize an online event that fall. "Black Utopia in a Post-Pandemic World" was the result. A lively zoom conversation between scholars and artists about Afrofuturism and its meaning included the powerful contributions of Alex Zamalin, whose vital book *Black Utopia: The History of an Idea from Black Nationalism to Afrofuturism*, was published in 2019. I was so pleased that Alex agreed to contribute to the volume with a powerful chapter coauthored with his colleague Alix Olson.

In 2021 David and the Institute's executive director, Christina Milletti, made the decision to organize a scaled-down version of the Humanities Festival with its utopian theme in September. We met at Silo City in the same environs where Daniel Shanahan stages his Torn Space public rituals, which you can read about in this volume. Masked and cautious, many of the contributors in this collection met to talk utopia and hope, while still suffering the impact of the pandemic and reeling from the tumultuous political and social climate. They included Jennifer Dorsey, Anita Butera, Richard D. Reitsma, Secil Ertorer, and Dalia Muller. I am grateful to all of them for being part of this volume. And I am also deeply grateful to the authors I reached out to for contributions following the festival, including Daniel Shanahan, Francis J. Butler, Marla Segol, Alexandra Leah Prince, Alix Olson, and Katelyn M. Campbell.

The contributors also have people and institutions to thank. Alexandra Leah Prince would like to extend their sincere gratitude to Rebecca Moore for her extensive and thoughtful feedback on their chapter. Katelyn Campbell thanks Smith College Special Collections for their support of her research through the Margaret Storrs Grierson Fellowship. Dalia Antonia Caraballo wishes to thank her mother and her mother-in-law and father-in-law, all of whom are educators who have given themselves to the critical work of learning from and with their students for many decades. Dalia says, "They are my enduring inspiration, and they continue to push my thinking." Marla Segol wishes to dedicate her chapter to the memory of Jody Myers, who shaped her thinking on queer and trans theory in the study of Jewish sex magic.

Francis Butler and Jennifer Dorsey want to acknowledge Siena College's Centers for Undergraduate Research and Creative Activity (CURCA) and Academic Community Engagement (ACE). Their scholarly collaboration would not have been possible without the funding and advocacy of faculty-led, community-engaged undergraduate research projects. Francis also thanks the Underground Railroad History Project of the Capital Region, Inc., whose support for research on New York's Black abolitionists contributed to this project. Jennifer thanks Cordell Reaves, coordinator of Community Affairs at NYS Office of Parks Recreation and Historic Preservation, for his friendship and encouragement of her scholarship and teaching. I want to give a personal thank you to my husband, Erik Seeman, who is both a prize-winning historian and supportive partner. And we are all grateful to David Castillo and Christina Milletti, whose leadership at the Humanities Institute made this volume possible.

SUNY Press has been a delight to work with. They've answered all my questions and have been supportive throughout the process. And finally to all the activists, scholars, teachers, and artists engaging in utopian practices and envisioning a different future, this volume is dedicated to you.

Introduction

Victoria W. Wolcott

"Sometimes that's all it takes to save a world, you see. A new vision. A new way of thinking, appearing at just the right time."[1] These words were spoken by a fictional character in N. K. Jemison's 2019 utopian novella *Emergency Skin*. But the idea of saving the world through utopian imaginings has a deep and profound history. At this moment of rupture, with the related crises of the pandemic, racial uprisings, and climate change, utopian thought and practice offer alternative paths to the future. Together the authors in this volume examine lived and imagined utopian communities from an interdisciplinary perspective. These are troubled utopias, not models of perfection, but they offer us insight and perspectives on the possibilities of utopian thinking and practice.

Utopia has never been contained in one discipline. Indeed, as a field, utopian studies is as anarchic and multivalent as utopias themselves. Many of scholars who study utopia are grounded in radical communities rather than elevated in ivory towers. And they draw from a panoply of sources, from science fiction to archives of intentional communities. They live temporally in the potential future as well as the deep past. And because utopia is most often defined as "social dreaming," imagination is at the center of utopian studies.[2] This volume contains contributions from historians, sociologists, and literary scholars, among others. And it ranges from discussions of medieval utopian religious practices to contemporary utopian projects and theories. However, this collection is not exhaustive. The chapters focus on Western concepts of utopia and do not engage with every aspect of utopian studies.

But three major themes tie the chapters together: the idea of utopia as a method, the rejection of blueprint utopias, and the practice of utopia as a collective project.

Deploying the concept of utopia comes with its own dilemmas, inherent in its coining by Sir Thomas Moore in 1516. Moore combined the Greek word for "good place" (eutopia) with the word for "no" (u) to construct "utopia" (no place).[3] Thus, from the term's inception, people considered utopias to be fantastical and out of reach, a world best left to fiction rather than lived reality.[4] But the social imagination necessary to envision utopia can also power dramatic social change. In the eighteenth and nineteenth centuries, for example, both religious and secular utopian communities proliferated in the United States, from cooperative towns founded by British utopianist Robert Owen to millenarian religious groups such as the Shakers. By the early twentieth century, utopian communities ranged from anarchist and single tax enclaves to student cooperatives and Christian socialist communities. And today there has been a resurgence of interest in utopian thought and practice. "Another world is possible," the slogan of the World Social Forum beginning in the early 2000s, is now a global refrain among progressives.

For progressive thinkers, utopianism has long been an arena of generative conflict. For example, debates between scientific and utopian socialism dominated left-wing discourse in the late nineteenth century. Self-described scientific socialists, including Friedrich Engels and Karl Marx, criticized the influential American utopian socialist and writer Edward Bellamy.[5] Utopian socialists such as Bellamy rejected conflict and violence as a path to revolution, embracing instead nonviolent revolution. For this reason, scientific socialists were disdainful of Bellamy, whose novel *Looking Backward* suggested that a peaceful but swift evolution of society would lead to a socialist utopia.[6] Marx decried Bellamy and his followers' lack of class analysis and their claims of universal emancipation, cooperation, and brotherhood. But because Bellamy posited a "velvet revolution," his ideas became popular among pacifists who feared the chaos of class conflict but still desired revolutionary change.[7]

The desire to prevent violence meant that some utopianists had an ambivalent relationship to strikes and other working-class political action. And they openly criticized the sectarian politics of the communist left. Despite that, the modern labor movement was deeply influenced by Bellamy and other utopian socialists' communal and hopeful vision of a utopian future. Many intentional communities actively supported organized labor and created cooperatives to offer an alternative to competitive capitalism.

These movements offered broad and inclusive visions of solidarity that went beyond trade unionism. And the idea of peaceful revolution was central to utopian socialists and radical pacifists well into the twentieth century. In 1940, for example, the famed white pacifist A. J. Muste called for "pacifism as a revolutionary strategy."[8]

Utopian socialists' framework for social change involved giving the ends and means of social struggle the same weight. The white British author Aldous Huxley, highly influential in pacifist and radical circles, was one popularizer of this model. Although best known for his dystopian novel *Brave New World*, Huxley was an active promoter of utopian thought and practice. While living in California during the 1930s, utopian socialists introduced Huxley to Vendanta mysticism, a philosophical branch of Hinduism, and he later wrote a utopian novel, *Island*.[9] His 1937 essay collection, *Ends and Means: An Inquiry Into the Nature of Ideals*, was widely read by political radicals. In this work he promotes nonviolent solutions to revolutionary change. On cooperatives, a key institution for utopian socialists, Huxley writes, "Co-operatives and mixed concerns already exist and work extremely well. To increase their numbers and to extend their scope would not seem a revolutionary act . . . In its effects, however, the act would *be* revolutionary; for it would result in a profound modification of the existing system."[10] Cooperatives provided a revolutionary end through peaceful means, ameliorating the worst excesses of capitalism and promoting egalitarianism.

The relationship between means and ends is also captured in the term "prefigurative," coined by the political scientist, Carl Boggs in 1977. "By 'prefigurative,'" stated Boggs, "I mean the embodiment, within the ongoing political practice of a movement, of those forms of social relations, decision-making, culture, and human experience that are the ultimate goal."[11] Like Huxley, Boggs identified movements where the means and ends converged. And he characterized the New Left of the 1960s and early 1970s as the recipient and popularizer of this tradition. Sociologist Wini Breines, in her 1982 work *The Great Refusal*, expands on the prefigurative nature of New Left politics. This politics encompasses "[t]he effort to build community, to create and prefigure in lived action and behavior the desired society, the emphasis on means and not ends, the spontaneous and utopian experiments that developed in the midst of action while working toward the ultimate goal of a free and democratic society . . ."[12] By balancing means and ends, linear time collapses as utopianists live society's future in the present.

Historians have largely overlooked the legacy of utopian socialism as the New Left's prefigurative politics emerged from what appeared to be a relatively conformist and contained post–World War II political world that rejected utopianism. In the late 1940s the twin horrors of fascism and Stalinism suggested to many liberals that utopian thinking was dangerous. Works such as Arthur Schlesinger Jr.'s *The Vital Center*, Daniel Bell's *The End of Ideology*, and Judith N. Shklar's *After Utopia* as well as political philosophers Hannah Arendt and Theodor Adorno argued that utopian thinking had led to totalitarianism.[13] These works emphasized the horrendous costs of "blueprint" utopias that were inflexible and dictatorial.[14] "The urge to construct grand designs for the political future of mankind," noted Shklar in 1957, "is gone. The last vestiges of utopian faith required for such an enterprise have vanished."[15] The anti-utopian thinking of the mid-twentieth century inaccurately tied totalitarian states to utopian communities. Indeed, cooperation, not domination, was a central tenet of communal utopianism. For example, most radical pacifists who lived in utopian communities generally defined themselves as socialists or anarchists, were deeply critical of the Soviet Union, and were among the first to speak out about the dangers of fascism.[16] The anti-utopianism in the post–World War II era has largely faded. But the concept of what a utopian vision in the West should look like has also gone through revision and transformation.

That transformation has led to even greater emphasis on means. Utopia has become less about achieving a goal and more about the process of getting to that goal, what Ruth Levitas calls a "method," the first theme in this volume.[17] We see this in utopian pedagogies that push students to imagine a different future or in a theatrical space where audience and players unite in utopian practice. Indeed, this book is part of a larger project in utopian studies of destabilizing, or troubling, ideas of modernity and progress. Because the idea of progress is central in Western thought, it can have a totalizing role in utopian practice with every experiment designed to achieve a final goal. In contrast, utopia in these chapters is always becoming, always in process. Troubled utopias question more simiplistic ideas of modernity and progress, and they bring to light problematic aspects of utopian experimentation. Settler utopianism, for example, in North America led to the displacement of Indigenous people as idealistic white reformers created intentional communities in spaces they perceived as untouched.[18] Even more troubling are utopianists who created experiments within the institution of slavery, as did Fanny Wright and Joseph Davis in the United States. History and literary imaginings, in this volume, are not simply a way station to an ever more perfect future. They are modes of thinking and doing that challenge Western notions of perfection.

The best example of modernity in Western utopias is the notion of a "blueprint" utopia, which provides fixed and rigid future plans. These chapters, in contrast, describe utopias in flux, always reimagined and rebirthed, the collection's second theme. Blueprint utopias are also static, lacking the flexibility and improvisation needed for change. But change is central to utopian methodology. As Octavia Butler memorably wrote in her 1993 utopian novel *Parable of the Sower*, "All that you touch you change. All that you change changes you. The only lasting truth is change."[19] Blueprints are immutable, but for Butler utopia *was* change.

This collection also reflects an engagement with what Laurence Davis defines as "grounded utopia" as a way to escape the trap of modernity. Davis asks, "can we imagine a form of radically refigured, 'down-to-earth' utopianism capable of staying with our contemporary troubles and contributing to transformative processes within them?"[20] He suggests that such an approach will release "greater imaginative awareness of neglected or suppressed possibilities for qualitatively better forms of living latent in the present," rather than a "transcendent utopia" that quests for absolute perfection.[21] To avoid a blueprint utopia imposed from the top, utopian methods must be practiced in interaction with others, in classrooms, on stages, on pages, and in the streets. Grounded utopia also centers the cooperative, as an economic organization and philosophy that offers alternatives to both competitive capitalism and individualism. Historical work that elevates the lives of working people engaged in such social imaginary methods offer a perspective on grounded utopias. Radical pedagogy and examination of contemporary movements, such as queer utopias, also drive this practice.

The final theme linking the chapters is the importance of the collective, rather than the individual. Classrooms, churches, and intentional communities all offer spaces that help us rethink the possible. Utopian experimentation challenges our understanding of how to raise children, what a family looks like, or how to sustain a local economy. As Tom Moylan suggests in his work *Becoming Utopian*, "Working collectively in comradely solidarity, those who consciously desire that better world have to find ways to tease out the tendencies and latencies that will enable all of humanity to build it, here and now, in the shell of the old."[22] Such a project requires flexibility and improvisation, again negating the rigidity of blueprint utopias. Utopia is about the journey rather than the destination.

The first section of the volume, "Toward a Utopian History," uses a historical lens to examine troubled utopias. Francis J. Butler and Jennifer Hull Dorsey explore the interracial utopia envisioned by the Reverend Thomas

James, a Black abolitionist whose vision for racial integration and equality failed in the aftermath of Reconstruction. During the antebellum period, James worked with white abolitionists who fully embraced the humanity and aspirations of African Americans. Born enslaved, James found the religious and political atmosphere of antebellum Western New York conducive to utopian thought and practice. These activists called not only for an end of slavery, but also for Black enfranchisement and desegregation.

Similarly, my chapter on Black cooperators examines the influence of Robert Owen on multiple generations of African Americans and white reformers, often with problematic outcomes. Fanny Wright and Joseph Davis attempted to create cooperative utopian plantations with enslaved labor. After emancipation, freedpeople on Davis's plantation used Owenite ideas to overcome economic deprivation and white racial violence. The legacy of Owenite cooperatives carried into the twentieth century when African American cooperatives thrived in the mid-twentieth century, most notably in the Father Divine movement. And they have found new life in cities such as Buffalo, New York, in the twenty-first century.

Katelyn M. Campbell takes us to the 1970s, arguably the height of prefigurative politics in utopian history. She traces the emergence of a feminist utopia at Sagaris, a radical feminist school that failed among conflict and controversy. Founded in 1975, Sagaris sought to create a physical and intellectual space for feminist theorizing. Campbell tells the story of their unrealized utopian dreams. By foregrounding the process of creating utopia, rather than judging its product, she gives us a window into radical feminist struggles with perfection. These "sites of failure" provide opportunities to evaluate radical feminist social dreaming and reclaim the discarded fragments of those dreams. But Sagaris had a lasting legacy in radical feminist circles as participants went on to form new communities and collectives.

The next section, "Toward a Utopian Method," brings together contemporary examinations of collective struggles that create utopian spaces. Secil E. Ertorer envisions the promise of utopia for migrants, an understudied area in utopian studies. Through her work in social research, she contrasts the seeking of utopia with the dystopia many migrants find upon arrival. Ertorer also explores her own role as a researcher in dialogue with refugees, who have conflicting emotions and narration regarding their experiences. From Syrian refugees in Turkey to Karens in urban Canada, utopia proved fleeting and unattainable.

Daniel Shanahan, the artistic director of Buffalo's Torn Space theater, offers another way to trouble utopia through public ritual. In the performance space, Shanahan seeks to create community and build trust. Following Foucault, Shanahan views these spaces as heterotopia, othered spaces where the "real" can be experienced and grappled with. Torn Space creates this heterotopia through public ritual that brings together performers, often with no formal training, and spectators who become participants in the ritual. Shanahan uses Creative Placemaking to displace the audience as passive observers and transform them into participants. I know from personal experience attending and participating in these public rituals that Silo City, the industrial site in which they exist, is transformed into a kind of sacred space. The ephemeral nature of the experience and the constructed site, which is dismantled, add to this feeling. Shanahan's utopia is not one of perfection, but rather a heterotopia where change happens in real time.

The third section of the volume, "Toward a Troubled Utopia," explores the ways that utopias can be both troubling and make trouble in our society. Alex Zamalin and Alix Olson provide a rich overview of Black/Feminist/Queer utopianism in political and literary thought. They give us an outline to envision how utopia can be liberated "from some of its most reactionary proclivities." By troubling utopia, displacing it from the heteronormative, masculine European tradition and centering Black, queer, and feminist thinkers, the authors liberate utopia for use in contemporary political thought and practice. Black intellectuals, such as Martin Delany, George Schuyler, Octavia Butler, W. E. B. DuBois, N. K. Jemisin, and Richard Wright, avoid the moral absoluteness of European modern utopian planning and reject a teleological movement toward perfection by creating a more disjointed temporality. For Octavia Butler and N. K. Jemisin, for example, utopia is found not in an imagined future, but in the struggles of the present. Feminist scholars also trouble utopia, putting the concept in motion as struggle rather than a mechanistic goal. They mapped out a world outside patriarchy with collective care and continual grassroots struggle. Finally, the chapter concludes with a discussion of queer and trans utopian struggle, which also disrupts the teleological temporality of classical utopian thought. Examining queer theorists such as Jose Munoz and Lauren Berlant, who challenge the assimilationist politics of mainstream LGBTQ struggles, constructs a queer utopia that places desire at the center. Together these scholars demonstrate that utopia is a resource for the dispossessed.

Alexandra Leah Prince explores possibly the most notorious intentional community in American history, Jim Jones's Peoples Temple, an interracial utopian religious movement that ended in wholesale massacre in 1978. But they refocus our lens from culpable adults to the role of children in cooperative and collective sites created by the community. Prince traces how Jones's creation of an interracial family reflected the broader communal vision of the Peoples Temple. And as the community grew children and their welfare were highly visible and active parts of the movement. Concern for children also framed the horrific end of the movement in Jonestown, Guyana.

Marla Segol also explores a religious utopia, but one embodied in ritual. Segol takes us back in time to examine how Kabbalistic sex magic rituals sought to restore the connection between human and divine. Regendering this process created what she terms a trans theology, and thus also a trans utopia. Segol's remarkable analysis of ancient texts centers sexuality and queer utopian ideas. She understands trans not as moving from one gender category to another, but rather as a process of movement without a focus on destination. The messianic utopian vision of a religious community required a series of rituals and practices in the kabbalistic tradition based on sex magic. These rituals epitomize the concept of utopia as method. Segol's analysis of the deep past resonates powerfully with more contemporary conversations about a queer and troubled utopia.

We end the volume with the theory that most effectively disseminates utopian thought and practice, "Toward a Utopian Pedagogy." In an act of utopian instruction, Richard Reitsma and his students explore the space between utopian dreams of migrants and the reality of their experiences. His pedagogy privileges the agency of students and the migrants they study to construct their own narratives. Reitsma interrogates the myths of utopia that are largely performative to uncover real utopian strivings. Reitsma calls this a "pedagogy of love" that reflects his deep engagement with utopian pedagogical experimentations across Latin America, but particularly in Cuba, through the practice of *concientización*. Similarly, Anita C. Butera's pedagogy questions the United States' image of utopia through the lens of immigration. Transforming the classroom into a "community of learning," Butera troubles utopia by teaching dystopia. Within her classroom, hierarchies are overturned to create a collective that explores the myths of a unified American identity, primarily through the personal stories of professors and students.

The volume culminates with Dalia Antonia Caraballo Muller's inspired pedagogical Impossible Project. Muller draws on numerous thinkers, including Paulo Freire and bell hooks, to make a call for immediate practice, rather than social dreaming of a distant future. Muller criticizes the neoliberal university for stifling such a project and creates collective spaces within the university that challenges its teachings. The Impossible Project also deploys Afrofuturist ideas of alternative outlooks to push students into acting collectively to move toward a more just future. Muller brings these ideas into the classroom by employing a critical pedagogy that centers hope. Thus, her Impossible Project is a praxis rather than a lesson plan.

This volume is based on a premise of hope. If not utopia, then what? Given the state of our world, from mass incarceration to the climate crisis, the question should be what will happen if we do not engage in utopian pedagogy and practice. We may, in that case, end up in Moore's "no place," or no place that we and other living creatures can easily live in. The collective, communal, and cooperative utopian practices reflected in this collection offer hope, but also a series of pathways. Through ritual, on stage, or in sex magic, through pedagogy and through intentional living, utopians stubbornly challenge the established conditions of the present to create an alternative future. Collectively they use the tools of the past to build our future, with focused intention on the process rather than the product.

Notes

1. N. K. Jemison, *Emergency Skin* (Seattle: Amazon Original Stories, 2019), 25.

2. The political scientist Lyman Tower Sargent defines utopianism as a form of "social dreaming" that "allows communities to envision a radically different society than the one in which the dreamers live." Lyman Tower Sargent, "The Three Faces of Utopianism Revisited," *Utopian Studies* 5, no. 1 (1994): 3.

3. Lyman Tower Sargent, *Utopianism: A Very Short Introduction* (New York: Oxford University Press, 2010), 2. Western concepts of utopia predated Moore, dating back to at least Plato's *Republic*. There are also powerful non-Western traditions of utopia. Overviews of utopian studies include Barbara Goodwin and Keith Taylor, *The Politics of Utopia: A Study of Theory and Practice* (New York: St. Martin's Press, 1982); Howard P. Segal, *Utopias: A Brief History from Ancient Writings to Virtual Communities* (London: John Wiley & Sons, 2012); Russell Jacoby, *Picture Imperfect: Utopian Thought for an Anti-Utopian Age* (New York: Columbia University Press, 2005); Ruth Levitas, *The Concept of Utopia* (London: Philip Allan, 1990); Ruth Levitas, *Utopia as Method: The Imaginary Reconstitution of Society* (New York: Palgrave, 2013); Vandana Singh, *Utopias of the Third Kind* (London: PM Press, 2022); Timothy Miller, *The Quest for Utopia in Twentieth-Century America* (Syracuse: Syracuse University Press, 1998); Tom Moylan, *Becoming Utopian: The Culture and Politics of Radical Transformation* (London: Bloomsbury, 2020).

4. As a result, some proponents of utopian thought and practice have preferred the term "eutopia." In his 1922 work *The Story of Utopias*, for example, the urbanist Lewis Mumford wrote about possible eutopias, planned communities

like the garden cities of England and later America (Lewis Mumford, *The Story of Utopias* (Gloucester, MA: Peter Smith, 1959, 1922). On Mumford's use of "eutopia," see Donald L. Miller, *Lewis Mumford: A Life* (New York: Weidenfeld & Nicolson, 1989), 167; Robert Wojtowicz, *Lewis Mumford and American Modernism: Eutopian Theories for Architecture and Urban Planning* (New York: Cambridge University Press, 1996), 35–40; and Casey Nelson Blake, *Beloved Community: The Cultural Criticism of Randolph Bourne, Van Wyck Brooks, Waldo Frank, & Lewis Mumford* (Chapel Hill: University of North Carolina Press, 1990), 207–11.

5. Friedrich Engels, *Socialism: Utopian and Scientific* (London: Swan Sonnenschein & Co., 1892). For a discussion of the relationship between scientific and utopian socialist, see Levitas, *The Concept of Utopia*, 41–67; and Goodwin and Taylor, *The Politics of Utopia*, 72–77, 163–68. Marx and Engels were primarily reacting to the popular mid-nineteenth century Owenite and Fourier movements.

6. Csaba Toth, "Resisting Bellamy: How Kautsky and Bebel Read *Looking Backward*," *Utopian Studies* 23, no. 1 (2012): 57–78. Toth argues, "The immediatism of this American utopia flagrantly violated the stagist view of history" (63).

7. Marc Stears, *Demanding Democracy: American Radicals in Search of a New Politics* (Princeton: Princeton University Press, 2010), 13.

8. A. J. Muste, *Non-Violence in an Aggressive World* (New York: Harper & Brothers, 1940), 51.

9. Aldous Huxley, *Island* (New York: Harper & Brothers, 1962). Huxley wrote several books on pacifism, including *An Encyclopedia of Pacifism* (London: Chatto & Windus, 1937). For a discussion of India's influence on Huxley, see Sumita Roy, Annie Pothen, and K. S. Sunita, eds., *Aldous Huxley and Indian Thought* (New Delhi: Sterling Publishers, 2003).

10. Aldous Huxley, *Ends and Means: An Inquiry Into the Nature of Ideals* (1937; repr., New Brunswick, NJ: Transaction Publishers, 2012), 96.

11. Carl Boggs, "Marxism, Prefigurative Communism, and the Problem of Workers' Control," *Radical America* 11 (November 1977): 100.

12. Wini Breines, *The Great Refusal: Community and Organization in the New Left: 1962–1968* (New York: Praeger, 1982), xiv. The historian Sheila Rowbotham uses the term in her 1979 essay "The Women's Movement and Organizing for Socialism," in *Beyond the Fragments: Feminism and the Making of Socialism* (Newcastle, New South Wales: Newcastle Socialist Center, 1979). See also Stears, *Demanding Democracy*, 185; Francesca Polletta, *Freedom Is an Endless Meeting: Democracy in American Social Movements* (Chicago: University of Chicago Press, 2002), 6–8.

13. Arthur M. Schlesinger, Jr., *The Vital Center: The Politics of Freedom* (Boston: Houghton Mifflin, 1949); Daniel Bell, *The End of Ideology: On the Exhaustion of Political Ideas in the Fifties* (The Free Press, 1960), esp. "The Exhaustion of Utopia," 275–409; Judith N. Shklar, *After Utopia: The Decline of Political Faith* (Princeton: Princeton University Press, 1957); Hannah Arendt, *Origins of Totalitarianism* (Cleveland, OH: World Publishing Company, 1958); Karl Popper, *The Origins of*

Totalitarian Democracy (New York: Praeger, 1960); and J. L. Tallmon, *The Origins of Totalitarian Democracy* (New York: Praeger, 1960). In *Picture Imperfect*, historian Russell Jacoby insists that totalitarian regimes should not be considered utopian. "Utopia has lost its ties with alluring visions of harmony and has turned into a threat. Conventional and scholarly wisdom associates utopian ideas with violence and dictatorship" (81). See also Stears, *Demanding Democracy*, 123–30; and Goodwin and Taylor, *The Politics of Utopia*, 18–19. Goodwin and Taylor argue that true utopias should benefit everyone within a society, which excludes totalitarian societies.

14. On "blueprint" utopias, see Jacoby, *Picture Imperfect*, x–xv.

15. Shklar, *After Utopia*, vii.

16. Victoria W. Wolcott, *Living in the Future: Utopianism and the Long Civil Rights Movement* (Chicago: University of Chicago Press, 2022).

17. Ruth Levitas, *Utopia as Method: The Imaginary Reconstruction of Society* (New York: Palgrave, 2013).

18. On settler utopianism, see Karl Hardy, "Unsettling Hope: Contemporary Indigenous Politics, Settler-Colonialism, and Utopianism," *Space of Utopia: An Electronic Journal* 1 (2012): 123–36; Lyman Tower Sargent, "Colonial and Postcolonial Utopias," in *The Cambridge Companion to Utopian Literature*, ed. Gregory Claeys (New York: Cambridge University Press, 2010): 200–22; and Susan Bruce, "Utopian Justifications: More's Utopia, Settler Colonialism, and Contemporary Ecocritical Concerns," *College Literature* (2015): 23–43.

19. Octavia Butler, *Parable of the Sower* (1993).

20. Laurence Davis, "Grounded Utopia" in *Utopian Studies* 32, no. 3 (November 2021): 553.

21. Davis, "Grounded Utopia," 571.

22. Moylan, *Becoming Utopian*, 15.

Part 1

Toward a Utopian History

1

From "Surcharged Sympathy" to a "Cold Current of Neglect"

The Rev. Thomas James, Abolitionism, and Black Expectations for a Racial Utopia in Reconstruction America

Francis J. Butler and Jennifer Hull Dorsey

At the end of his 1886 memoir, the Reverend Thomas James, a Black minister in Rochester, New York, acknowledged the limits of the interracial antislavery activism that had defined his life and ministry. He celebrated that the abolitionist movement had achieved Black emancipation in the 1860s, but also despaired that racial discrimination persisted in the 1880s. He described his white contemporaries in the postwar era as willfully ignoring "the ways 'social prejudices' discriminate against younger African Americans" and "are inclined to leave us to our own resources." It was a depressing reality for James, who had come of age in an "atmosphere" that he described as "surcharged with sympathy for our race." Now, Black Americans were "again as isolated as in the days before the wrongs of our race touched the heart of the American people." James acknowledged that his youthful dreams of integration had become an apparently unattainable objective in the present because of "the cold current of neglect which seems to have chilled against us even the enlightened and religious classes of the communities among which we live, but of which we cannot call ourselves a part."[1]

This atmospheric shift from "surcharged sympathy" to "the cold current of neglect" shapes the structure and content of Thomas James's autobiography, *Life of Rev. Thomas James, by Himself* (1886). His object was not only to document his life, but also to explain how he came to believe that the campaign for Black emancipation would be accompanied by integration and civil rights for Black Americans. The memoir celebrates the interracial antislavery activism of the antebellum era and testifies to white Americans' "active and generous sympathy for the free colored man of the North as well as for his brother in bondage." It identifies and celebrates his white allies in antebellum "Antislavery agitation" with the object of impressing on this audience that he had personally "felt the good effect of that sympathy" in his relationships with white activists.[2] James's memoir can also be read as abolitionist apologetics. It argues that while his expectations of racial integration were unrealized as of 1886, his expectations were nevertheless grounded in real experiences in interracial antislavery activism between 1830 and 1864. As recently as 1870, with the passage of the Fifteenth Amendment, both Black and white abolitionists had good reason to believe that a racial utopia was on the horizon.

This chapter argues that the effect of this racial sympathy on Black abolitionists is evident in Thomas James's memoir. His multiple encounters with white allies with seemingly Black hearts raised his expectations for a racially inclusive postwar America. For James and his Black abolitionist contemporaries, their utopian vision was a United States without slavery and with enfranchisement and integration for all. The chapter analyzes key events in his narrative to explain the development of this utopian thinking and demonstrate that his experiences in interracial activism encouraged him to imagine that a postwar community committed to racial and social equality was within reach. Moreover, it argues that Thomas James's experiences with authentic racial inclusion, working alongside seemingly Black-hearted allies in the Civil War era, gave rise to his expectations for a postwar racial utopia.[3] Historian John Stauffer coined the term Black-hearted men to describe antebellum white allies who had understood "what it was like to be black" and renounced "their belief in skin color as a marker of aptitude and social status."[4] Prominent Black intellectuals and activists, including James McCune Smith and Frederick Douglass, asserted that white Americans had to undergo such a transformation before they could fully abolish slavery and racial discrimination. They also professed to have witnessed such a transformation in key allies including John Brown and Gerrit Smith, two white abolitionists who worked tirelessly in the 1850s for Black social uplift and emancipation.⁵

While James does not use the phrase Black-hearted to describe his white allies, his narrative is replete with examples of men and women who exhibited Black-hearted qualities. While living in New York in the 1830s, James worked alongside the prominent antislavery activists Beriah Green (1795–1874), Alvan Stewart (1790–1849), and William C. Bloss (1795–1863), a man whom Frederick Douglass expressly identified as someone who "cheered on and supported" Black Americans in their "demands for equal rights."⁶ His account of interracial abolition activism in Massachusetts in the 1840s celebrates the Massachusetts Supreme Court Associate Justice Samuel Sumner Wilde for his defense of personal liberty laws. James further identifies Black-hearted women, noting that he proudly "made the acquaintance" of Prudence Crandall, who had championed integrated education for Black women. Most significantly, James's memoir devotes considerable attention to Black-hearted Union officers who oversaw the Kentucky camps for Black refugees where James ministered in the 1860s.⁷ In short, while his expectations of a postwar racial utopia went unrealized, James's life experience offers a window into the development of the utopian thinking widely held by the generation of Black activists and their Black-hearted white allies who had secured abolition, citizenship, and enfranchisement for Black Americans by 1870.

In contrast with other nineteenth-century African American narratives, James's memoir offers an abbreviated account of his life in slavery. He was born a term slave in Montgomery County, New York, in 1804. According to the letter of New York's 1799 Gradual Emancipation Act, James was eligible for manumission in 1832, but his early life experiences were indistinguishable from those of other enslaved people in America. As an eight-year-old, he was effectively orphaned when slaveholder Asa Kimball sold his mother and siblings. James remembered both his mother's resistance and Kimball's determination to sell her when she protested. He dispatched men who bound her "hand and foot" and delivered her to the purchaser. James never saw his mother again. When Kimball unexpectedly died in 1821, seventeen-year-old James was sold at auction. Purchased by a speculator, he was resold within a few months to George Hess, a man James described as uniquely brutal. He remembered that Hess "worked me hard" and "undertook to whip me." Hess also proposed to trade James to a new purchaser "in exchange for a yoke of steers, a colt, and some additional property." The combination of physical violence, forced displacement, and social isolation sparked James's decision to flee to Canada. That same year, he escaped by walking more than 200 miles alongside the route of the Erie Canal—a route subsequently followed by untold numbers of enslaved people seeking freedom. When James reached the village of Lockport, an anonymous Black man showed him the way to the Canadian border.[8]

After three months abroad, James returned to the United States and settled in the vicinity of Rochester, an area undergoing both an economic boom and a historic religious revival. Both phenomena profoundly shaped the trajectory of James's life. Only a decade earlier, Rochester (then Rochesterville) was a new settlement composed of New England immigrants in search of affordable homesteads. The opening of the Erie Canal's eastward route between the Genesee River at Rochester to Albany and Lake Champlain in the 1820s brought a surge of migrants who worked in the emerging shipping and flour-milling industries. Unsurprisingly, James discovered that in such a competitive labor market, white employers were unlikely to interrogate him about his legal status. He readily found employment in the 1820s, built a solid resume of work experience, and established good working relationships with his employers and colleagues. At the same time, Rochester attracted the attention of Christian missionaries representing multiple Protestant denominations. These evangelists, who had followed the original New England migrants into Central and Western New York, aspired to Christianize the frontier. They preached in open fields and makeshift meeting houses. In emotional exhortations, they urged their audiences to confess their sins and seek divine repentance in anticipation of the second coming of Christ (millenarianism). They also preached Christian perfection, a doctrine holding that by the grace of God, Christians can achieve a state of holiness in their lifetime.[9]

Historians have documented that these dual doctrines of millenarianism and Christian perfection had a marked effect on the social and cultural development of Central and Western New York. In time, many of the regions' Christian converts came to the logical conclusion that they should not limit their quest to personal holiness but extend it to society writ large. After all, what value was personal redemption in a society that remained steeped in sin? Their faith inspired them to organize moral purity campaigns and social reform movements to address seemingly intractable social problems. As a consequence, Central and Western New York would give rise to some of the nation's most renowned champions of abolitionism and civil rights in the antebellum era.[10] Other Christians opted to separate themselves altogether from the wickedness of the world, joining together with fellow millenarians in communal settlements where they could enact their utopian visions. The Shaker Villages at Watervliet, New York, and New Lebanon, New York, are among the best known utopian experiments, but antebellum New York was home to several other intentional communities including the Skaneateles Community, the Sodus Bay Phalanx, the Oneida Community, and Modern Times.[11]

Thomas James was both a beneficiary and an agent of this Christian evangelism. As a slave, he had "never been inside of a school or a church, and I knew nothing of letters or religion," but as a free Black man he found both in Rochester in the 1820s. He learned how to read with the help of a "Mr. Freeman, who had opened a Sunday school of his own for colored youths." The white clerks in the warehouse encouraged him in his studies, and he made such strides in his education that he advanced from worker to a supervisor of "the freight business of the warehouse, with full direction over the landing of boats." Regarding his spiritual development, James likely attended revivals led by white Christian missionaries, but it is evident that he also encountered Black evangelists. By 1823, James had become affiliated with a missionary outpost of the AME Zion Church of New York City. He subsequently organized a Sunday school for Black children in Rochester and began holding prayer meetings, presumably for the towns' growing population of Black settlers. In 1829, AME Zion licensed James to preach, and he leveraged his connections with area businessmen to secure a site for a "religious edifice." In May 1833, AME Zion Bishop Christopher Rush ordained James to the priesthood, and it was on that occasion—what James called his "manhood"—that he sealed his new identity with a new name. In 1886, he remembered: "I had been called Tom as a slave and they called me Jim at the warehouse. I put both together when I reached manhood and was ordained as Rev. Thomas James."[12]

James entered ministry at a critical juncture in the development of the abolitionist movement in America. Increasingly in the 1820s and 1830s, white and Black activists were working together to achieve their shared goal of ending slavery. They were also more vocal in their demands for immediate and total abolition.[13] This trend toward radicalism played out in the fall of 1835 when several prominent Christian antislavery dissidents from the American Colonization Society met in Utica to organize a New York branch of the American Anti-Slavery Society. Nearly 500 conventioneers participated, including the Rev. Thomas James. The object of their first meeting was to draft a constitution, elect officers, and adopt resolutions to advance their mission, but a mob forced its way into the hall just as the participants were moving into committee work, forcing the meeting to adjourn for the day. In response, Gerrit Smith urged the conventioneers to reconvene at his estate in Peterboro to complete their businesses.[14]

At the conclusion of their 1835 meeting, the New York State Anti-Slavery Society articulated a threefold mission: to abolish slavery, "to elevate the character and condition of the people of color," and to correct "the prejudice of public opinion" against Black Americans.[15] One year later, the Society went even further by affirming its commitment to work toward the desegregation of public spaces, churches, and transportation networks. Segregation, the resolutions affirmed, "is the very spirit of slavery, is nefarious and wicked, and should be practically reprobated and discountenanced." The Black and white delegates also committed to advocate for Black youth in their pursuit of advanced education and "honorable employments."[16]

In the 1840s, white abolitionists in New York had also joined with Black abolitionists in advocating for Black enfranchisement.[17] This had been a key goal of Black activists since 1821, when the revised New York State Constitution instituted new property requirements for Black voters that effectively disenfranchised them. Through the 1840s and 1850s, Black abolitionists gathered in conventions to develop strategies for reforming the constitution. At the Convention of the Colored Inhabitants of the State of New York in 1840, they expressly attacked the New York State Constitution as "a violation of every principle of justice, anti-republican, and repugnant to the assertion of man's equality upon which our government is founded."[18] The following year, the New York State Convention of Colored Citizens published an address in which they labeled the disenfranchisement of Black men a "blow directly crushing the native energies of him whom it directly affects; the full development of all of whose powers is essential for his healthy existence, whether we regard him in his intellectual, moral, or physical being."[19]

The white abolitionists Thomas James knew in New York State were unequivocal in their demands for abolition, desegregation, and even voting rights. They collaborated with Black activists to add measures to repeal the property requirement in 1846 and again in 1860. These measures failed, but the margin of voters who voted *in support* of repealing the property requirements grew by 8.8 percent. Moreover, in Central and Western New York—where James had first engaged in abolition activism—a majority of the electorate cast ballots *in favor* of Black suffrage, evidence for James and others in his interracial coalition that their efforts were having a practical effect on the New York electorate.[20]

Equally important, many of his white allies advanced these goals of abolition, enfranchisement, and integration through politics. As an example, his trusted partner William C. Bloss was elected to the New York State Assembly in 1844, where he advocated for Black voting rights and the desegregation of public education for three years. He protested segregated seating in the visitors' gallery of the New York State Assembly and refused to worship in churches with segregated seating.[21] Over the next two decades, it was James's Black-hearted allies in Central New York who spearheaded the Liberty Party (1840–48), the National Liberty Party (1852), and the Radical Abolition Party (1855–56). Moreover, it was at a Syracuse-based convention in 1855 that the delegates of the Radical Abolition Party resolved "to remove slavery from the national territories by means of our national power and to remove it from the States also, by means of the same power, whenever the States themselves shall refuse to remove it."[22] In short, the Black-hearted allies the Reverend Thomas James knew in New York State repeatedly affirmed their commitment in words and in action to the utopian goals of abolition, enfranchisement, and integration.

When he moved to Massachusetts in 1838, James found more likeminded allies committed to ending slavery and advancing integration, from whom he would learn the power of protest, civil disobedience, and affirmative law for achieving their shared goals of Black freedom and integration. James's memoir dwells on his involvement in two direct-action campaigns. The first involved a concerted effort among Black and white abolitionists to secure freedom for Lucy Faggin, a Virginia slave brought to New Bedford by slaveholder Henry Ludlam in 1841.[23] James encountered Faggin on a train ride from New York City and struck up a conversation, "as I was in duty bound to do" in his capacity as the newly appointed pastor of the New Bedford AME Zion Church. Learning she would be in New Bedford indefinitely, James "asked her to come to my church." Weeks later, when Faggin still had not attended services, James and his Black congregants went to Ludlam's dwelling "to call on her and learn, if we could, why she did not attend the services." According to James, Ludlam responded: "Lucy is my slave, and slaves don't receive calls." But James refused to let the matter rest. On the advice of unidentified "friends," he appealed to New Bedford police judge Henry J. Crapo for a writ of habeas corpus. When the judge refused, James took his request to the Massachusetts Supreme Court, where Associate Justice Samuel Sumner Wilde issued the requested writ that "his judicial brother in New Bedford had denied us." On returning to New Bedford, the local sheriff promptly served Henry Ludlam, but, according to James, the slaveholder proposed to post bail for Faggin rather than present her to the court. When the sheriff asked James if he would accept this arrangement, James chided him: "Mr. Sheriff, you were directed to take the person of the girl, Lucy, and I call up on you to do your duty."[24]

James worked in concert with the Rev. Joel Knight, a Methodist pastor and abolitionist, as well as the larger New Bedford Black community to protect Lucy. According to James, "twenty men from the colored district" stationed themselves outside Knight's home and succeeded in repelling an attempted "rescue" by a mob of a dozen white men. When the white community learned of these aggressive tactics, "the entire town was now agog over the affair." More important, the same sheriff who had previously hesitated to take Faggin from Ludlam now called the local police who "escorted" Lucy to the train station so she could travel unbothered to Boston to meet with Justice Wilde. By James's account, Wilde explained that "if she wanted her freedom she should have it."[25] Lucy's liberation was an absolute victory for Black freedom, prompting the Bostonian Black journalist William C. Nell to report to William Lloyd Garrison that on her release a crowd gathered to pray and sing hymns of "Praise for her escape from the '*delectable land of slavery.*'" In his memoir, James simply noted with pride that the efforts of this biracial coalition had meant that "Lucy's master was forced to return to his slave home without his human chattel."[26]

The second action that James celebrates in his memoir is his participation in the abolitionists' campaign to desegregate the Eastern Massachusetts railroad lines. James was part of a biracial cohort of civil rights activists that included Black abolitionists Frederick Douglass and David Ruggles as well as Black-hearted activists William Lloyd Garrison, John Collins, and Wendall Phillips to desegregate the Eastern Railroad.[27] The campaign was deliberately provocative. White allies secured first class tickets for their Black colleagues and then, on boarding, the conductors would inevitably direct the Black passengers to move to the other car. James remembered the conductors' direction that "our rules forbid your occupation of seats in this car. We want no trouble, and you had better go out peaceably." When Black passengers refused to move, the conductors faced a dilemma: either hold the train until the passengers voluntarily moved and thus delay everyone's departure or remove the passengers by force. The latter was James's experience. He returned to Judge Henry Crapo to levy charges of assault and battery on the railroad crew, but the judge "handed down a long, written opinion" in which he ruled "that custom was law, and by custom colored persons were not allowed to ride in cars in the company of white people."[28]

Over time, the activists appealed to the Massachusetts legislature to consider if the discriminatory practices of the railroad violated the Massachusetts Constitution. In 1842, a Joint Special Committee issued a report that effectively affirmed the petitioners' claims, but the committee did not go so far as to vote on legislation to prohibit discrimination.[29] The government's refusal to act infuriated William Lloyd Garrison, who responded by stepping up the direct-action campaign. He published a "traveler's directory" in *The Liberator* to help activists identify which train lines extended "equality of privileges" and which made "an odious distinction on account of color, and a bullying propensity to carry it out."[30] The abolitionists' civil disobedience persisted until the legislature agreed to take up the drafted legislation. By 1843, the railroad company saw the writing on the wall and agreed to voluntarily desegregate the Jim Crow cars rather than submit to state regulation. Forty years later, when James reflected on this milestone in racial integration, he remembered it as a heady experience. In his own words, the legislative report affirmed the recognition that in antebellum Massachusetts, "the youngest colored child had the same rights as the richest white citizens."[31]

But James's most prolonged and concrete opportunity to work with Black-hearted men for emancipation and civil rights came in the context of the Civil War. To abolitionists schooled in the theology of Christian millenarianism, 1861 surely looked like the dawn of a divinely ordained era. The Republican Party had taken control of both the White House and Congress. Longtime white allies including William H. Seward, Hannibal Hamlin, Benjamin Wade, and Thaddeus Stevens now levered the powerful engines of the state.[32] With the first and second Confiscation Acts, Congress expressly directed the Union Army to liberate enslaved men and women, and the Reverend Thomas James followed in their wake to minister to Black refugees.[33] The American Missionary Association, an abolitionist organization of Northern ministers, dispatched James and dozens of other Black and white clergy and lay ministers to the Union-run refugee camps to evangelize, educate, and advocate for the displaced Black men, women, and children who found themselves out of bondage but not quite free.[34] When James arrived in Louisville, Kentucky, he discovered that "the government took me out of the hands of the Missionary Society" and gave him an explicit task: to "take charge of freed and refugee blacks, to visit the prisons of that commonwealth, and to set free all colored persons found confined without charge of a crime."[35] In effect, the American government had commissioned James an agent of Black freedom.

James's identity as a Black abolitionist and Union chaplain made him an easy target for assault. While traveling on a train through Missouri, he was harassed and robbed by white "ruffians," but James also remembered the conductor's efforts to protect him until "government officers" from another railcar came to his rescue.[36] During his time in Louisville, Kentucky, James took direction from two Union commanders: General Stephen G. Burbridge and his successor, General John M. Palmer. They tasked him with attending to the needs of Black refugees in camps, but also empowered him to emancipate any slaves he encountered beyond the camps. Burbridge expressly guaranteed he would protect James in the administration of his duties, and he had an opportunity to make good on this promise. When James reported to the general that he had received death threats from a local official for liberating refugees detained in "slave pens," Burbridge put the local authorities on notice. James relates in his memoir that the general warned: "If James is killed, I will hold responsible for the act every man who fills an office under your city government. I will hang them higher than Haman was hung, and I have 15,000 troops behind me to carry out the order. Your only salvation lies in protecting this colored man's life." Thereafter, James traveled with a Union soldier who served as his personal guard, "a necessary precaution in view of the threats of violence of which I was the object." Burbridge had proven himself to be a trustworthy ally, and perhaps even a Black-hearted man, willing to expose himself to ridicule and danger to protect Black people, not unlike the Black-hearted men James had known in New York and Massachusetts. Over the next three years, he moved about Louisville in relative safety with a "squad of guards" rescuing Black people who had been locked up in private homes or detention centers or had been unable to get to camp. By his own count, he liberated hundreds of people, and some he "sent north to find homes."[37]

In 1865, General John M. Palmer succeeded General Burbridge, but the change in leadership did not derail the Reverend James's mission among Black refugees. In fact, Palmer seemed to share James's enthusiasm for the cause of Black freedom. In 1901, Palmer published his own wartime recollections, and he recounted in detail the conundrum of advancing emancipation in the border state of Kentucky that technically was not subject to the Emancipation Proclamation. He remembered that the Black refugees in Kentucky came to the Union camps at Louisville believing that "I would declare them free." Palmer knew this was not precisely accurate, but he also did not correct them, notwithstanding pressure from fellow officers. On July 4, 1865, Palmer presided over a ceremony before a field full of refugees. A clergyman read the Declaration of Independence, and Palmer announced, "My countrymen, *you are free,* and while I command in this department the military forces of the United States will defend your right to freedom." Palmer reflected that he knew he was acting without authorization, but he made the pronouncement with a determination to "'drive the last nail in the coffin' of the 'institution' even if it cost me the command of the department."[38]

James also remembered the events of that day in his memoir. He recalled the reading of the Declaration of Independence and that Palmer read to the crowd "a number of abusive anonymous letters he had received, because of his course in this and other matters where the interests of the colored people were concerned."[39] He also remembered Palmer's efforts to advance freedom for Black women. It was Palmer who ordered James to "marry every colored woman that came into the camp to a soldier unless she otherwise objected to such proceeding," using his authority as the leader of the camp and a minister to do so.[40] From James's telling, this was not just an exercise in white officers imposing their Christian values or Yankee values on Black refugees, as some historians have argued, but a legal strategy to extend freedom to Black women.[41] James believed that "Congress passed a law giving freedom to the wives and children of all colored soldiers and sailors in the service of the government," and so marriage became the speediest method for securing freedom and mobility for Black women living in a state of legal limbo within these camps.[42]

Perhaps most important, the Reverend Thomas James remembered both Generals Palmer and Burbridge as white allies who created a safe space for James to attend to injured Black souls. Within the refugee camp, James established and offered a "Sunday school and day school," and he "held religious services twice a week as well as on Sundays." He also offered pastoral care to the grieving. James remembered

> the mother bereaved of her children who had been sold and sent farther south lest they should escape in the general rush for the federal lines and freedom; children, orphaned in fact if not in name, for separation from parents among the colored people in those days left no hope of reunion this side of the grave; wives forever parted from their husbands, and husbands who might never hope to catch again the bright-eye and the welcoming smile of the helpmates whose hearts God and nature had joined to theirs.[43]

Up to this point in his life, white allies had been a persistent presence in James's activist life. He had learned to read in New York with the help of white clerks in the warehouse where he worked. He partnered with white lawyers and judges to subvert the rights of slaveowners to bring the people they enslaved into free states, and he fought against segregation on railcars in Boston alongside white abolitionists. Each of these endeavors would have been impossible without the aid of white allies, and so it stands to reason that James, coming to Civil War Kentucky and receiving orders to free enslaved people and recruit them into the Union army, would view and interpret Burbridge and Palmer as two of many white allies who had an "active and generous sympathy for the free colored man of the North, as well as for his brother in bondage."[44]

Figure 1.1. The Fifteenth Amendment (1870). Thomas Kelly published this lithograph to celebrate the ratification of the Fifteenth Amendment. Surrounding the central image of a celebratory parade are idealized representations of postwar Black life and portraits of prominent Black and white abolitionists. *Source*: Library of Congress, Prints and Photographs Division, Washington, DC. https://www.loc.gov/item/93510386/

In October 1864, Thomas James took leave from his post in Louisville, Kentucky, to attend the National Convention of Colored Men at the Wesleyan Methodist Church in Syracuse, New York. It was a familiar venue for abolitionists. It had hosted past Negro Conventions where Black activists had strategized to resist colonization schemes and advance abolition, enfranchisement, and integration. It had also hosted meetings of the biracial Radical Abolitionist Party. But this 1864 Convention was uniquely charged with excitement. It was an opportunity for Black abolitionists to celebrate emancipation, however precarious; to pressure Congress to officially pass the Thirteenth Amendment; and an opportunity to think about the future, to envision the world they wanted to build going forward.[45] The timing was also significant. The activists had agreed to meet one month *before* the consequential 1864 presidential election. Since the last National Convention of Colored People held in 1855, the Supreme Court had denied citizenship to Black Americans, the South had plunged the nation into Civil War for the express purpose of maintaining slavery, and nearly half a million slaves had forced the federal government to take deliberate steps to emancipate enslaved people as a war measure to defeat the Confederate cause.[46] One month before the presidential election, there was a consciousness among the delegates that the Democratic candidate, George B. McClellan, could win the presidency and accept a peace settlement that would derail the march toward Black freedom.[47] Suffice to say, there had never been a more important moment for the nation's Black leaders to coordinate their efforts to reelect Lincoln and, more importantly, establish what it was that Black people saw as the just ends for their service in arms and support for the Union cause: "the freedom, progress, elevation, and perfect enfranchisement of the entire colored people of the United States."[48]

These fears notwithstanding, the conventioneers were exuberant and resolved. The speech delivered by New York City abolitionist Dr. P. B. Randolph was the longest recorded among all the convention's orators. Randolph seized the mood of the convention and offered a blissful vision of the near future:

> My very soul leaps onward a full century; and its visions fall on the fertile fields, with no slave driver there . . . Ay! My soul listens already to the glad prelude of a song of triumph welling up from myriad hearts, and swelling into a paean that fills the concave of heaven itself with the deep-toned melodies of jubilee . . . we are here to prove our right to manhood and

justice, and to maintain these rights . . . by the divine right of brains . . . of manhood, of womanhood, of all that is great and noble and worth striving for in human character. We are here to ring the bells at the door of the world; proclaiming to the nations, to the white man in his palace, to the slave in his hut, kings on their thrones, and to the whole broad universe that WE ARE COMING UP! Yes; we are, at last; and going up to stay.[49]

Randolph's enthusiasm for the future reflects the devotion of all the conventioneers for the promise of "justice and freedom." Each delegate, however cognizant he was of the potential perils of McClellan's victory in the 1864 presidential election, anticipated that the advancements in Black freedom and civil rights had placed Black Americans at the dawn of a new era of freedom and inclusion. The delegates had every good reason to expect that their prewar utopian aspirations would now be realized in the postwar era. Their view of the moment, as they interpreted it to one another at the 1864 National Convention, was providential: "God had interfered mercifully for the oppressed and offset the nation's acts against the Black man by meeting them at every point."[50] Their fervor and hope for that future solidified their view that "every day seems almost an era in the history of our country." "We have at last reached the dividing line," John S. Rock pronounced, and the fervor of the moment even inspired young women to address the convention and exhort to its delegates "to trust in God and press on, and not abate one jot or tittle [sic] until the glorious day of jubilee shall come."[51]

The official addresses and resolutions of the 1864 National Convention of Colored Men were staider in their tone than the biblically inspired speeches delivered by the likes of John S. Rock or Dr. P. B. Randolph. Yet the convention's "Declarations of Wrongs and Rights" and "Address of the Colored National Convention to the People of the United States" make evident that James's prior utopian thinking was not singular. James functioned in a community that anticipated that abolition would lead to two concrete goals. First, the 1864 conventioneers explicitly echoed the goals articulated at his very first antislavery convention in Utica. Echoing the resolutions of 1836, the 1864 Convention's "Address of the Colored National Convention" stated its mission: "to complete the emancipation, enfranchisement, and elevation of our race."[52] Second, the convention affirmed Black Americans as possessing "the same rights as other citizens" with respect to "the full enjoyment of enfranchised manhood, and its dignities" as well as their "fair share of the public domain."⁵³ This was a community of like-minded Black men and women filled with hope for freedom, citizenship, and equality.

Just as noteworthy, the Black leaders of the convention made time to acknowledge the contributions of their white allies, Black-hearted men and women, to this seeming turning point in history. The resolutions thanked President Lincoln and the abolitionist-led Congress for passing laws that empowered Black men to carry US mail, recognized the sovereignty of Haiti and Liberia, retaliated in just measure to Confederate policies that led to the massacre or execution of Black Union soldiers, and revised statutes with discriminatory language.⁵⁴ Such acknowledgments indicate the delegates' conviction of the strength of their biracial collaboration and their expectation for its endurance. In fact, this convention was still hopeful enough and prophetically minded enough to reconstitute itself as an organization ready for the next frontier: enfranchisement and integration. One of the more lasting achievements of this convention was the establishment of the National Equal Rights League, which the convention expressly charged with the goal to "promote everything that pertains to a well-ordered and dignified life" and "to obtain by appeals to the mind and conscience of the American people, or by legal process, when possible, a recognition of the rights of the colored people of the nation as American citizens."⁵⁵

It is not difficult to imagine this moment in 1864 with the Reverend Thomas James sitting on the convention floor, discussing the hopes he had manifested in the lives of the refugees to whom he ministered in Kentucky or measuring the anxiety the conventioneers exuded in their exhortations for Union voters to reelect Lincoln with their own faith in God's providential intervention to achieve a "year of jubilee."⁵⁶ However, in actuality, the post-racial America that Reverend Thomas James and his fellow delegates anticipated in 1864 stalled in the 1870s. Reconstruction died as white supremacist organizations engaged in domestic terrorism against Black citizens and white Republicans in the South. Although Southern Republicans and the federal government enacted measures designed to suppress and destroy organizations like the KKK, the costs of those measures, white Southern recalcitrance, and a prevailing Northern Republican belief that "the troublesome 'Negro question' had been removed from national politics" with the successful adoption of the Fifteenth Amendment combined to end concerted, unified federal efforts to secure any meaningful vestige of Black freedom other than the end of bondage itself.⁵⁷ Thus, the hopes James and his fellow conventioneers expressed in 1864 gave way to the racial segregation that became normative in the 1880s.

Reflecting on the past to make sense of the present, James rightly understood the importance of cross-racial collaboration and utopian thinking for achieving social change. The Black-hearted men with whom James had labored for decades had been replaced by coldhearted men. This reality likely informed both the structure and content of his autobiography. After all, at eighty-two years of age, blinded by cataracts and enfeebled by bodily pains, Thomas James knew his memoir was likely his last best chance to shape the future. He avoided drafting a conventional "slave narrative," opting instead to write a memoir that testifies to the power of interracial activism and utopian thinking. *Life of Thomas James, by Himself* defied the emerging thesis of the "Lost Cause" that the antebellum goals of abolition, enfranchisement, and integration were either unrealistic or impossible. In fact, James was so confident in the hopeful lessons to be learned from his activist life that he retitled a subsequent edition *Wonderful Eventful Life of Rev. Thomas James, by Himself* (1887). While the millennium he had anticipated in the 1830s had not yet arrived in the 1880s, Thomas James remained ever confident in the power of cross-racial collaboration and utopian thinking for achieving social change.

Notes

1. Rev. Thomas James, *Life of Rev. Thomas James, by Himself* (1886; repr., Chapel Hill: University Library, University of North Carolina at Chapel Hill, 2000), 23, https://docsouth.unc.edu/neh/jamesth/jamesth.html.

2. James, *Life of Rev. Thomas James*, 23.

3. For a complete explanation of why the American government and electorate abandoned the quest for Black civil integration, see Heather Cox Richardson, *The Death of Reconstruction: Race, Labor, and Politics in the Post-Civil War North, 1865–1901* (Cambridge: Harvard University Press, 2004) and Eric Foner, *A Short History of Reconstruction, 1863–1877*, updated ed. (New York: Harper Perennial Modern Classics, 2015).

4. John Stauffer, *The Black Hearts of Men: Radical Abolitionists and the Transformation of Race* (Cambridge: Harvard University Press, 2002), 1.

5. Stauffer, *The Black Hearts of Men*, 1–2, 4, 6–7.

6. James, *Life of Rev. Thomas James*, 7–8. Thomas James and Frederick Douglass often crossed paths in Rochester, New York, and again in New Bedford, Massachusetts; and, unsurprisingly, they collaborated with many of the same white allies in both locations. Frederick Douglass, *Life and Times of Frederick Douglass, Written by*

Himself (1892; repr., Chapel Hill: University Library, University of North Carolina at Chapel Hill, 1999), 333, https://docsouth.unc.edu/neh/dougl92/dougl92.html.

7. James, *Life of Rev. Thomas James*, 10–11 (Justice Wilde); 16 (Crandall), and 17–19 (Kentucky).

8. James, *Life of Rev. Thomas James*, 5–6.

9. On the economic and social development of central New York, see Joanne Reitano, "The Empire State, 1790–1830," in *New York State: People, Places, and Priorities: A Concise History with Sources* (New York: Routledge, Taylor & Francis Group, 2016), 66–96.

10. For more on the significance of economics and revivalism and the development of abolition activism in Central and Western New York, see Judith Wellman, *Grass Roots Reform in the Burned-over District of Upstate New York: Religion, Abolitionism, and Democracy* (New York: Routledge, 2011); Milton C. Sernett, *North Star Country: Upstate New York and the Crusade for African American Freedom* (Syracuse: Syracuse University Press, 2002), and Spencer W. McBride and Jennifer Hull Dorsey, eds., *New York's Burned-over District: A Documentary History* (Ithaca: Cornell University Press, 2023).

11. On communal and utopian societies, see Robert S. Fogarty, *All Things New: American Communes and Utopian Movements, 1860–1914* (Chicago: University of Chicago Press, 1990).

12. James, *Life of Rev. Thomas James*, 6–7.

13. On the radicalization of the interracial abolition movement, see Richard S. Newman, *The Transformation of American Abolitionism: Fighting Slavery in the Early Republic* (Chapel Hill: University of North Carolina Press, 2002); Manisha Sinha, *The Slave's Cause: A History of Abolition* (New Haven: Yale University Press, 2016), 195–98, 226–28; and Paul J. Polgar, *Standard-Bearers of Equality: America's First Abolition Movement* (Chapel Hill: University of North Carolina Press, 2019).

14. For a historian's account of these events, see Stauffer, *Black Hearts of Men*, 100–1. James is listed as delegate "T. James" in the published proceeding of the convention. New York State Anti-Slavery Society, *Proceedings of the New York Anti-Slavery Convention, Held at Utica, October 21, And New York Anti-Slavery State Society, Held at Peterboro, October 22, 1835* (Utica, NY: Printed at the Standard & Democrat Office, 1835), 47.

15. *Proceedings of the New York Anti-Slavery Convention*, 10.

16. New York State Anti-Slavery Society, *Proceedings of the First Annual Meeting of the New-York State Anti-slavery Society: Convened at Utica, October 19, 1836* (Utica, NY: Pub. For the Society, 1836). 10.

17. On the disenfranchisement of Black voters in New York State, see David N. Gellman and David Quigley, "The Convention of 1821 and the Politics of Disenfranchisement," in *Jim Crow New York: A Documentary History of Race and Citizenship, 1777–1877*, ed. David N. Gellman and David Quigley (New York:

New York University Press, 2003), 75–77 and Phyllis F. Field, *The Politics of Race in New York: The Struggle for Black Suffrage in the Civil War Era* (Ithaca: Cornell University Press, 2009), 35–36.

18. Convention of the Colored Inhabitants of the State of New York (1840: Albany, NY), "Minutes of the State Convention of Colored Citizens, Held at Albany, on the 18th, 19th, and 20th of August, 1840, for the Purpose of Considering Their Ppolitical Condition," *Colored Conventions Project Digital Records*, 8, https://omeka.coloredconventions.org/items/show/620.

19. New York State Convention of Colored Citizens (1841: Troy, NY), "New-York State Convention of Colored Citizens, Troy, August 25-27, 1841," *Colored Conventions Project Digital Records*, 28, https://omeka.coloredconventions.org/items/show/231.

20. Moreover, according to Field, voting rights activists succeeded in keeping Black enfranchisement at the forefront of every legislative session between 1855 through 1860. Field, *Politics of Race in New York*, 137–40.

21. Joseph Blossom Bloss, *A Tribute to William C. Bloss at the Unveiling of a Monument to His Memory at Brighton Cemetery, September 22, 1893, by His Son* (Rochester, NY: Post Express Printing Company, 1893), 11–13.

22. "Proceedings of the Convention of Radical Political Abolitionists, Held at Syracuse, N.Y., June 26th, 27th, and 28th, 1855: Slavery Is an Outlaw, and Forbidden by the Constitution, Which Provides for Its Abolition" (New York: Central Abolition Board, 1855), Cornell University Library Digital Collections, 3, https://digital.library.cornell.edu/catalog/may818307.

23. The following events are detailed in James, *Life of Rev. Thomas James*, 9–10. See also Kathryn Grover, *The Fugitive's Gibraltar: Escaping Slaves and Abolitionism in New Bedford, Massachusetts* (Amherst: University of Massachusetts Press, 2001), 160–67.

24. James, *Live of Rev. Thomas James*, 10.

25. James, *Life of Rev. Thomas James*, 11. Historian Thomas D. Morris has concluded that Associate Justice Wilde was acting on a 1785 anti-kidnapping provision in the Massachusetts habeas corpus statue. According to Morris, "This law eliminated state recognition of the so-called right of reception, a right that had been recognized by Pennsylvania in its gradual abolition act. The Massachusetts law provided that persons lawfully residing in the state (a judicial question) could not be removed unless "by due course of law, to answer for some criminal offense committed in some other of the United States of America." See *Free Men All: The Personal Liberty Laws of the North, 1780–1861* (Baltimore: Johns Hopkins University Press, 1974), 42.

26. Although James offers different details in his account of the Faggin rescue, Black and white abolitionists alike understood the significance of these events. William Lloyd Garrison subsequently published Nell's account of the Fagan rescue in the *The Liberator*. See "Document 43. The Rescue of Lucy Faggins" in Peter C.

Ripley, Roy E. Finkenbine, and Michael F. Hembree, *Witness for Freedom: African American Voices on Race, Slavery, and Emancipation* (Chapel Hill: University of North Carolina Press, 1993), 137–38.

27. For a comprehensive account of this desegregation campaign, see Louis Ruchames, "Jim Crow Railroads in Massachusetts," *American Quarterly* 8, no. 1 (1956): 61–75 and Steve Luxenberg, *Separate: The Story of Plessy v. Ferguson, and America's Journey from Slavery to Segregation* (New York: W. W. Norton & Company, 2019), 3–25.

28. James, *Life of Rev. Thomas James*, 15.

29. Evidently, the General Court drafted legislation to force desegregation but then delayed voting on the matter. See Massachusetts General Court, *In Senate, Feb. 22 1842: The Joint Special Committee to Whom Was Committed the Petition of Francis Jackson and Others, and Sundry Other Petitioners, for a Law Securing to Colored Persons Equal Rights in Rail-Road Accommodation . . . Report:* . . . [Boston, MAass. : s.n.], 1842, http://archive.org/details/insenatefeb2218400mass.

30. Garrison cited in Luxenberg, *Separate*, 21.

31. James, *Life of Rev. Thomas James*, 15.

32. Known abolitionists within the president's cabinet included Secretary of State William H. Seward and Vice President Hannibal Hamlin. Additionally, abolitionists had assumed power of important congressional committees, including Senator Benjamin Wade, who chaired the committee on Federal Territories, and Congressman Thaddeus Stevens, who chaired the House Ways and Means Committee. Fergus M. Bordewich, *Congress at War: How Republican Reformers Fought the Civil War, Defined Lincoln, Ended Slavery and Remade America* (New York: Knopf, 2021), 64, 68. James M. McPherson, *Battle Cry of Freedom: The Civil War Era* (Oxford: Oxford University Press, 1988), 260.

33. Amy Murrell Taylor, *Embattled Freedom: Journeys through the Civil War's Slave Refugee Camps* (Chapel Hill: University of North Carolina Press, 2018), 72–77; Richardson, *The Death of Reconstruction*, 1–13.

34. Taylor, *Embattled Freedom*, 13–14.

35. James notes that the American Missionary Association had originally dispatched him to Louisiana and Tennessee, but it seems that he never served in either location. James, *Life of Rev. Thomas James*, 17.

36. James, *Life of Rev. Thomas James*, 17. Confederate guerillas swarmed through the Union-occupied territories at the time that James and other missionaries were dispatched to work among Black refugees. The guerillas raided refugee camps, Union supply depots, and reconstituted cotton plantations worked by wage-earning freedmen. They also recaptured Black refugees for reenslavement in Confederate territory. While James's encounter with "ruffians" happened early in the Civil War, it is not unthinkable that he and his adult daughter, with whom he was traveling, could have been abducted, brutalized, or enslaved by guerillas. See Taylor, *Embattled Freedom*, 118–19, 133–34, 136–39.

37. James, *Life of Rev. James*, 18, 22–23.

38. John McAuley Palmer, *Personal Recollections of John M. Palmer: The Story of an Earnest Life* (Cincinnati: R. Clarke Company, 1901), 240–42. At the time that General Palmer presided over these activities, Congress had passed the Thirteenth Amendment, but the ratification process would not be completed until December 6, 1865. In the meantime, neither the Emancipation Proclamation nor the Congressional Confiscation Acts applied to the enslaved people of Kentucky, a Union state governed by citizens who had sworn allegiance to the Constitution. Palmer's careful language makes clear he understood this complicated political-legal environment. It also explains his hesitancy to prounce emancipation. Palmer likely knew that earlier in the war, Abraham Lincoln had fired or countermanded orders from other Union generals in border states that sought to dismantle slavery for the express reason that those orders injured Unionist slave owners, not Confederate ones. McPherson, *Battle Cry of Freedom*, 352–54, 497–99.

39. James, *Life of Rev. Thomas* James, 19. It is worth noting that Palmer also mentioned James in his memoir, identifying him as the clergyman he had charged with investigating the illegal imprisonment of Black men seeking wage labor in Louisville. Palmer, *Personal Recollections of John M. Palmer*, 234.

40. James, *Life of Rev. Thomas James*, 19.

41. On this rationale for Black marriage, see Amy Murrell Taylor, who argues that Union officers saw marriage as "an incubator of good social and political values" where "future citizens developed the character and morals necessary to . . . act as responsible citizens." *Embattled Freedom*, 78.

42. James, *Life of Rev. Thomas James*, 18. Amy Murrell Taylor points out that these marriages were encouraged by the American Missionary Association and Union military officers as a way to control refugees and regulate the spaces they occupied in these refugee camps, not necessarily to grant freedom to Black women married to Black soldiers in Union uniform. See Taylor, *Embattled Freedom*, 34–35, 78.

43. James, *Life of Rev. Thomas James*, 21. In fairness, it is not evident that these generals would have identified themselves as Black-hearted allies. Palmer, as an example, may have identified as an enemy of slavery and slave power more than as a Black-hearted man. Nevertheless, James's memoir offers them up as exemplary allies and models for the postwar generation of white leaders.

44. James, *Life of Rev. Thomas James*, 23.

45. This was also the first Negro Convention to include delegates from the Union-occupied states of Virginia, North Carolina, Louisiana, Mississippi, Tennessee, Missouri, and the District of Columbia. National Convention of Colored Men, *Proceedings of the National Convention of Colored Men; Held in the City of Syracuse, N.Y.; October 4, 5, 6, and 7, 1864; with the Bill of Wrongs and Rights; and the Address to the American People* (1864: Syracuse, NY), *Colored Conventions Project Digital Records* 2022, 4–6, https://omeka.coloredconventions.org/items/show/282.

46. Fergus M. Bordewich argues that the convention delegates had additional concerns about federal progress toward their key goals. The 1864 Convention addressed the issues of unequal pay for Black soldiers, unanswered questions about Reconstruction, and the news of the Fort Pillow Massacre. Moreover, at the time of this convention in October 1864, emancipation still looked precarious because the national amendment to abolish it had been defeated in the House of Representatives. There was a real fear at the convention that Lincoln would abandon emancipation to win reelection or end the war, something that Frederick Douglass himself addressed at the convention. See *Congress at War*, 357–65, 379–85, 399–400.

47. McClellan's views on prosecuting the war were somewhat vague and ill-defined. However, the Democratic Party's platform in 1864 made clear that if McClellan won, the party would push for an armistice and an initial peace agreement to bring the South back into the Union. Either policy—McClellan's or the Democrats'—would mean the nation would likely abandon a constitutional amendment to end slavery. Bordewich, *Congress at War*, 399–400, 404–8, 411–14.

48. *Proceedings of the National Convention of Colored Men*, 9.

49. *Proceedings of the National Convention of Colored Men*, 21–22.

50. *Proceedings of the National Convention of Colored Men*, 14.

51. *Proceedings of the National Convention of Colored Men*, 15, 22–23.

52. *Proceedings of the National Convention of Colored Men*, 45.

53. *Proceedings of the National Convention of Colored Men*, 42. The reference to the public domain is twofold. First, it refers to the lands opened for American colonization in the West through the consequential Homestead Act of 1862. Second, it refers to the lands administered by the War Department in Southern states that many ardent abolitionists wanted redistributed to Black refugees from slavery and freedmen in the aftermath of the war. See both Bordewich's *Congress at* War, 182–84 and Murrell's *Embattled Freedom*, 212–15.

54. *Proceedings of the National Convention of Colored Men*, 34–35.

55. See "Preamble and Constitution of the National Equal Rights League" in the *Proceedings of the National Convention of Colored Men*, 36–39. This organization was the nation's premier civil rights organization in the postwar era and a precursor to the National Association for the Advancement of Colored People. See Christi M. Smith, "National Equal Rights League (1864–1921)" (*Black Past*, December 18, 2009), https://www.blackpast.org/african-american-history/national-equal-rights-league-1864-1915/; and "The Equal Rights League and Suffrage," Falvey Memorial Library, Villanova University, https://exhibits.library.vlllanova.edu/institute-colored-youth/community-moments/equal-rights-league-and-suffrage.

56. *Proceedings of the National Convention of Colored Men*, 22–23.

57. Foner, *A Short History of Reconstruction*, 193. For a full discussion of the KKK, domestic terrorism, and the Union retreat from Reconstruction, see Foner, *A Short History of Reconstruction*, 184–98 and Richardson, *The Death of Reconstruction*.

2

Black Cooperators

Owenism and Utopia in Black America

VICTORIA W. WOLCOTT

> I know that society may be formed so as to exist without crime, without poverty, with health greatly improved, with little, if any misery, and with intelligence and happiness increased a hundredfold; and no obstacle whatsoever intervenes at this moment except ignorance to prevent such a state of society from becoming universal.
>
> —Robert Owen, Address to the inhabitants of New Lanark, 1816

> Individuals will be born in cooperative health centers, will live in cooperative houses, will meet their needs from cooperative stores, will be protected by cooperative law, and, in the end, will be buried by cooperative burial associations.
>
> —Samuel Lloyd Myers, 1942

In the wake of a mass shooting in Buffalo, New York, on May 14, 2022, when a white supremacist gunned down fourteen African Americans at a local grocery store, the community turned toward a set of practices that had its origins in nineteenth-century utopian experiments. The massacre temporarily shut down the only large grocery store in Buffalo's segregated

East Side, limiting the neighborhood's access to fresh and healthy food. The Buffalo Food Equity Network and Cooperation Buffalo mobilized after the shooting to help organizations such as the Buffalo Freedom Gardens, African Heritage Food Coop, and Food for the Spirit develop cooperative and community-oriented solutions to the food crisis.[1] These cooperative organizations, like the visions offered by Robert Owen and Samuel Lloyd Myers, draw from a legacy of utopian experimentation in the Black community. That experimentation drew from white ideals of a perfect society, what Lyman Tower Sargent calls "social dreaming," an opportunity to both envision and enact an alternative model of society.[2] But for African Americans, utopian thought and practice came out of struggle and survival. Thus, Robin D. G. Kelley's concept of "freedom dreams" better describes what has happened in Buffalo. "I have come to realize," says Kelley, "that once we strip radical social movements down to their bare essence and understand the collective desires of people in motion, freedom and love lay at the very heart of the matter."[3]

Robert Owen, the white industrialist and reformer, and Samuel Lloyd Myers, the Black economist and educator, both embraced a cooperative vision. For them, cooperation was more than an economic strategy; it signified a comprehensive and idealistic vision of the future. For African Americans in slavery and freedom, this vision inspired utopian experiments in communalism, small-scale capitalism, and consumer and producer cooperatives. For African Americans experiencing segregation, discrimination, and white supremacist violence, dreaming was vital for survival. Their experiments ranged from separatist colonies that emphasized the growth of Black businesses outside white influence to interracial utopian communities with a profound spiritual commitment to full equality. But central to all these groups was the idea of the cooperative, both the broad concept of cooperation propagated by Robert Owen and the practical application of cooperative economics. Black cooperators tilled fields, opened cooperative stores, fought segregation, and brought their dreams from the world of imagination to the reality of racial struggle.

Owenite Dreams

In the mid-summer of 1826 in an idyllic Indiana hamlet, two men strolled garden paths and shared their vision of a different world. One was a Scottish industrialist, far from his home, and the second a plantation master intrigued by the idea of utopia. This encounter in New Harmony would launch a series of utopian experiments in the Mississippi Delta that would draw praise and support from Booker T. Washington and Theodore Roosevelt, among others, but would also highlight the limitations of an Owenite model of paternalistic utopianism.[4] Joseph Davis, the planter and older brother of the Confederate President Jefferson Davis, first encountered Robert Owen in a stagecoach while traveling across Pennsylvania in 1825. Owen was on his way back to Great Britain to raise more funds for his new utopian community, New Harmony.[5] The community would only survive for two short years, but its experiments in progressive education, communalism, and cooperation would live on and shape the utopian experimentation of African Americans in the nineteenth and twentieth centuries.

Robert Owen, the Scottish industrialist, gained fame as one of the major thinkers behind the development of utopian socialism in the nineteenth century, along with the French philosophers Charles Fourier and Henri de Saint-Simon. In 1799, Owen took over his father-in-law's sprawling mill in New Lanark, Scotland, determined to create a community there that lifted up workers through education, decent housing, health care, and other social services. New Lanark's mill workers were better housed and educated than the average industrial worker, but Owen maintained a paternalistic control over them. He restricted their access to alcohol and demanded that families keep high moral standards. By 1825, Owen's outspoken views on religion, private property, and marriage made him increasingly unpopular in Great Britain. Like other utopianists, he set out for America in 1825 to find a more welcoming reception and a society more open to radical ideas. In the United States, he was a popular lecturer who traveled widely, including throughout the South. Seeking to create a true utopian community, he purchased property from the religious Rappite society, which established Harmonie in Indiana but wished to return to its original colony in Western Pennsylvania. Harmonie was the result of settler utopianism, because that the federal government took the land from the Miami Confederation of Indigenous tribes and sold it to Rapp. Renamed New Harmony, Robert Owen's utopia was not long lasting, but its impact on American utopianism was profound.[6]

Another admirer of Owen and fellow immigrant from Scotland, Frances "Fanny" Wright, was also a regular visitor to New Harmony. Owen's communitarianism and radical views on religion and marriage shaped Wright's plans, particularly her creation of a remarkable community that sought to emancipate enslaved people by harnessing their labor. Wright carried to America the idea that the young nation was an ideal society, a utopia already in the making. She had a romantic vision of the United States as a progressive nation that fulfilled the promises of republicanism. Wright published her observations in an 1821 volume of letters, *Views of Society and Manners in America*, which elevated her profile among European and American radicals. The one flaw in American society, imported from Great Britain in her view, was the institution of slavery. Although an abolitionist, her views on slavery were deeply problematic; she was convinced that given the right economic incentives, white Southern planters would be eager to emancipate their enslaved workers.[7] Wright, like most white abolitionists at the time, also embraced colonization as the ultimate solution to the system of slavery. After emancipation, freedpeople would be transported to Liberia or Haiti, leaving white Americans to fulfill their Jeffersonian destiny as farmers in the New Republic.

Wright published her utopian blueprint, "A Plan for the Gradual Abolition of Slavery in the United States, without Danger of Loss to the Citizens of the South," in the *New Harmony Gazette*.[8] Her principal idea was to allow enslaved people to purchase their freedom through their labor, ensuring that their masters would not lose capital because of their emancipation. With the support of Owen and his son Robert Dale Owen, who had more progressive attitudes toward emancipation than his father, Wright founded Nashoba, a two-hundred-acre plantation near Memphis, Tennessee, in 1825. In an echo of New Harmony's settler utopianism, this land had recently been confiscated from the Chickasaw Indians. Wright named the community Nashoba after a Chickasaw word for the local river. She purchased ten enslaved people whose labor would, ideally, allow them to purchase their own freedom. The following year she purchased a family of enslaved people, a mother and her six children. The fact that these transactions made her a slaveowner did not seem to trouble Wright. This was a scaled-down version of her initial plan because of the lack of financial backing, including from those planters who initially had expressed some support but never followed through with funds or enslaved workers. The experiment began to unravel almost immediately, as the land was difficult to clear and did not yield sufficient crops to sustain the community.[9]

Wright returned to New Harmony the following year during a period of uncertainty and crisis in her utopian start-up. At this point she began to adapt some of Owen's more controversial teachings, particularly his rejection of religion and criticisms of the institution of marriage. Hoping to revive Nashoba as an interracial utopia, albeit one with subordinate roles for African

Americans, in December 1826 Wright invited like-minded white intellectuals to join the Tennessee experiment as "trustees" of the community. The white trustees would continue to oversee the enslaved laborers, although Wright suggested that the next generation of Nashoba residents, both Black and white, would receive an identical education leading to racial equality. One of those trustees, James Richardson, brought infamy to the project when he revealed the extent of Nashoba's free-love practices. Richardson kept records of his experiences at Nashoba, which he then published in an abolitionist journal, the *Genius of Universal Emancipation*. Richardson reported that one of the enslaved women, Isabel, had complained about a sexual assault. She was told "that we consider the proper basis of the sexual intercourse to be the unconstrained and unrestrained choice of *both* parties." This progressive stance was undermined by the next statement. "Nelly having requested a lock for the door of the room in which she and Isabel sleep, with the view of preventing the future uninvited entrance of any man; the lock was refused, as being, in its proposed use, inconsistent with the doctrine just explained."[10] Clearly Richardson, and the other white trustees, expected the enslaved women to make themselves sexually available. And their view that slavery and utopia were compatible rendered the experiment unworkable from the start.

Wright defended the trustees' behavior and went on to be one of the foremost defenders of both free love and free thought.[11] But the Nashoba experiment failed. When she and Robert Dale Owen returned in the summer of 1828, few trustees remained, and the community was in disarray, so they agreed to abandon the communitarian experiment. In January 1830, Wright emancipated the remaining enslaved families and brought them to freedom in Haiti. The president of the island nation, Jean Pierre Boyer, settled the freedpeople on his own land and promised them permanent lots. Nashoba had evolved from a grand scheme to abolish slavery and colonize freedpeople to a small utopian experiment that failed within two years, around the same length of time that New Harmony survived. And although Wright sought to embrace Owen's progressive education and communalism at Nashoba, the colony was never designed to be a fully egalitarian and interracial community. The enslaved members could not be trustees, and when they had earned enough to buy their freedom, the expectation had always been that they would leave for Liberia or Haiti, not remain at Nashoba as fully equal members.[12]

Fanny Wright was not the only Owenite to apply communitarian principles to an enslaved community. Joseph Davis, a prosperous planter, met Wright at a reception for the Marquis de Lafayette in Natchez, Mississippi, in 1825. The two immediately bonded over their interest in Owenite ideas. Wright sang Owen's praises and recommended a visit to New Harmony, while Davis educated her on the plantation system, knowledge that she used to develop her plans for Nashoba.[13] Davis visited New Harmony the following year, meeting with Owen and admiring the cooperative labor system and progressive education in the colony. He returned to his plantation along the Mississippi south of Vicksburg, known as Davis Bend, determined to apply Owenite principles to his enslaved workforce in ways that paralleled Owen's treatment of the New Lanark mill workers. Central to these ideas was cooperation in the broadest sense, as workers laboring in harmony for the good of the community. But for Owen and Davis, it was also about control, of morality, family life, and, in the case of those enslaved, freedom itself. Owen, in fact, referred to his workers as "living machines," which is also an apt description of planters' perception of enslaved workers on a Southern plantation.[14] Despite Owen and Davis's idealism, New Lanark and Davis Bend were both very much capitalist endeavors, designed to make profits rather than create a fully socialist and egalitarian society.

Joseph Davis's application of Owenite ideas did improve the daily lives of his growing enslaved population. Davis provided them with larger cabins and encouraged them to grow their own food and raise livestock, leading to better-than-average diets and the ability to sell or barter surplus produce. At least some of the enslaved children received enough education to become literate, although when Davis briefly opened an interracial school on the plantation, his white neighbors insisted it be closed. Enslaved men and women had the opportunity to learn skills such as smithing and running a cotton gin. Most remarkably, Davis set up a plantation court system run by the enslaved, meaning that the white overseers, figures of terror on most plantations, had little power to punish the workers. But the cooperation that Davis tried to instill in his community was a means to an end, and that end was profit.[15]

Into this community came a remarkable African American man, Benjamin Montgomery, who would be instrumental in developing Black Owenite ideas into the twentieth century. Montgomery was born enslaved in Virginia in 1819 and was purchased by Davis in 1836. He attempted to escape the plantation when he arrived, but Davis brought him back and, noting that he was literate and highly intelligent, gave him a leadership role within the enslaved community. In 1842 Montgomery began operation of a mercantile store at Davis Bend that served both Black and white customers, keeping the profits to benefit his family. His son, Isaiah Montgomery, became Joseph

Davis's personal secretary, exposing him to Owenite ideals as he transcribed correspondence and read in Davis's vast library. But the grimmest reality of enslavement remained even in this model Owenite plantation. Davis Bend's enslaved families lived with the fear of being sold away when Joseph Davis died and with the knowledge that there was little opportunity for escape in the Mississippi Delta.[16]

The best evidence for their discontent came at the outbreak of the Civil War, when the enslaved population of Davis Bend refused to follow Joseph Davis as he fled the plantation, despite his pleas. In his absence, the enslaved families ransacked his mansion, carrying his linens, clothing, and cookware to their own cabins.[17] The Montgomery family, who had accumulated money from the mercantile store, took the opportunity to flee to safety, spending much of the war years in Cincinnati. During the war, the Union General Ulysses S. Grant was eager to use Davis Bend, now occupied by union troops, as a model Black colony, calling it a "Negro Paradise."[18] The Freedman's Bureau oversaw the plantation, setting up schools and medical clinics for the freedmen and women. The Bureau leased land to freedpeople, and the court system that had been initiated by Davis continued under their control.

During the occupation Ben Montgomery and his family returned to Davis Bend and quickly reasserted their leadership in the community.[19] Remarkably, in 1866 Davis sold the plantation to Montgomery for $300,000 to be paid off over ten years with yearly interest payments. Montgomery, now fully in charge of the plantation without the supervision of his former master or the Freedmen's Bureau, printed leaflets advertising Davis Bend as a Black colony where freedpeople could live independently. For much of the next decade the plantation flourished, becoming the third-largest cotton producer in Mississippi by the early 1870s.[20] In 1871 the African American writer Frances Ellen Watkins Harper visited the plantation and marveled at its success. "They are building up a future which if exceptional now I hope will become more general hereafter," she wrote in a letter.[21] Montgomery ran the court system, oversaw the mercantile, and enticed former enslaved Davis Bend workers who had fled during the war back to the plantation. But the extended Davis family, including disgraced Confederate President Jefferson Davis, constantly threatened the Montgomerys with possible foreclosure, particularly after Joseph Davis's death in 1870. After a series of devastating floods, plummeting cotton prices, and infestations of boll weevils and army worms, the Montgomery family finally foreclosed in 1881. By this point Ben Montgomery, the family's patriarch, had died. His son Isaiah opened a store in downtown Vicksburg and traveled to Kansas to explore the Black towns that had developed in the 1870s where some Davis Bend freedpeople had migrated. Trained under Davis and his father, Isaiah was envisioning another Owenite community, but one entirely outside white control.[22]

Black Owenites in Freedom

Influenced by the Kansas settlements, Isaiah Montgomery got his opportunity to form his own Black Owenite utopia in 1887. Another Montgomery son, William Thornton Montgomery, had had significant economic success setting up an agricultural community in North Dakota along a railroad line.[23] When Isaiah Montgomery heard of the opportunity to purchase undeveloped land at a low price along the Louisville, New Orleans, and Texas Railroad, he jumped at the chance, hoping to replicate his brother's success. The railroad company was eager to find willing workers to clear the land and believed, as one former resident put it, "the Negro was held, then as now, to hold some peculiar and natural adaptation to life in this semi-tropical country and to enjoy to some extent a large degree of racial immunity from the ills imagined to be always attendant on life in the delta."[24] Montgomery choose land between Memphis and Vicksburg and named it Mound Bayou after the large Indian mound at the center of the property. Joining Montgomery were numerous Davis Bend freedpeople who spent the early years of the settlement clearing land and building makeshift homes. Thanks in part to plentiful lumber and a profitable mill, by 1907 Mound Bayou housed 800 Black families.[25] Isaiah's leadership in Mound Bayou reflected the same leadership style of Robert Owen and Ben Montgomery, a paternalism that reinscribed social hierarchies while enforcing strict moral norms. This was done through education, policing, particularly of alcohol and prostitution, and religion.[26]

In the early twentieth century, Mound Bayou became a symbol of the potential of Black capitalism to uplift the race.[27] At the center of that campaign was the educator Booker T. Washington, the director of the Tuskeegee Institute and influential African American thinker whose 1901 memoir, *Up From Slavery*, became a bestseller. Isaiah Montgomery, himself a former slave, accompanied Washington to the Atlanta Exposition in 1895, where Washington gave his infamous "Atlanta Compromise Speech," calling for economic solidarity between the races at the expense of political power or social equality. Montgomery, and the prosperous Mound Bayou banker Charles Banks, became prominent members of the National Negro Business League, which often held Mound Bayou up as a model of Black capitalism and self-sufficiency. Booker T. Washington argued that, "Isolated from whites . . . the black town acted as a laboratory, proving that under the correct circumstances the race was hard working, law abiding, and capable of self-government."[28] Mound Bayou was his premier example of this philosophy. Washington also connected Montgomery and Banks with white philanthropists who could step in when the local economy faltered. Both Julius Rosenwald and Andrew Carnegie loaned money to keep Banks's businesses solvent and built local institutions, including a Carnegie-sponsored library.[29] Mound Bayou's educational institutions, including its Normal and Industrial Institute, also embraced the industrial education of Washington's Tuskeegee Institute.[30]

But most significantly, Montgomery embraced Washington's separation of Black economic power and Black political power. This was demonstrated in a shocking way at the 1890 Mississippi Constitutional Convention, the culmination of the use of white vigilante terror to wrest control from Black Republicans in the wake of Reconstruction. It was the protection of the Freedmen's Bureau and Republican control of Mississippi during Reconstruction that had allowed the Davis Bend community, under Ben Montgomery's control, to flourish for a time. But that time had passed. Attending the convention as a representative of the county's Republican Central Committee, Isaiah spoke out in support of the disenfranchisement of all African Americans and many poor whites in the state. He later justified his decision, which was roundly criticized by both W. E. B. DuBois and Frederick Douglass, as an attempt to ensure that Mound Bayou would be left alone to flourish as a Black colony.[31] Mound Bayou resident Aurellius Hood echoed that sentiment in his 1909 pamphlet on the town: "There has never been any suggestion of the question of social equality and it has been utterly impossible for any such troublesome and unreal phantasm to even approach the Mound Bayou situation."[32] Social and political equality were the sacrifices Mound Bayou residents paid to be left alone.

Mound Bayou's economic strength began to decline after 1915 as the result of a failed cotton seed oil venture and declining crop prices.[33] However, it remained a source of pride for African Americans in Mississippi and served as a haven for civil rights activists during the height of the movement in the early 1960s. The students who came to Mississippi during Freedom

Summer in 1964, for example, resided in Mound Bayou for security.[34] But the Mound Bayou story is more about the triumph of Black capitalism than Black communalism. The Davis Bend and Mound Bayou experiments were not egalitarian cooperatives or interracial utopias. Rather, they were paternalistic capitalist endeavors that reflected Robert Owen's successes and limitations in his original New Lanark experiment. But the idealism of a self-governed and prosperous Black community should not be overlooked. As Aurellius Hood declared, "If only one man shall be brought to discover for himself the roadway to the betterment of his own condition and be induced from consideration of the facts herein set out to follow the path thus blazed we shall feel that our labor shall not have been altogether in vain."[35] The labor of cutting the dense brush, growing and milling cotton, and building community institutions was done with common goals and outside the purview of white Mississippians. It was cooperative in the sense of having a common purpose.

Robert Owen's utopian plans also impacted northern communities in the antebellum period, where white abolitionists set up communes to aid free Black families. In New York, the progressive white real estate baron Gerrit Smith worked with the radical abolitionist John Brown to create a community that provided land ownership for African American families. The discriminatory 1821 New York State Constitution required African American men to own property of at least $250 in value in order to vote. In response, Smith purchased 120,000 acres of land in the Adirondacks that he divided into forty-acre plots and distributed to three thousand African Americans. John Brown purchased land near the settlement and named the community Timbuctoo. The experiment lasted only a decade. Like so many agricultural utopias, such as Nashoba, the land proved difficult to clear and farm, and the Black settlers were largely from cities without the needed agricultural experience.[36] A more successful Northern endeavor was the Northampton Association of Education and Industry in Western Massachusetts, an abolitionist community between 1842 and 1846. Northampton more resembled communal utopias like Oneida and New Harmony, with families living, eating, and working together. Ten families, both Black and white, joined Northampton, including two of the most prominent Black abolitionists of the antebellum period, Sojourner Truth and David Ruggles. The residents ran a silk mill as a workers' cooperative, providing an alternative to Southern cotton. Although the communal aspect of Northampton lasted only four years, the radical politics and interracialism survived much longer.[37]

Building a Cooperative Commonwealth

The abolitionists at Northampton adopted a critical aspect of communal utopias that was not fully embraced by Joseph Davis or Isaiah Montgomery, the cooperative. By the mid-nineteenth century, consumer and producer cooperatives had gained popularity in the United States. Most American cooperatives were based on the writings of a group of British weavers who were followers of Robert Owen, the Rochdale Society of Equitable Pioneers. In the 1840s the group drew up a set of rules, which allowed their cooperative to be replicated internationally. Rochdale cooperatives were voluntary groups that refused to discriminate in their membership. Proponents of Black cooperatives saw this as an essential element of their success. Writing in 1942, Samuel Lloyd Myers wrote, "there should exist no actual limitation of membership to those of a particular race or occupation, for as the cooperative grows, the tendency for concentration of membership will tend to make the organization clannish, thus causing it to stand aloof from the cooperative movement and preventing it from growing and expanding in the sense suggested above."[38] Rochdale consumer cooperatives sold their wares to the community at market prices and gave their members periodic rebates and discounts on goods. Members invested in the cooperative equally and received dividends based on their purchases. Workers founded the first American cooperatives based on Rochdale's rules in 1863, and they proliferated throughout the late nineteenth century. They were particularly popular among freedpeople, who could combine their scarce resources to run cooperatives rather than become dependent on plantation owners or exploitative white-owned stores that charged exorbitant prices. For Myers and many other African American scholars and activists, the Rochdale cooperatives were not just an economic entity, but a transformative social movement.[39]

The most significant proponent of cooperatives in the early twentieth century was W. E. B. DuBois. Although DuBois was critical of Isaiah Montgomery's accommodationism in the political sphere, he admired the tenacious economic achievements of Mound Bayou. In 1907 he published a study on "Economic Cooperation Among Negro Americans," which was compiled at Atlanta University's "Conference for the Study of the Negro's Problems." This study defined cooperation broadly, much as Robert Owen did, and included Davis Bend and Mound Bayou as examples because those community members worked together to build Black economic wealth.[40] Over time DuBois's commitment to cooperation only grew. In 1918 he founded the Negro Cooperative Guild and traveled the country promoting cooperatives as a solution to economic marginalization.[41] For the next two decades DuBois continued to champion cooperatives. In 1933 he explicitly invoked nineteenth-century utopian socialist communities as a model for African Americans suffering at the height of the Great Depression. "Going back to the preaching of Robert Owen and Charles Fourier," wrote DuBois, "we can by consumers and producers cooperation, by phalansteries and garden cities, establish a progressively self-supporting economy that will weld the majority of our people into an impregnable, economic phalanx."[42] And in his 1940 book *Dusk to Dawn*, DuBois reflected on the possibility of building "a co-operative commonwealth" that would begin in African American neighborhoods and, when economically secure, would seek alliances with white cooperatives.[43]

DuBois was joined in his efforts at promoting cooperatives by a young Ella Baker, the highly skilled civil rights activist and organizer. George Schuyler, editor of the *Pittsburgh Courier*, hired Baker to run the Young Negroes' Cooperative League (YNCL) in 1930. The YNCL was a coalition of local cooperatives that offered workshops and training sessions nationwide. Baker won a scholarship to a Cooperative Institute held at New York's Brookwood Labor College in 1931, part of the workers' education movement central to the spread of cooperatives.[44] Progressive workers' education and folk schools actively pursued cooperatives, most notably at Brookwood and the Highlander Folk School in Tennessee. Workers' education was developed by working- and middle-class women who embraced an expansive version of organized labor, which prefigured the "culture of unity" of the Congress of Industrial Organizations (CIO) in the 1930s.[45] Called "social unionism," it tied the growth of the labor movement to a larger movement of social change to create a more egalitarian world, including cooperatives.[46] Workers' education also promoted labor interracialism, a philosophy that elevated racial cooperation among the working classes as integral to a more egalitarian future.[47]

During the Great Depression, the height of labor interracialism, Black Owenites moved decisively away from the Black capitalism of the Montgomery family and Booker T. Washington toward a more socialist orientation that centered Rochdale cooperatives. Indeed, it was during the Great Depression that the cooperative movement was at its strongest. The economic crisis motivated African Americans to pool their assets and search for alternatives to free market capitalism. Popular among socialists and small entrepreneurs alike, cooperatives provided much-needed resources to urban Black residents. And rural cooperatives provided safety and hope to displaced sharecroppers, both white and Black agricultural workers. Unlike the separatist communities such as Mound Bayou, many Depression-era cooperatives were interracial, reflecting the left-wing popular front politics of the time. Participants at a 1938 study tour of Nova Scotia's cooperatives organized by the Cooperative League of the USA, for example, were one-third Black. One of those who attended that tour was the Black educator Alethea Washington, who argued in 1939, "The cooperative movement is based on the deep and abiding religious principles of honesty, justice, equality, brotherhood, and love. The cooperative movement is inter-faith, inter-class, and inter-race. Therefore, it gives us that common meeting ground which produces the best setting for working together."[48] For Washington, DuBois, and many others, cooperation went beyond economic necessity to embrace a utopian vision of a better, more egalitarian future.

As Black urban communities grew in the Great Migration era following World War I, they began to form cooperatives that, in many cases, flourished into the 1950s. In Buffalo, New York, for example, two prominent African Americans, Jesse Taylor and E. E. Nelson, formed the Citizens Cooperative Society in 1928. Their goal was to "revolutionize the living and working conditions among the working classes."[49] By 1931 they opened their first store, a cooperative grocery, and worked to educate Black Buffalonians that Rochdale cooperatives could both elevate racial pride and provide economic security. In 1939, the newly renamed Buffalo Cooperative Economic Society opened another grocery store and a federal credit union. With the proceeds, they were able to purchase a building in 1944 that, along with the store, housed two apartments and a recreation center.[50]

Similar Rochdale cooperatives promoting self-sufficiency emerged in Gary, Indiana; Kansas City, Missouri; New Haven, Connecticut; and Chicago, Illinois.[51] Jacob L. Reddix, a leading proponent of cooperatives during the 1930s and 1940s, built a particularly successful network of cooperatives in Gary. "I concluded from my studies that a cooperative system might well be a way out for black people who were entrapped by unemployment, poor wages, and economic exploitation in the United States," remembered Reddix. "If the black workers could pool their purchasing and productive power they might lift themselves by their own boot straps."[52] In Washington, DC, a group of Black women, led by the educator Nannie Helen Burroughs, organized the "Cooperative Industries," a producer and consumer cooperative designed to provide employment for "unemployed workers and home-makers."[53] Black women such as Burroughs and Ella Baker were important figures in the cooperative movement during the Great Depression. They used their power as consumers to support Black businesses, including cooperatives, and boycott white stores that refused to hire African Americans by forming "housewives leagues" in cities like Detroit and Harlem.[54]

Writing in 1940, John Hope II, an African American economist and civil rights activist, pointed out that racism sometimes stymied cooperatives' success. "We see a serious potential threat to a strong movement in those areas where he is not given his full citizenship rights."[55] Those areas included both the sharecropping counties in rural Mississippi, where white supremacists worked to undermine Black cooperatives, and the burgeoning cities of the Midwest, which were deeply segregated. But despite these limitations, Rochdale cooperatives offered a form of resistance more potent than more isolated Black capitalist strategies, which emphasized private profit rather than community cooperation. As Alethea Washington suggested, "Through consumers' cooperation we will build a cooperative economic society. Its principle of open membership will give us economic brotherhood. Its principle of 'one person, one vote' will give us economic democracy."[56] Similarly, Samuel Myers argued, "Consumers' cooperation is not only an economic plan. It is educational, social, and in a sense religious as well."[57] This was a utopian vision of a new society that reached beyond economic nationalism to community transformation. Myers's invocation of religion as an aspect of cooperation is best seen in the most visible African American utopian movement in the twentieth century, Father Divine's Peace Mission, an intentional community that created a cooperative empire.

Father Divine was, arguably, the most successful Black Owenite.[58] He built an economic empire in Harlem and elsewhere during the 1930s and 1940s, with hundreds of cooperative businesses from gas stations and restaurants to boarding houses and retail stores. His Peace Mission drew from multiple legacies, including the entrepreneurship promoted by Booker T. Washington and socialist utopian communities such as Llano del Rio in California. Similarly, Divine's religious teachings are an amalgamation of white Protestant beliefs, most importantly New Thought, and the African American prophetic tradition. These beliefs led to a profoundly disruptive politics, as Divine preached that all humans, across race and gender, were fully equal and should live this reality in interracial homes and communities. The Divinites embraced a present and future entirely free of racial categories, practicing utopian interracialism.[59] By the mid-1930s, Father Divine's Peace mission was the largest realty holder in Harlem, with three apartment houses, nine private houses, fifteen to twenty apartments and meeting halls, twenty-five restaurants, six groceries, ten barber shops, ten cleaning stores, twenty-four wagons, and a coal business, all run as cooperatives. By the end of the Depression, the Peace Mission was handling millions of dollars annually and had savings reportedly in excess of $15 million.[60] This economic success suggests that tying Rochdale cooperatives to a utopian vision better fulfilled the Owenite dream of a new society than isolated urban cooperatives alone.

The cooperative labor Divinites provided at the Peace Mission's restaurants, resorts, and groceries was rewarded with communal housing, plentiful food, and security from the ravages of the Great Depression. Divine's followers changed their names; many practiced celibacy, and the abundant healthy food and renouncing of tobacco and alcohol often transformed their physical health. As stated in a manual on church discipline, "It shall be a violation of the Discipline of this Church for any Member to smoke, chew tobacco, gamble, use profane language, indulge in intoxicating liquors, indulge in the lusts of the flesh, or participate in any of the vices, fancies, tendencies and unwholesome pleasures of the world."[61] There was plenty of food, music, and dancing at Peace Mission settlements, but "the vices of the world" were set aside in this earthly heaven. The Father Divine movement is the premier example of the economic efficiency of utopian communalism. In the nineteenth century, Owenite communities such as New Harmony, Economy, and Amana had success as farmers and small-scale industrialists. The Oneida community, for example, achieved prosperity manufacturing silverware and other products in the mid- to late nineteenth century. But at its height, the Peace Mission boasted thousands of properties and supplied low-cost housing and food for hundreds of thousands.

Initially the Peace Mission cooperatives were located in urban centers, primarily Harlem and later Philadelphia. But in 1935 Divine established an interlocking system of rural cooperatives in Ulster County, New York, which Divine called the Promised Land. It was situated about one hundred miles due north of Harlem and was accessible by steamboat, train, and car. It was an overwhelmingly white community, but for Divine this was an asset rather than a drawback. As he built his cooperative empire, he deliberately sought out opportunities to racially integrate communities despite threats of violence. At its height, the Promised Land consisted of thirty communities that housed twenty-three hundred people and was spread across about two thousand acres. In addition to farms with cows, chickens, and garden vegetables, the Promised Land boasted cooperative gas stations, restaurants, and tourist residences. Two large docks with lavish boathouses welcomed excursion steamers from the city. As with Divine's urban cooperatives, the Promised Land ran only on cash, and all the goods were sold below market rate.⁶² Father Divine's Promised Land attracted a significant amount of attention. The *New York Times*, for example, reported in 1939, "In this huge community that has facilities for feeding and lodging perhaps 10,000 persons at one time, where no person may smoke, drink or curse, there are cultivated farms, resort hotels, country clubs, estates, scores of houses and dormitories, all manner of restaurants, stores, gasoline stations, tailor shops, barber shops, garages and even two large docks with boathouses on the Hudson River, capable of accommodating the largest excursion steamers."⁶³ This was a new society that Robert Owen or Fanny Wright could admire, although a fully egalitarian and interracial community was never part of their vision.

Rural Owenites

The Promised Land was far from the only rural cooperative that benefited Black Owenites during the Great Depression. Although we often associate rural communes with the romantic ideals of middle-class whites, African Americans had a deep connection to the land. The ability to grow one's own food and live independently has been an aspiration for Booker T. Washington in the late nineteenth century to Black Nationalists in the late twentieth century.⁶⁴ As African Americans became increasingly urbanized during the Great Migration era, their previous rural homes could be an alluring alternative when faced with the urban North's housing and employment discrimination. That was true for the Divinites and vacationers who frequented the Promised Land. And in the South, creating rural cooperatives could protect the most vulnerable farmers and sharecroppers from economic and physical insecurity during the height of the Great Depression.

In the decades following emancipation, freedpeople like Isaiah Montgomery prioritized land ownership and building businesses, goals that continued into the twentieth century. In the 1880s, for example, in the midst of the Populist era, landless Black people and a small group of whites formed biracial lodges of the Cooperative Workers of America (CWA) in South Carolina to offer cooperative stores and schools.⁶⁵ In 1922 the National Federation of Colored Farmers provided education, financial assistance, and support to African American farmers and advocated "cooperative buying, production and marketing" to improve their lives.⁶⁶ This was particularly important for sharecroppers, who could undercut the overpriced plantation stores by buying goods at wholesale. These buying clubs and small cooperatives were less effective during the height of the Great Depression, when landowners threw Black and white sharecroppers off their land and refused to share government payments with them.[67] Thus, cooperatives were a partial remedy to a capitalist system that was brutalizing Southern workers. Organized labor was another, and sharecroppers fought back, creating the socialist-run Southern Tenant Farmers Union (STFU) in Arkansas and the communist-run Alabama Sharecroppers Union (ASU). One experiment epitomized the power of blending the cooperative and labor movements. The Delta Cooperative, which later expanded to a second farm, was a model producer and consumer cooperative and utopian community that sheltered displaced sharecroppers who had been evicted because of their activism in the STFU.[68]

Sherwood Eddy, a white Protestant missionary, established the Delta cooperative in 1936. After traveling to Arkansas to investigate racial violence against displaced Black and white STFU members, Eddy purchased land in rural Mississippi and transported twenty-four families to the new interracial community. "The great object of the Cooperative Farms," argued Eddy, "is to build a new type of manhood and a new social order amid the decay of the old system."[69] In recognition of the important heritage of Rochdale cooperatives, the Delta cooperators christened their new post office, store, community center, and school as "Rochdale."[70] A year later they developed a second farm, Providence. Black members of the cooperatives, which were located near Mound Bayou, had long memories of cooperative planning and resistance to white supremacy. And the Delta farm became an important destination for Christian socialists to meet and plan. Delta also was a model for New Deal administrators, particularly from the Farm Security Administration (FSA), which created large-scale cooperative communities in a similar model, although most of the New Deal cooperatives were segregated.[71] Cooperation, across racial lines and against a corrupt agricultural system, fueled a successful utopian experiment that lasted two decades before virulent white backlash brought it down.

Decline and Renewal

In the postwar period, cooperative communities of all kinds experienced significant decline. The Delta and Providence farms had always been targeted by white supremacists, but in the wake of the *Brown v. Board of Education* decision in 1954 these attacks increased dramatically. Faced with white harassment and terror, the trustees liquidated the cooperative and sold the land to individual families in 1956.[72] Like other New Deal Programs, the FSA fell victim to the growing congressional conservatism during and after the war years. Although conservatives had always attacked the FSA as radical, the patriotism behind the war effort escalated this rhetoric. Conservative congressmen claimed the communities were copies of Soviet Kolkhozy, collective farms built in Soviet Russia. Bowing to this pressure, during the war Congress ordered the liquidation of the FSA.[73] Urban cooperatives met a similar fate. The Buffalo Cooperative Society's businesses flourished during the 1940s; however, by 1961 they had gone bankrupt. Massive urban renewal projects in the city displaced the African American community, and chain supermarkets challenged the viability of the cooperatives.[74] Father Divine's Peace Mission also failed to flourish after World War II. Wartime employment largely ended the Great Depression, which also lessened the movement's appeal. Fewer people needed the low-cost cooperative housing, restaurants, and resorts. The farms and businesses in the Promised Land began to close rapidly, declining from twenty-five in 1942 to nine in 1950.[75] And in the broader society, many intellectuals and activists during the Cold War era became disenchanted with utopianism, linking it to the horrors of totalitarianism in Nazi Germany and the Soviet Union.[76]

But the dream of Black Owenites did not die with the Cold War. At the height of the civil rights movement in the 1960s, Mississippi again became a hotbed of cooperative experimentation. Mechanization of agriculture had largely taken away the few agricultural jobs left. In response, African American activists from civil rights organizations began to organize agricultural workers. One such project was the Mississippi Freedom Labor Union (MFLU) founded in 1965 to help cotton choppers and tractor drivers demand higher wages from plantation owners. They soon attracted the support of hundreds of workers and their families. When a dozen families on a single plantation demanded higher wages, the plantation owner swiftly evicted them. In an echo of the STFU, the MFLU set up a small community for displaced families that became known as "Strike City."[77] The successor to the FSA, the Farmers Home Administration, funded the start-up costs for a group of Black farmers in Panola County to purchase land and equipment and develop a successful cooperative. In a similar venture, an African American activist from Boston, Owen Brooks, developed the North Bolivar County Farm Cooperative, which housed 900 families producing food for themselves and the market. The legendary Mississippi activist Fannie Lou Hamer also built a cooperative she named Freedom

Farm, which included a "pig bank" that poor families could use to begin to raise their own livestock. In 1966 another civil rights legend, John Lewis, began to work with the Southern Regional Council's Community Organizing Project to run cooperatives.[78] Today the Mississippi Association of Cooperatives (part of Federation of Southern Cooperatives) includes ten cooperatives with a largely Black membership, "building from a tradition steeped in the civil rights movement."[79]

Black Nationalists also embraced cooperatives as a means of creating separate self-sufficient communities, similar to Isaiah Montgomery's Nationalist vision for Mound Bayou. The Republic of New Afrika moved to Mississippi in 1970 and established the "Provisional Government of the Republic of New Afrika," which they envisioned as a "*a new society* built with no color, class, gender and physical ability discrimination."[80] Although their efforts were stymied by local law enforcement and white resistance, in 2013 one of the activists, Chokwe Lumumba, was elected as mayor of Jackson, Mississippi, and helped to spearhead a project known as Cooperation Jackson. Under Lumumba's leadership, the citizens of Jackson engaged in participatory democracy to determine the city's budget and priorities. And, cognizant of the long history of Black Owenites, they launched a series of cooperatives that included agriculture, commerce, arts and culture.[81] A less successful attempt to create a utopian community based on Black Power principals was the establishment of Soul City in North Carolina. This was the brainchild of civil rights activist and lawyer Floyd B. McKissick. In contrast to the independent Father Divine Peace Mission or Delta Cooperative Farm, McKissick sought out federal funding for his utopia, which was to be built from scratch in a sparsely populated and economically depressed region. In 1972 he obtained a fourteen million dollar guarantee from the Department of Housing and Urban Development, working closely with the Nixon administration to obtain the funding. His plans were ambitious, including eight residential villages with schools, recreational facilities, and light industry. But only one of the villages was built, and McKissick struggled to get capital investment in the community. By 1979 the federal government withdrew all support for Soul City, and McKissick's plans never reached full fruition.[82]

McKissick's alliance with the Nixon administration is reminiscent of Isaiah Montgomery's willingness to accommodate the white supremacist Democratic Party in Mississippi. Both men sacrificed political autonomy for economic self-sufficiency. Other Black Power advocates who were strident critics of capitalism embraced cooperatives as a central aspect of economic nationalism without making the same compromises. Historian Joshua Clark Davis notes that in the 1960s and 1970s "activist entrepreneurs," including Black Power activists running bookstores and other businesses, "viewed their businesses as 'prefigurative institutions' that served as models for the democratic society that social movements hoped to build."[83] Many embraced the term *Ujamaa*, a Kiswahili word popularized by Tanzania's first Black president Julius K. Nyerere that promoted socialism through community. Maulana Karenga, the leader of the Black Power organization US and creator of the *Kwanzaa* holiday, popularized the term in the United States. Karenga explained that *Ujamaa* reflected a "commitment to the practice of shared social wealth," which included a cooperative economic model that would benefit the Black community.[84] Black Panther Party members and the Congress of African Peoples (CAP), led by poet and artist Amiri Baraka, also developed cooperative businesses in numerous cities during the late 1960s and 1970s.[85] This blending of Owenite cooperation and Black capitalism in the late twentieth century demonstrates the endurance of utopian dreaming.

Conclusion

In recent decades there has been something of a resurgence of utopian thought along the lines of Robert Owen's vision. The popularity of the Democratic Socialists of America resonates with nineteenth-century utopian socialism, the social unionism of the Progressive era, and the 1930s blending of labor and civil rights. Interest in building new cooperatives, both in rural Black communities and in segregated cities, has experienced a growth. For example, in the wake of George Floyd's murder, a group of African American women founded the Freedom Georgia Initiative, an intentional community in rural Georgia that was established "out of an extreme sense of urgency to create a thriving safe haven for Black families in the midst of racial trauma, a global pandemic, and economic instabilities across the United States of America brought on by COVID-19."[86] The freedpeople of Davis Bend sought a similar safe haven when they founded Mound Bayou. In Buffalo, the newly formed Cooperation Buffalo promotes and supports the creation of worker-owned cooperatives in the city, explicitly building on the legacy of mid-century Black coops.[87] Black Owenite experiments in cooperation ranged in their durability and commitment to a radically new society. But they all were committed to a form of self-determination, and they differed dramatically from the efforts of Wright and Davis to blend enslavement and utopian communalism. "The central idea of cooperation as a plan for the Negro," argued Myers, "is simply that the group may by united action free themselves from their precarious dependence on others and by their own resources improve their economic and social status."[88] African Americans' utopian vision always entailed this definition of cooperation, freedom from dependence, and freedom to dream.

Notes

1. Buffalo Food Equity Network, "Buffalo Food Justice Advocates and Partners Call for End to White Supremacy and Anti-Blackness," May 17, 2022, *Food for the Spirit*, https://www.cooperationbuffalo.org/about-us.

2. Lyman Tower Sargent, "The Three Faces of Utopianism Revisited," *Utopian Studies* 5, no. 1 (1994): 1–37.

3. Robin D. G. Kelley, *Freedom Dreams: The Black Radical Imagination* (New York: Beacon Press, 2002), 12. For an exploration of Black utopias from a literary perspective, see Alex Zamalin, *Black Utopia: The History of an Idea from Black Nationalism to Afrofuturism* (New York: Columbia University Press, 2019).

4. On the encounter between Owen and Davis, see Joel Nathan Rosen, *From New Lanark to Mound Bayou: Owenism in the Mississippi Delta* (Durham, NC: Carolina Academic Press, 2011), ix; Janet Sharp Hermann, *Joseph E. Davis: Pioneer Patriarch* (Jackson: University Press of Mississippi, 1990), 43–45.

5. Hermann, *Joseph E. Davis*, 43; Rosen, *From New Lanark to Mound Bayou*, 83.

6. Joel Nathan Rosen, *From New Lanark to Mound Bayou: Owenism in the Mississippi Delta* (Durham, NC: Carolina Academic Press, 2011), 8–15; Bestor, *Backwoods Utopia*, 60–132; Mark Holloway, *Heavens on Earth: Utopian Communities in America, 1680–1880* (New York: Dover Publications, 1966), 104–15; Edward K. Spann, *Brotherly Tomorrows: Movements for a Cooperative Society in American, 1820–1920* (New York: Columbia University Press, 1989), 17–49. Owen's most significant work, which was in Joseph Davis's library, was *A New View of Society*, published in 1816. For the influence of Fourier on American communal utopias, see Carl Guarneri, *The Utopian Alternative: Fourierism in Nineteenth-Century America* (Ithaca, NY: Cornell University Press, 1991).

7. In "Revisiting Nashoba: Slavery, Utopia, and Frances Wright in America, 1818–1826," *American Literary History* 17, no. 3 (2005): 438–59, Gail Bederman argues that Wright's travels with the Marquis de Lafayette in 1824, when she met and corresponded with illustrious planters such as Thomas Jefferson and James Madison, gave her an incomplete picture of how entrenched slavery was in America. On Wright's admiration of Owen, see Morris, *Fanny Wright*, 116–18; Holloway, *Heavens on Earth*, 114–15.

8. Frances Wright, "A Plan for the Gradual Abolition of Slavery," *New Harmony Gazette* I, no. 4–5 (October 1, 1825).

9. On Nashoba, see William H. Pease and Jane H. Pease, *Black Utopia: Negro Communal Experiments in America* (Madison: The State Historical Society of Wisconsin, 1963), 17, 22–35; Bederman, "Revisiting Nashoba"; Bestor, *Backwoods Utopias*, 220–26; Rosen, *From New Lanark to Mound Bayou*, 46, 81–82; and Celia Morris, *Fanny Wright: Rebel in America* (Chicago: University of Illinois Press, 1984), 108–40.

10. Quoted in Bestor, *Backwoods Utopias*, 224. See also Morris, *Fanny Wright*, 136–38. In Wright's absence, Richardson also punished the enslaved people at Nashoba with beatings and separated enslaved mothers from their children (Morris, *Fanny Wright*, 141–45).

11. Lori D. Ginzberg, "'The Hearts of Your Readers Will Shudder': Fanny Wright, Infidelity, and American Freethought," *American Quarterly* 46, no. 2 (1994): 195–226.

12. Morris, *Fanny Wright*, 164–66, 198; 207–8, 211–13.

13. Rosen, *From New Lanark to Mound Bayou*, 81. Rosen reports that Davis agreed to purchase one of Wright's "recalcitrant" enslaved workers and that the two remained friends (82). On Wright's influence on Davis, see also Hermann, *The Pursuit of a Dream*, 8–9; Hermann, *Joseph E. Davis*, 39–41.

14. Rosen, *From New Lanark to Mound Bayou*, 58.

15. Rosen, *From New Lanark to Mound Bayou*, 86–93; Hermann, *The Pursuit of a Dream*, 12–34; Eric Foner, *Reconstruction: America's Unfinished Revolution, 1863–1877* (New York: Harper & Row, 1988), 58–59.

16. Rosen, *From New Lanark to Mound Bayou*, 96–105; Hermann, *The Pursuit of a Dream*, 17–22.

17. Hermann, *The Pursuit of a Dream*, 38; Steven Hahn, *A Nation Under Our Feet: Black Political Struggles in the Rural South from Slavery to the Great Migration* (Boston: Harvard University Press, 2003), 80.

18. Foner, *Reconstruction*, 59. Isaiah Montgomery spent much of the war serving with the Union Navy.

19. Hermann, *The Pursuit of a Dream*, 46–64.

20. Rosen, *From New Lanark to Mound Bayou*, 111; Foner, *Reconstruction*, 162.

21. "Truth Is Stranger Than Fiction," July 5, 187, in *A Brighter Coming Day: A Frances Ellen Watkins Harper Reader*, ed. Frances Smith Foster (New York: The Feminist Press, 1993), 132. Harper was particularly impressed by the work done by women on the plantation and befriended one of Montgomery's daughters. I am grateful to James Holstun for alerting me to this source.

22. Rosen, *From New Lanark to Mound Bayou*, 105–14; Hermann, *The Pursuit of a Dream*, 104–95, 209; Ronald Love, "Community in Transition: A Study of Mound Bayou, Mississippi" (PhD diss., Boston University, 1982), 11–12; Norman L. Crockett, *The Black Towns* (Lawrence: University Press of Kansas, 2021), 10–12.

23. Rosen, *From New Lanark to Mound Bayou*, 121; Hermann, *The Pursuit of a Dream*, 220. William Thornton eventually abandoned this endeavor to join his brother in the warmer climate of Mississippi.

24. Aurellius P. Hood, "The Negro at Mound Bayou: Being an Authentic Story of the Founding, Growth, and Development of the "Most Celebrated Town in the South" (A.P. Hood, 1909), 6. On the belief that Black people were immune to malaria, see also Love, "Community in Transition," 13; and Hamilton, *Black Towns and Profit*, 45.

25. Hermann, *The Pursuit of a Dream*, 223; Hood, "The Negro at Mound Bayou," 9–15; Love, "Community in Transition," 16–18.

26. Rosen, *From New Lanark to Mound Bayou*, 131–35; Hermann, *The Pursuit of a Dream*, 219–35; Kenneth Marvin Hamilton, *Black Towns and Profit: Promotion and Development in the Trans-Appalachian West, 1877–1915* (Urbana: University of Illinois Press, 1991), 43–98; Hamilton, *Black Towns and Profit*, 55–56.

27. Black capitalism is a growing historical subfield. For representative works, see Laura Warren Hill and Julia Rabig, eds., *The Business of Black Power: Community Development, Capitalism, and Corporate Responsibility in Postwar America* (Rochester: University of Rochester Press, 2012); Marcia Chatelaine, *Franchise: The Golden Arches in Black America* (New York: Liverwright, 2020); and Nathan Connolly, *A World More Concrete: Real Estate and the Remaking of Jim Crow South Florida* (Chicago: University of Chicago Press, 2016).

28. Booker T. Washington, "Law and Order and the Negro," *Outlook* (November 6, 1909): 547.

29. Hood, "The Negro at Mound Bayou," 50; Love, "Community in Transition," 20; Hahn, *A Nation Under Our Feet*, 454–55; Crockett, *The Black Towns*, 129–31.

30. On the relationship between Booker T. Washington and Mound Bayou, see August Meier, "Booker T. Washington and the Town of Mound Bayou," *Phylon* 15, no. 4 (1954): 396–401; Rosen, *From New Lanark to Mound Bayou*, 137–38; Hermann, *The Pursuit of a Dream*, 232–34; Hood, "The Negro at Mound Bayou," 12–14, 26; Crockett, *The Black Towns*, 126–27; Hamilton, *Black Towns and Profit*, 56–61.

31. Rosen, *From New Lanark to Mound Bayou*, 139–44; Hermann, *The Pursuit of a Dream*, 230–31; Hahn, *A Nation Under Our Feet*, 447; Hamilton, *Black Towns and Profit*, 55.

32. Hood, "The Negro at Mound Bayou," 116.

33. Rosen, *From New Lanark to Mound Bayou*, 147.

34. Love, "Community in Transition," 29–32.

35. Hood, "The Negro at Mound Bayou," 1.

36. On Timbuctoo, see Sally V. Svenson, *Blacks in the Adirondacks: A History* (Syracuse: Syracuse University Press, 2017), 19–29; "Timbuctoo African American History in the Adirondacks," *Adirondack Journal*, https://www.theadkx.org/timbucto-

african-american-history-in-the-adirondacks/. The settlement area is entirely reforested, and there are no remnants of the community surviving.

37. Christopher Clark, *The Communitarian Moment: The Radical Challenge of the Northampton Association* (Ithaca, NY: Cornell University Press, 1995); Arthur E. Bestor Jr., "Fourierism in Northampton: A Critical Note," *New England Quarterly* 12 (1940): 110–22; Holloway, *Heavens on Earth*, 127–28.

38. Myers, "Consumers' Cooperation," 39.

39. Jessica Gordon Nembhard, *Collective Courage: A History of African American Cooperative Economic Thought and Practice* (University Park: Pennsylvania State University Press, 2014), 22, 49, 71–77; John Hope II, "Rochdale Cooperation Among Negroes," *Phylon* 1, no. 1 (1940), 39–52; Myers, "Consumers' Cooperation," 4–9; John Curl, *For All the People: Uncovering the Hidden History of Cooperation, Cooperative Movements, and Communalism in America* (Oakland: PM Press, 2009), 56–57.

40. W. E. B. DuBois, *Economic Cooperation Among Negro Americans; Some Efforts of American Negroes for their Own Social Betterment* (Atlanta: Atlanta University Press, 1907), 38–39, 171–72. Myers argues that the list of businesses, including those at Mound Bayou, in DuBois's study were not actually cooperatives but private businesses "attempting to solve the economic problems of the group of which they were a segment" (Myers, "Consumers' Cooperation," 46). A similar Atlanta University study was published a decade later; see Thomas I. Brown, ed., *Economic Co-operation among the Negroes of Georgia* (Atlanta: Atlanta University Press, 1917).

41. Nembhard, *Collective Courage*, 32, 103–6. See also Lizabeth Cohen, *A Consumers' Republic: The Politics of Mass Consumption in Postwar America* (New York: Alfred A. Knopf, 2003), 49.

42. W. E. B. DuBois, "The Right to Work," *Crisis* (April 1933): 93.

43. W. E. B. DuBois, *Dusk of Dawn: An Essay Toward an Autobiography of a Race Concept* (Oxford University Press, 2007, 1940), 108.

44. Nembhard, *Collective Courage*, 89–91, 113–20; Cohen, *Consumer's Republic*, 50; Barbara Ransby, *Ella Baker and the Black Freedom Movement: A Radical Democratic Vision* (Chapel Hill: University of North Carolina Press, 2003), 82–91; Victoria W. Wolcott, *Living in the Future: Utopianism and the Long Civil Rights Movement* (Chicago: University of Chicago Press, 2022), 21–23.

45. On the "culture of unity," see Lizabeth Cohen, *Making a New Deal: Industrial Workers in Chicago, 1919–1939* (New York: Cambridge, 1990).

46. Daniel Katz, *All Together Different: Yiddish Socialists, Garment Workers, and the Labor Roots of Multiculturalism* (New York: New York University Press, 2011), 20; Susan Stone Wong, "From Soul to Strawberries: The International Ladies' Garment Workers' Union and Workers' Education, 1914–1950," in *Sisterhood and Solidarity: Workers' Education for Women, 1914–1984*, ed. Joyce L. Kornbluh and Mary Frederickson (Philadelphia: Temple University Press, 1984), 43; Richard J. Altenbaugh, *Education for Struggle: The American Labor Colleges of the 1920s and*

1930s (Philadelphia: Temple University Press, 1990). See also the special issue on Workers' Education in *International Labor and Working-Class History* 90 (fall 2016).

47. Victoria W. Wolcott, "Networks of Resistance: Floria Pinkney and Labor Interracialism in Interwar America," *Journal of African American History* 105, no. 4 (fall 2020): 567–92.

48. Alethea H. Washington, "Section B: Rural Education—The Cooperative Movement," *Journal of Negro Education* 8, no. 1 (January 1939): 105. On the tour there were nineteen African Americans and thirty-five whites.

49. Quoted in Monroe Fordham, *The Buffalo Cooperative Society, 1928–1961* (Buffalo: Buffalo State College, 1975), 1.

50. Fordham, *The Buffalo Cooperative Society*, 8–12. On the Buffalo Cooperative Economic Society, see also Myers, "Consumers' Cooperation," 59; Nembhard, *Collective Courage*, 122. Nembhard notes that the original Citizens Cooperative Society was a branch of Baker's Young Negroes Cooperative League.

51. Hope, "Rochdale Cooperation Among Negroes," 40–43. On the Gary cooperatives, see J. L. Reddix, *The Negro Seeks Economic Freedom Through Cooperation* (Chicago: Central States Cooperative League, 1936), 9–10; Myers, "Consumers' Cooperation," 51–53; "Consumers' Cooperation Among Negroes in Gary, Indiana," *Monthly Labor Review* 42, no. 2 (February 1936): 369–71. Nembhard, in *Collective Courage*, also points to Rochdale cooperative stores in Memphis and Harlem (76–77, 133).

52. Jacob L. Reddix, *A Voice Crying in the Wilderness* (Jackson: University Press of Mississippi, 1974), 118. Reddix became an "advisor on cooperatives" for the Farm Security Administration in 1939 (122).

53. Hope, "Rochdale Cooperation Among Negroes," 46; Nembhard, *Collective Courage*, 151.

54. Victoria W. Wolcott, *Remaking Respectability: African American Women in Interwar Detroit* (Chapel Hill: University of North Carolina Press, 2001), 176–83; Cohen, *Consumer's Republic*, 50–53.

55. Hope, "Rochdale Cooperation Among Negroes," 52.

56. Washington, "Section B: Rural Education," 105.

57. Myers, "Consumers' Cooperation," 87.

58. Biographical works on Father Divine include Robert Weisbrot, *Father Divine and the Struggle for Racial Equality* (Urbana: University of Illinois Press, 1983); Jill Watts, *God, Harlem U.S.A.* (Berkeley: University of California Press, 1992); Harris, *Father Divine*; and Kenneth E. Burnham, *God Comes to America: Father Divine and the Peace Mission Movement* (Boston: Lambeth Press, 1979). The Father Divine movement is recognized by scholars as a utopian community. See Timothy Miller, *The Quest for Utopia in Twentieth-Century America* (Syracuse: Syracuse University Press, 1998), 83–84; Robert Weisbrot, "Father Divine and the Peace Mission," in *America's Communal Utopias*, ed. Donald E. Pitzer (University

of North Carolina Press, 1997), 432–44; Robert S. Fogarty, *Dictionary of American Communal and Utopian History* (Westport, CT: Greenwood Press, 1980), 31–32; Wolcott, *Living in the Future*, 87–116.

59. Wolcott, *Living in the Future*, 88, 96, 106, 109, 115–16, 118.

60. Weisbrot, "Father Divine and the Peace Mission," 436; Charles Samuel Braden, *"These Also Believe": A Study of Modern American Cults and Minority Religious Movements* (New York: MacMillan, 1956), 13–15; Weisbrot, *Father Divine*, 122.

61. "Church Discipline, Constitution and By-Laws," c. 1941, 8, folder 1, "Circle Mission, Inc.," Box One, Father Divine Collection, Schomburg Library, New York, NY.

62. For the history of Promised Land, see Carleton Mabee, *Promised Land: Father Divine's Interracial Communities in Ulster County, New York* (Fleischmanns, NY: Purple Mountain Press, 2008); Weisbrot, *Father Divine*, 6, 124–34; Watts, *God, Harlem U.S.A.*, 137–38; McKay, *Harlem*, 50–53. See also "'Father Divine' Rides High: Angels Own $212,000 Worth of Real Estate," *Chicago Defender*, July 8, 1939, 2.

63. "Robert S. Bird, "Father Divine's Movement Expands," *New York Times*, July 2, 1939, E10.

64. On Booker T. Washington, see Dona Brown, *Back to the Land: The Enduring Dream of Self-Sufficiency in Modern America* (Madison: University of Wisconsin Press, 2011), 51; Monica M. White, *Freedom Farmers: Agricultural Resistance and the Black Freedom Movement* (Chapel Hill: University of North Carolina Press, 2018), 28–62. On Black Nationalist agrarianism, see Russell Rickford, "'We Can't Grow Food on All This Concrete': The Land Question, Agrarianism, and Black Nationalist Thought in the late 1960s and 1970s," *Journal of American History* 103, no. 4 (March 2017): 956–80; Steven Conn, *Americans Against the City: Anti-Urbanism in the Twentieth Century* (New York: Oxford University Press, 2014), 266–69. On the "whiteness" of nature, see Paul Outka, *Race and Nature: From Transcendentalism to the Harlem Renaissance* (New York: Palgrave Macmillan, 2008).

65. Nembhard, *Collective Courage*, 52–53; Hahn, *A Nation Under Our Feet*, 418–19.

66. Hope, "Rochdale Cooperation Among Negroes," 48–49. On rural cooperatives, see also Nembhard, *Collective Courage*, 172–88; Curl, *For All the People*, 186–86; and White, *Freedom Farmers*.

67. When Roosevelt came to office in 1933, he sought to aid farmers by passing the Agricultural Adjustment Act (AAA), which paid landowners for voluntarily reducing their crops. The federal government instructed landowners to share these payments with their tenants, but they often simply refused or evicted tenants altogether. See Nan Elizabeth Woodruff, *American Congo: The African American Freedom Struggle in the Delta* (Cambridge: Harvard University Press, 2003), 157–58; Robert H. Craig, *Religion and Radical Politics: An Alternative Christian Tradition in the United States* (Philadelphia: Temple University Press, 1992), 152–53; Mark

Fannin, *Labor's Promised Land: Radical Visions of Gender, Race, and Religion in the South* (Knoxville: University of Tennessee Press, 2003), 91; Howard Kester, *Revolt Among the Sharecroppers* (New York: J. J. Little and Ives Company, 1936), 27–54.

68. For a comprehensive history of the Delta and Providence Cooperative Farms, see Robert Hunt Ferguson, *Remaking the Rural South: Interracialism, Christian Socialism, and Cooperative Farming in Jim Crow Mississippi* (Atlanta: University of Georgia Press, 2018). See also Fannin, *Labor's Promised Land*, 123–25; Anthony P. Dunbar, *Against the Grain: Southern Radicals and Prophets, 1929–1959* (Charlottesville: University Press of Virginia, 1981), 114–20; Fred C. Smith, *Trouble in Goshen: Plain Folk, Roosevelt, Jesus, and Marx in the Great Depression South* (Oxford: University Press of Mississippi, 2014), 114–42; Vaneesa Cook, *Spiritual Socialists: Religion and the American Left* (Philadelphia: University of Pennsylvania Press, 2019), 56, 62–68; Rick L. Nutt, *The Whole Gospel for the Whole World: Sherwood Eddy and the American Protestant Mission* (Macon, GA: Mercer University Press, 1997), 275–80; and Wolcott, *Living in the Future*, 55–86.

69. Sherwood Eddy, *A Door of Opportunity or An American Adventure in Cooperation with Sharecroppers* (New York: Eddy and Page, 1937), 58.

70. Sam H. Franklin Jr. to Dr. Alfred Lee Wilson, September 24, 1937, folder 14, box 2, Delta and Providence Cooperative Farm Papers, Southern Historical Collection, University of North Carolina, Chapel Hill, North Carolina; Sam H. Franklin Jr. to Dr. Alfred Lee Wilson, September 24, 1937, folder 14, box 2, Delta and Providence Cooperative Farm Papers.

71. Donald Holley, *Uncle Sam's Farmers: The New Deal Communities in the Lower Mississippi Valley* (Chicago: University of Illinois Press, 1975); Paul Conkin, *Tomorrow a New World: The New Deal Community Program* (Ithaca, NY: Cornell University Press, 1959); Brian Q. Cannon, *Remaking the Agrarian Dream: New Deal Rural Resettlement in the Mountain West* (Albuquerque: University of New Mexico Press, 1996); Sidney Baldwin, *Poverty and Politics: The Rise and Decline of the Farm Security Administration* (Chapel Hill: University of North Carolina Press, 1968). FSA communities explicitly modeled themselves after utopian communities. Planners studied the nineteenth-century Shaker, Rappite, and Oneida colonies. New Deal agencies built nearly one hundred communities, fifty-two of which were fully cooperative. Nine of the cooperative communities were African American.

72. Sam H. Franklin Jr., "Early Years of the Delta Cooperative Farm and the Providence Cooperative Farm," 87, 88–89, 90–91, undated, p. 83, folder 188, box 19, Delta and Providence Cooperative Farm Papers; Ferguson, *Remaking the Rural South*, 123–26. A summer camp and health clinic, run by talented Black educator Fannie Booker, ran at the former Providence farm into the 1970s.

73. Baldwin, *Poverty and Politics*, 3; Holley, *Uncle Sam's Farmers*, 137; Grubbs, *Cry from the Cotton*, 160. The cooperative associations canceled their leases and gave farm families a mortgage to their land and homes. In 1946, President Truman

abolished the FSA and replaced it with the Farmers Home Administration, which subsidized private land ownership rather than communal and cooperative projects.

74. Fordham, *The Buffalo Cooperative Society*, 15.

75. Carleton Maybee, *Promised Land: Father Divine's Interracial Communities in Ulster County, New York* (New York: AbeBooks, 2008), 201–2; 209–10. Divinites sold the last Promised Land property, Kingston Mansion, in 1985 (217).

76. Arthur M. Schlesinger Jr., *The Vital Center: The Politics of Freedom* (Boston: Houghton Mifflin, 1949); Daniel Bell, *The End of Ideology: On the Exhaustion of Political Ideas in the Fifties* (New York: The Free Press, 1960), esp. "The Exhaustion of Utopia," 275–409; Judith N. Shklar, *After Utopia: The Decline of Political Faith* (Princeton: Princeton University Press, 1957); Hannah Arendt, *Origins of Totalitarianism* (Cleveland: World Publishing Company, 1958); Karl Popper, *The Origins of Totalitarian Democracy* (New York: Praeger, 1960); and J. L. Tallmon, *The Origins of Totalitarian Democracy* (New York: Praeger, 1960).

77. John Dittmer, *Local People: The Struggle for Civil Rights in Mississippi* (Chicago: University of Illinois Press, 1994), 365.

78. Dittmer, *Local People*, 365; Nembhard, *Collective Courage*, 178–80, 218; White, *Freedom Farmers*, 65–87.

79. http://www.mississippiassociation.coop/about-us/.

80. Edward Onaci, *Free the Land: The Republic of New Africa and the Pursuit of a Black Nation-State* (Chapel Hill: University of North Carolina Press, 2020), 79–112; Kali Akuno and Ajamu Nangwaya, *Jackson Rising: The Struggle for Economic Democracy and Black Self-Determination in Jackson, Mississippi* (Ottawa: Daraja Press, 2017), xii. They changed the spelling of Africa to the Swahili spelling, Afrika. On the role of Southern cooperatives for Black nationalists, see Rickford, "'We Can't Grow Food on All This Concrete.'"

81. "Cooperation Jackson," https://cooperationjackson.org/; Akuno and Nangwaya, *Jackson Rising*.

82. Christopher Strain, "Soul City, North Carolina: Black Power, Utopia, and the African American Dream," *Journal of African American History* 89, no. 1 (winter 2004): 7–74; Thomas Healy, *Soul City: Race, Equality, and the Lost Dream of an American Utopia* (New York: Metropolitan Books, 2021); Floyd McKissick, *Three-Fifths of a Man* (New York: Macmillan Company, 1969); Floyd B. McKissick, *Soul City North Carolina* (Soul City, NC: The Company, 1974).

83. Joshua Clark Davis, *From Head Shops to Whole Foods: The Rise and Fall of Activist Entrepreneurs* (New York: Columbia University Press, 2017), 22.

84. Maulana Karenga, "The Seven Principles," in *Modern Black Nationalism: From Marcus Garvey to Louis Farrakhan*, ed. William L. Van Deburg (New York: New York University Press, 1997), 282; Scott Brown, *Fighting for Us: Maulana Karenga, The Us Organization, and Black Cultural Nationalism* (New York: New York University Press, 2003), 14–15.

85. Nembhard, *Collective Courage*, 219–20.

86. "The Freedom Georgia Initiative," https://thefreedomgeorgiainitiative.com/.

87. On Cooperation Buffalo, see "Cooperation Buffalo," https://www.cooperationbuffalo.org/.

88. Myers, "Consumers' Cooperation," 83.

3

"The Women Activists Found Little Peace at Bucolic School"

Utopian Dreams, Radical Feminist Nightmares, and the Pedagogical Potential of Sagaris

KATELYN M. CAMPBELL

Sagaris. The word hisses as it flows off of my tongue, unfamiliar, when I first stumble upon it in the archive. I am an eager first-year graduate student visiting the papers of Rita Mae Brown—a famous radical and lesbian feminist activist and novelist whose documents are housed in Special Collections at the University of Virginia. I traveled to Charlottesville not knowing what I would find but feeling some sense of urgency to see what Brown's papers had to show me. And here, in a letter tucked in a folder of correspondence between Brown and Gloria Steinem, this new term appeared.[1]

Sagaris was a radical feminist school conceived by Brown and a host of some of the most famous radical feminists of her day in the mid-1970s. Organizers, many of whom were part of the creation of the field of Women's Studies, were interested in creating a space where women could travel for further study and training in feminist philosophy that went beyond consciousness-raising while building an institution that would be able to withstand the test of time. The Institute hosted a successful first session of its summer school in 1975 before erupting into conflict and controversy during the second session several weeks later when a controversy split the school in two. A group of defectors split off into a separate camp in response to allegations by radical feminist group the Redstockings that Steinem, whose Ms. Foundation was a major funder of the school, had been a CIA collaborator.[2] This conflict was the subtext of Brown's letter exchange with Steinem that brought the Institute to my attention in the archive.

Despite Sagaris's wide advertisement, superstar roster, and subsequent controversy, the Institute seldom appears in histories of 1970s feminisms. When I began seeking out more information about Sagaris, it seemed that much of movement historiography had engaged in an act of collective non-remembrance when it came to the Institute—occasionally it might appear in a footnote or was mentioned offhand, but outside of the archive I rarely if ever saw Sagaris referred to beyond a whisper.[3] The failed promise of Sagaris's utopian experiment—that it would be the site from which the feminist revolution would finally spring forth—had become a source of embarrassment.

In the nearly five decades since the dissolution of Sagaris, feminisms have continued to shift and change. Particularly in the wake of the emergence and proliferation of anti-identitarian modes of theorizing,[4] the feminisms of Sagaris are often regarded to be what theorist Elizabeth Freeman has called a "temporal drag" for queer theory especially, tying the field to an essentialist past it would rather forget.[5] However, despite the changes in feminisms alongside the emergence of "queer" grammars, the question of how to bring about feminist revolution remains pertinent and urgent, particularly amid the resurgence of neofascist and misogynist politics in the United States and around the world. At the time of this writing, the Supreme Court has just overturned *Roe v. Wade* (1973), removing guarantees residents of its states and territories once had to the right to abortion. In the wake of the decision, amid my own feelings of helplessness, I observed hundreds of people in my broader social media networks posting online about their confusion about what steps to take. In a moment when millions of people were eager to take some kind of action, it seemed that the only option available was to send money to organizations and collectives providing direct support to patients. While these financial contributions support critical work, I could not help but think of Sagaris's long-ago call for a need to ready the ground for feminist revolution so there would be a broad enough network of activists to receive people when it came time to fan a nascent spark into a flame. I know I was not the only person longing for some in-person place to do that kind of work after the end of *Roe*.

What do unrealized utopian dreams like Sagaris have to teach us about the futures we desire and how we might build them? In keeping with Heather

Love's call in *Feeling Backward* (2007) to make space for negative affects within queer history, I felt myself continuously drawn back to Sagaris in spite of the fog and red flags that surrounded it, sifting through boxes and keyword searches to find a way back to some version of the truth through the veil of shame.[6] In the years since my initial encounter with Sagaris in Virginia, I have slowly pieced together some of the broken shards of the story of what happened through archival research across several geographically disparate collections to try to understand what it meant. This chapter seeks to speak to the question of what there is to learn from the Institute's fiery ending by engaging with this reassembled archive. Drawing from José Esteban Muñoz's (2010) concept of utopia as something that exists on a horizon we long for but may never reach, I argue that Sagaris can serve as a portal for us to better understand utopianisms as works of *process* rather than products.[7]

Into the Portal

In her 2020 essay "Two Rivers," Black feminist poet, thinker, and facilitator Alexis Pauline Gumbs draws our attention to Tougaloo, Mississippi—a storied place in civil rights history. Tougaloo is a place where two rivers meet; where Audre Lorde worked as a poet in residence, arrived a librarian and left a teacher, and fell in love with a woman she called "my sunflower"; where Fannie Lou Hamer received an honorary doctoral degree before returning to the Delta to start her Freedom Farm Cooperative, which sought to feed Black Mississippians whom white supremacist farmers in Sunflower County had long forced to go hungry.[8] For Gumbs, this meeting place of two rivers is a portal—a place that connects those whose revolutionary spirit also yearns for the utopian dreams Lorde and Hamer's projects aspired to make real. A portal is a site where past, present, and future can flow together, and where radicalisms of the present can be in conversation with radicalisms of the past.

An important part of Gumbs's historical work and artistic practice is the genre of collage—a medium that Gumbs marries with archival research to build altars for Black feminists whose teachings, as Gumbs puts it, show us how "we can mother ourselves."[9] A collage requires the artist to assemble a new whole from pieces gleaned from different contexts—in DIY spaces, this often involves snippets from repurposed magazines, solidified with glue stick construction. Gumbs's collages are careful assemblies of bits and pieces that help us see how important these women's stories, which serve as portals, really are. They suggest a kind of affective relationship between those coming into consciousness of their own place within revolutionary possibility and those who arrived at that convergence before. In thinking with Sara Ahmed's concept of orientation from *Queer Phenomenology* (2006), portals serve as spaces we can orient ourselves toward from which we can see the world as we are meant to see it.[10] We thus look for portals so what seems unclear about the future (and whether there is any hope for us in it) can become clear.

How do we find our way to portals? SaraEllen Strongman has written of the importance of what she terms the "archaeological impulse" of Black feminism to seek out the work of those who came before to plot out one's path to the future.[11] This impulse, Strongman argues, is undergirded by an "animating affect" that is composed of an urge to seek out and share Black women's writing from the past in ways that move beyond typical academic archival work.[12] Strongman writes that this impulse was of particular importance to Black feminists in the 1970s and 1980s for reclaiming the power of Black womanhood. This work of sifting and sorting through material that historically has been cast aside can reveal a trail of breadcrumbs back to the portals seekers are searching for if they are moved to look for them.

The methodological impulse Strongman describes motivates the work of this project; however, the application of the method to a project like Sagaris further requires an engagement with material that, in its ability to help provide a kind of knowing of self, simultaneously lays bare forms of shame and embarrassment that have long motivated silence around the topic. I am reminded here of the *New Yorker*'s 2013 quasi-obituary for radical feminist thinker Shulamith Firestone, who died alone in her apartment at age sixty-seven after years of suffering from schizophrenia and poverty. This piece also served as a dark reflection on where the movement stood forty years after radical feminist had first emerged in the late 1960s and early 1970s. Reflecting on Firestone's funeral service, journalist Susan Faludi wrote, "It was hard to say which moment the mourners were there to mark: the passing of Firestone or that of a whole generation of feminists who had been unable to thrive in the world they had done so much to create."[13] When I first read this assessment of the state of 1970s radical feminisms it gave me pause. As I turned it over in my mind repeatedly over the months that followed, I found the source of my disagreement with Faludi: that the disappointment presented was rooted not in a newly created world having been thwarted, but rather that a generation of feminists had not found the way to create the necessary tools they needed to build the utopian vision they imagined before the groundswell of radical energy of the movement's heyday was squashed. But even as the radical feminist revolutionary dream that motivated many activists never quite came into being, its fragments live on tucked in memories, basements, sound waves, and archival boxes awaiting appraisal to understand what went wrong amid the wreckage. These sites of failure offer opportunities for understanding the limitations of the tools at hand, and certainly a place like Sagaris is such a site fertile for excavation.

What's more, Sagaris was an experiment dominated by white women, many from middle-class backgrounds, who had the means to pursue graduate-level education. One of its featured professors was Mary Daly—a feminist theorist and scholar who served as the advisor to Janice Raymond, whose attacks on Sandy Stone in her book *The Trans-sexual Empire* (1979) and elsewhere helped to create a powerful crucible from which trans-exclusionary radical feminism proliferated.[14] Excavating our way toward the portal to Sagaris requires understanding methodologically that what is revealed may not exclusively produce feelings of positive kinship, but rather may evoke negative affects that we would rather ignore. But these negative affects offer their own pedagogy—one that asks white women feminists who are committed to anti-racist work and scholarship, myself included, how we can understand the prefigurations of the past as sites from which we can envision counter-cartographies toward a different kind of utopian imagining for the future. To do so, we have to allow ourselves to find our way back to the portal, where two rivers meet, to begin.

Two Rivers Converge at Sagaris

The Passumpsic River converges from two branches, East and West, that flow together through the town of Lyndonville, Vermont, where a group of several hundred feminists converged for the first meeting of the Sagaris Institute in 1975. Sagaris first emerged in the feminist press in 1974, about nine months prior to the opening of its first session on the campus of Lyndon State College in Lyndonville. Convened by a majority-white collective of leading feminist thinkers, including Blanch Boyd, Rita Mae Brown, Jan Corwin, Lynn Corwin, Judy Cohen, Kathryn Kilgore, Sandy Lucas, Ada McAllister, Jane Myers, Joan Peters, and Marilyn Webb, Sagaris was intended to provide a space for feminist thought outside the constraints of the patriarchal university.[15] The group was a band of radical feminists and veteran movement activists from a variety of backgrounds—early advertisements for the Institute note that their occupations ranged from college professor to waitress-playwright to babysitter. In addition to the organizing committee, the Institute received backing from a number of noteworthy feminists of the day, such as Gloria Steinem, as well as a host of feminist college professors including Mary Daly, Catharine Stimpson, and Phyllis Chesler.

In the years leading up to Sagaris, much of radical feminist theory had been developed outside the academy within smaller groups and collectives and disseminated through a wide range of newsletters and other publications. The early years of radical feminism saw the rise in recognition of groups such as Cell 16, The Feminists, the Radicalesbians, and the Furies. Alice Echols, one of the first scholars to write a history of the movement, described this period as having begun in 1967, growing wildly before splits over tactics and orientation brought its heyday to a close around 1975.[16] Indeed, by the founding of Sagaris, all of the aforementioned groups had broken up, with Rita Mae Brown and Charlotte Bunch, two Sagaris teachers, leaving the Furies a year prior. With the movement seemingly under threat, activists such as Brown felt it was necessary to build a place for radical feminist theorizing that could be more permanent to build toward feminist revolution in ways that autonomous collectives alone did not allow.

Although feminist theory had found its way into the more permanent structures of universities through the early days of the institutionalization of Women's Studies, organizers of Sagaris were not content with the notion that existing institutions could be reformed. Co-founder Joan Peters declared in an interview that "Present courses leave something to be desired. In many schools the women's studies are controlled by men or locked into a system that does not allow adequate freedom for maximum intellectual growth. . . . Our institute, which we call an institute to allow ourselves the intellectual freedom not possible in establishment colleges, is meant to be a feminist-humanist alternative to existing patriarchal society schools of higher education."[17] Feminist newspaper *Big Mama Rag* further described the Institute as "answer[ing] the need for the study of unadulterated feminist philosophy."[18]

While organizers like Peters identified extant universities as embedded within the patriarchal establishment, the institutional *form* of the university remained one to which they returned as a model for radical feminist education. Despite its imperfections, the structure of the university as a locus for learning was convenient and familiar for Sagaris founders, many of whom had attended college for an undergraduate education and a large portion for graduate school. Some organizers were already living in Vermont at the time of the Institute's inception, with a few teaching at nearby Goddard College. The group decided to rent out buildings on the campus of Lyndon State College, which would provide ample space for classes in an environment they were already familiar with for teaching. The early schedule for Sagaris looked not unlike one a first-year student might receive when scheduling her first semester of classes.

The choice of the structure of the university as the model for radical feminist education was a risky one—the challenge before organizers was the question of whether the groundswell of radical feminist energy they hoped they could transform into the vanguard could be contained within that institutional form.[19] Rita Mae Brown was an early dissenter in the shift within the collective toward the model of the university for the institute as opposed to something more akin to a think tank. In an interview, Brown stated that she left the collective at that time because she did not want to give so much of her energy to a project that seemed destined to create a white middle-class institution; however, she did opt to remain as a teacher.[20]

Public critiques of the university structure and the costs associated with Sagaris emerged early. In an editorial in *Big Mama Rag*, Linda Fowler criticized the Collective for what she saw as a classist fee structure, arguing that it would be impossible for most women who made the material sacrifices necessary to fully commit to movement work to afford the $700 bill.[21] She argued that faculty salaries, which were set at $1,500 per five-week session, were far too high considering the lack of scholarship funds available.[22] Fowler further argued that Sagaris seemed to cling too tightly to institutional forms more representative of capitalism than with the socialist ideals expressed in advertisements for the Institute, writing that "If [the Collective is] seeking to produce a feminist Harvard you can count a lot of women out. Radical feminists are not seeking a shelf of leather-bound feminist classics starting with *Sisterhood is Powerful*. We do not want tenure on the NOW national board. We do not seek to change life's projectionist while leaving the same film on the reel. We are not after a piece of the pie."[23]

Sagaris Collective members responded in a letter published in the next edition of *Big Mama Rag*, writing that they understood that the Institute was unequal and had been working without pay themselves to bring it together, noting that they had applied to foundations for funds to support more scholarships and fund the Institute.[24] This shift toward appealing to foundations for funds was a marked difference from the initial goals of organizers, who stated in an earlier interview with magazine *The Lesbian Tide* that their goal was to avoid institutional funds entirely and instead be funded by small donations from women around the country in order to maintain their independence.[25] Ultimately, Sagaris received funding from the Ms. Foundation, the Carnegie Corporation, and the Lucius and Eva Eastman Family Fund.[26] Their reported largest expense was the more than $60,000 required to rent out space for the Institute, which was mostly subsidized by participant fees.

Money problems would prove to be the spark that would go on to ignite a fire at Sagaris later in the summer. Just before the start of the first session of the Institute in June, a newly reconfigured group organized under the banner of the Redstockings released a report in early May demonstrating ties they had uncovered between Gloria Steinem and the CIA.[27] In the report, the Redstockings trace Steinem's emergence within the political realm after college through her selection as founder of a research institute funded by the CIA, which produced reports on leaders within global youth movements, particularly those associated with socialism. The Redstockings then pointed toward Steinem's meteoric rise within feminism despite her lack of radical credentials, the paradoxical level of support for Steinem's *Ms. Magazine* as opposed to other feminist publications more favorable to radical feminism than the liberal feminism of *Ms.*, and Steinem's involvement in projects such as the Women's Action Alliance that collected and consolidated information about feminist groups. The allegations raised by the Redstockings reverberated throughout the radical feminist community in the United States, setting the stage for a confrontation at Sagaris.

Building and Breaking Sagaris

Despite the controversy proceeding the first days of Sagaris, on June 9, 1975, about 150 women descended upon the campus of Lyndon State College to attend the Institute. Participants gathered on the muggy New England campus for nine hours of classes each day, beginning with an hour of "Body Development" in the morning, followed by two and a half hours of political theory, electives in journalism, education, creative writing, and psychology in the afternoon before evening courses in economics.[28] Students packed into tight college dorm rooms, which left little room for privacy but provided a brief respite from the school's grueling schedule.[29] Women who brought children along with them were provided with free childcare, led by a long-time elementary schoolteacher and a graduate student in counseling.[30]

Big Mama Rag continued its coverage of Sagaris throughout the first session of the Institute, sending writer Jackie St. Joan to Vermont from Denver to report on the proceedings. In a dispatch published that July, St. Joan described Sagaris as being composed of a broad group of women from a number of backgrounds—most from the Midwest rather than larger cities, more than half lesbians, most aged twenty-two to thirty-two (with a nonetheless strong contingent of older or more experienced women). She further relayed that "most were from middle class backgrounds, although a strong working class caucus developed. All but five women were white. Seven women brought nine children with them. . . . With the tempo of a beehive (credit: Mary Daly) and the intensity of a love affair, the session was exciting and exhausting, with a cramping of personal time/space, hard work, meetings, conflicts, and learning."[31]

A critical aspect of learning at Sagaris was the merging of theoretical work with embodied knowledge. In addition to time devoted to bodywork such as karate, instructors like Marilyn Webb integrated movement work and theater games into their classes. Webb, whose journalism class focused on writing skills, developed this integrated approach while teaching feminist studies at Goddard College, believing that it helped students clear their mental blocks and become better writers.[32] There were also regular dances in the evenings at Sagaris where participants could mingle and break out of the seriousness of each day of classes. The emphasis on movement practices at Sagaris served purposes both practical and political: evening dances and in-class movement helped to shake out the mental and physical stiffness accumulated during hours of seated coursework with the added benefit of facilitating student mingling, while the general emphasis on embodiment further underscored the Institute's commitment to moving beyond theorizing and toward making feminist revolution.

Among the participants in the first session was forty-two-year-old activist Marilyn Murphy—a six-year veteran of the women's movement and PhD candidate from Irvine, California. Murphy learned about the Institute from a brochure given to her by a friend. She regarded Sagaris as one of the most pivotal moments of her life—her experience at the Institute prompted her coming out as a lesbian and lifelong commitment to lesbian feminism. As she recalled in a 2013 memoir,

> I was overwhelmed by a feeling of destiny, a feeling hard to integrate for a person who believes in a random universe. I couldn't

shake it though and made arrangements to spend $2000 of my husband's money for room and board and tuition and plane fare for an event I knew next to nothing about. My plans shocked everyone in my family, including me. In my whole life, I had never gone *anywhere, overnight* without at least one member of my family going with me. . . . Yet, I was determined to do all those things I never did because of a compulsion I couldn't explain.[33]

Murphy turned forty-three while at Sagaris, which the group celebrated with "cake for 150."[34] Although her session at Sagaris was "mostly lesbians," she still identified as straight, attending the Sagaris prom with Rita Mae Brown (because "Lesbians made sure all us non-Lesbians had dates."[35]) She reported loving all of her classes, except for the daily bodywork ones, which she forewent in order to rest, as sleep was in short supply.

Murphy's journey to Sagaris in some ways embodied the critique levied by Linda Fowler in her early indictment of the Institute's costs. Murphy, who had access to funds through her husband and had already had access to extensive higher education, was able to travel to Sagaris without much trouble in spite of the expense. Murphy's remembrance of the significance of her decision to travel alone to Sagaris marks its place as a transformational moment for her while also presenting a moment of defiance of fairly typical standards for her white and upper middle-class sociality. However, Murphy's example was not representative of the Institute's full student population. A young Dorothy Allison was also drawn to Sagaris from afar, traveling north from Tallahassee, Florida, with members of her feminist collective and the emergent feminist bookstore Herstore. Unlike Murphy, Allison had grown up poor in South Carolina. Her upbringing had been indelibly marked by incest and abuse, which she would later recount in her memoir *Trash* (1988).[36] Allison had been out as a lesbian for some time by the time she arrived at Sagaris, living in a house with other Women's Movement organizers and dating widely within Tallahassee. Each day was a battle for Allison—as she ramped up her resistance to her passing as middle-class and straight, adorning her car with a DYKE bumper sticker, she faced increased discrimination. Her car was defaced and smashed. Fellow collective members marginalized her for dating a Black woman. She faced further backlash when the University of Florida threatened to close down the Women's Center with which she collaborated for its connection to the waitress union she was helping to organize. Middle-class members of the collective could not understand Allison's own working-class perspective on why the union mattered. By the time she got to Sagaris, Allison was approaching a breaking point, but didn't have the words to describe it.[37]

In a 2007 oral history, Allison reflected fondly upon her time at Sagaris at some length, remarking that "the women that ran it—put it together—just did a remarkable thing, and they caught a lot of hell for it."[38] Sagaris was a place where Allison could finally talk about class difference—something she felt deeply but which had been marginalized in her collective. She remembered convening with other socialist lesbians at Sagaris and the ways their conversations about class opened up her conceptions of herself and what was possible for feminist politics. Allison recalled, "Up in Vermont, all of a sudden that dorm, with people talking about language and what made you uncomfortable. And all of a sudden it was like another light came on in the room, and I could see another corner that I hadn't really been paying much attention to, but which I had been dealing with for years. . . . That deep sense of shame that I was born with, I did not actually have to continue to carry."[39]

Allison left Sagaris with a renewed sense of energy and purpose, along with a newfound connection with Charlotte Bunch. She returned to Tallahassee with one of the members of her collective, moving back into the house they'd begun renting in a rundown neighborhood not long before they'd left for Vermont. When things turned sour in Tallahassee, it was Bunch who helped find Allison work in Washington, DC, which served as a springboard for the acclaimed career she went on to build as a writer.

Although the first session of Sagaris proved fruitful in terms of making connections between feminists and cultivating a sense of belonging, it was not without conflict. One can imagine how the discomfort of sitting in packed classrooms and dorm rooms in the muggy New England summer without air conditioning and pushing through weeks of nearly nonstop classwork and socialization could produce discord and discomfort. Murphy described a gay-straight split and class divisions that arose and dissipated after the first two weeks. However, accounts of the first session seem to reflect a net positive experience of the Institute. That positivity would prove to be short-lived.

As the debate over the Redstockings' allegations reached Sagaris, the second session was underway. Participants were split over Sagaris's acceptance of a grant from the Ms. Foundation—a fissure that erupted into a six-hour debate between Ti-Grace Atkinson and Joan Peters over whether accepting the funds would corrupt Sagaris.[40] After the public confrontation, which took place in front of the full school after an announcement that the Institute had received an additional $10,000 from the foundation, participants took a vote and agreed to accept the funds. However, Atkinson's protest continued. On August 7, 1975, a group of twenty-nine women led by Atkinson that would eventually include fellow instructors Alix Kates Schulman, Susan Sherman, and Marilyn Webb convened in a separate space on campus under the banner of the August 7th Survival Community and began to unpack what had happened. By August 11, they had written a preliminary declaration of their independence from Sagaris and the official formation of their own community for the remainder of the Institute. The participants eventually drafted a lengthy report on their experience at Sagaris—an abridged version of which was published in a 1976 edition of the journal *her-self*. Members said that the split at Sagaris had occurred for two reasons—the reformist approach of the Sagaris Collective and the radical feminist commitments of some of its community—which they argued represented the contrast between the vision of Sagaris and its reality.[41]

That the members of the August 7th Survival Community chose to remain on campus, albeit separated from the rest of the Institute, to do the painful work of dissecting what had happened and writing it down for others to learn from it reflects a feminist sensibility developed through consciousness-raising of self-study and public reflection. Even as they resisted the institutional orientation of Sagaris, the members of the Survival Community created their own oppositional archive of the school to make it clear to others what they saw as its failings. This work proved to be exhausting and further divisive. In part because of their physical proximity, life in the August 7th Survival Community sat in a state of prolonged tension with Sagaris. Former members of the Sagaris faculty lost two weeks of pay and the cost of two weeks of the costly room and board. Childcare was similarly cut off for the five children whose mothers had left Sagaris proper. Rushed to process their experiences at Sagaris while attempting to write a newsletter and publish their report, members cordoned off from one another, working frantically but not collectively in a community center nearby that they'd rented for eight dollars per day. Reflecting on their two weeks of work, members of the Community wrote, "As the dissenting minority, we found ourselves with little money, and outside the realm of established authority. A few women left our group and Lyndonville. Often we didn't know why or take the time to work out difficulties. We often reacted to our own anger in indirect, traditional female ways. . . . From our experiences, it seems that we must pay attention to our process at all times. We must guard against using old modes of behavior, such as relying on expertise instead of continuing our commitment to sharing skills. We must work to provide a revolutionary feminist environment."[42]

Despite their own diagnoses of their collective's imperfections, the perspectives of members of the August 7th Survival Community present an important counterpoint to remembrances of Sagaris that focus only on the drama of its schisms. Participants in the Survival Community did not wholly reject the vision of Sagaris; rather, they saw the Institute's struggles as being representative of the limitations of a politics that relied too heavily on past institutional forms. Members of the Sagaris Collective themselves remarked in their report on the first iteration of the Institute that, while practical, the use of a traditional university setting as its backdrop undermined the revolutionary intentions of the feminist thought on the syllabus by creating a learning environment in which patriarchy had already conditioned participants to act subservient.[43] The August 7th Survival Community's conclusion that careful consideration rather than pure expediency should be the organizing strategies for feminist work foreshadows a turn toward care in radical feminist thinking. In the wake of the rush of the past half-decade or more of radical feminist organizing, perhaps the strategy for sustenance was not the harried churning out of newsletters and manifestoes that had become the norm. Perhaps the longer-term strategy for sustenance would come from organizing strategies that were as radical in their commitment to caretaking as they were in their militancy.

Leaving Sagaris

After the end of the second session of Sagaris, organizers of the Institute took some time away before reconvening. News of the rift had made the news even in the mainstream press—the *New York Times* headline in late August read "The Women Activists Found Little Peace at [Their] Bucolic School."[44] The spectacle of a group of movement celebrities erupting into infighting during their trip to the countryside easily lent itself to such teasing coverage. Several months later, they reconvened to work through feedback from the first year, generating a report that made its way into the papers of Mary Daly, one of the instructors. In the report, organizers reflected on the feedback they'd received with regard to the high cost of the institute, as well as issues participants had with the tight accommodations and lack of flexibility in housing and food options. And they digested the rift that had caused the August 7th Survival Community to break off, maintaining their position that they were right to keep the funds from the Ms. Foundation, despite understanding those who critiqued them.

Exhausted but not defeated, the women made plans for Sagaris II in 1977 while also preparing a series of collaborative workshops with the National Black Feminist Organization, set to take place in 1976.[45] A later pamphlet for Sagaris II described it as a "Multiracial Feminist Institute," set to convene for four two-week sessions from June to August 1977 at a YWCA Camp twenty minutes outside Minneapolis, Minnesota, at a much-reduced price per session from the first convening and at a location far different from the space of the patriarchal university.[46] The National Black Feminist Organization, which shared office space with *Ms. Magazine*, folded its national organization in 1975 with some local chapters continuing to operate until 1980, suggesting that the partnership with Sagaris was short-lived.[47] Although ads for Sagaris II surfaced in a handful of feminist publications, further coverage of the event was sparse, standing in stark contrast to the firestorm of articles writing in response to the first convening. After the pamphlet for Sagaris II, the Institute seems to have disappeared from the archive. It is unclear whether the collective disbanded formally or went on an extended hiatus, leaving members more time to work on other feminist projects they deemed pressing or to recover from the fatigue often brought on by extended movement work.

Although the Sagaris Collective's dream of a permanent radical feminist institute was not realized, the effects of their work nonetheless persisted residually in the lives of the women who'd found themselves there, circled on those dorm room floors in Vermont, making sense of their lives and envisioning a radical feminist future outside of the patriarchal cage. Tracing the threads of Sagaris through two of its participants—Marilyn Murphy and Dorothy Allison—leads to two important throughlines for radical feminism. For Murphy, the lessons she learned at Sagaris about the limitations of traditional educational structures in radical feminist work went on to influence the school back in California she went on to co-found, Califia. For Allison, Sagaris facilitated her move out of Tallahassee to Washington, allowing her to begin her career as a writer. I trace their post-Sagaris stories here in the spirit of returning to Gumbs's concept of accessing the portal—how we come to know the knowledge we carry with us that connects us to a utopian sense of justice that moves across time.

Marilyn Murphy's return to California from Sagaris was an emotional one—though her husband waited for her with flowers, she did not share his sense of celebration. Her return trip was filled with the day-to-day experiences of patriarchy from which she'd felt a reprieve for the first time in her life while at Sagaris. On her way to the airport, a woman in her shuttle initiated a flirtation with the driver that outraged her; a man seated next to her on her connecting flight to Boston took pleasure in making sure his leg touched hers and the leg of the other woman seated next to him for the entire flight; five men eyed her at the newspaper stand while she purchased a pack of cigarettes. She felt a new uneasiness about the way her body was surveilled in ways that she'd previously accepted as normal.[48] The male gaze now felt invasive, inescapable. She remembered, "If I were that unconscious of the effects, in my body, of men's gaze, what else could I be doing, unconsciously, in response to the presence of the men in my life and in the world at large? The bars of that cage that comprise women's oppression, those bars that I had learned to look between, to keep peripheral, had moved without my knowing during those five women-only weeks at Sagaris. Now, those bars were in my sight, in my consciousness, *in my face*. Now I *knew* I was living in a man-made cage."[49] Matters did not improve in the weeks that followed. She began exchanging letters with lesbians she'd met at Sagaris who were experiencing similar feelings after leaving the campus—that their lives couldn't truly be theirs living in men's spaces on patriarchy's terms. Murphy left her marriage, came out as a lesbian, and committed herself to political work supporting women. She went on to co-found Califia Community—a radical feminist education and action organization that sought to replicate the structure of Sagaris through women-only week-long and long weekend camps. She later moved to the feminist community Pagoda in St. Augustine, Florida—a lesbian separatist project that served as host to, among other artists, a long-standing rotation of lesbian musicians and performers.

The founding of Califia serves as an example of the importance of Sagaris, even amid its struggles, for the utopian values of radical feminist pedagogy. Murphy had been involved with a group of women in California who were interested in building a feminist school prior to attending Sagaris and, upon her return, was quick to put the lessons she'd learned in Vermont to work. Along with several other Califia co-founders who'd attended Sagaris, they reached out to every lesbian or feminist group they could think of in Southern California to collaborate to build Califia, putting together shorter week- or weekend-long conferences at campgrounds using peer education models not dissimilar from the Highlander Institute of civil rights and labor activism. This model allowed for much lower costs, particularly for working-class women who could not afford to take time off from work, and resisted the hierarchical design of Sagaris. Murphy later described Califia as "the daughter of Sagaris and, like most daughters, is very like and very unlike her mother."[50] Murphy's invocation of familial lineage as a way of relating Califia and Sagaris provides a model for understanding the Institute not as an isolated experiment but rather as an actress[51] within a continuum of radical feminist activity. This continuum, linked with a radical feminist network, was critical for supporting movement workers such as Dorothy Allison.

Upon returning to Tallahassee, it quickly became clear to Allison that matters had not improved since her departure some weeks prior. The house her collective rented in town had become increasingly dangerous. She and fellow collective member Flo determined that it was time to leave. When Charlotte Bunch called to offer her a position with *Quest* in Washington, DC, she jumped at the chance to move and headed north. There she joined a feminist collective composed of a mixture of lesbian and straight women, many of whom were middle-class and/or affiliated with the radical think tank Institute for Policy Studies. *Quest* had some financial resources at its disposal but nonetheless required significant fundraising. Allison did much of this work through direct mail and solicitations—something she hated but did because it was necessary for the magazine's survival. At *Quest*, Allison found a new kind of family, filling some of the gap left by the biological family from whom she'd become estranged after leaving for college and moving in with her collective in Florida.

Allison recalled, "*Quest* was Amazing. And some of the women that I met there, in terms of working class theorists, were just marvelous. It's just like constantly being 'Wake up, girl!' You know? 'Wake up! Can't you see what's going on?' Wonderful, astonishing, but at the same time, operating out of an institution that was an old Left program."[52] Despite her affinity with the women of *Quest*, Allison and fellow working-class collective member Bev Fisher began to notice the ways class and careerism inflected the ways wealthier women within the group approached their work. While she and Fisher struggled financially, running the magazine and cycling on and off unemployment, wealthier collective members were building their own niches within feminist theory and pursuing security through tenure and other institutional means.[53] This class difference was a source of both tension and support. As Allison remembered, "If I hadn't been living in the lesbian collective, I would have starved doing the work I was doing and never earning any money. But we never really talked about that some of them were building tenure and building a career in publishing books; and then some of us were doing all of the foot soldier work and getting no attention, getting by on the satisfaction of the work we were doing, and feeling like we were making a revolution, but some of the revolutionaries were prospering."⁵⁴

At *Quest*, as at Sagaris, the presence of a collective produced new possibilities through the sharing of resources; however, the possibility of permanence in terms of financial security while doing feminist work remained profoundly raced and classed, similar to the concern Rita Mae Brown expressed during the planning for Sagaris. Allison's concern further points toward what later came to be called the nonprofit industrial complex.⁵⁵ The accompanying issues regarding competition for funding, reminiscent of those expressed by the Redstockings in their reported concerns about Gloria Steinem's role in the movement, continue to raise issues in radical and feminist spaces today.

Listening Back to Sagaris

Years after this project's inception, I stumbled upon a preserved radio documentary produced by the New York City station WBAI documenting what happened at Sagaris in real time. Forty-six summers after the Institute in 1975, I plugged in my headphones and listened to the crackle of classroom sounds. A young Alix Kates Shulman, who taught a class on feminism and anarchism at the Institute, speaks urgently into the recorder about the trepidation many of her students felt about studying earlier feminisms, thinking them to be obsolete. But, Shulman states, in her own study she found that earlier feminists had encountered nearly every issue that had come up at Sagaris in the past and produced extensive analysis to understand it that was waiting to be picked up and used. Shulman asserts, "It was a very strong lesson to learn that you could lose it! You could lose all of that knowledge!"⁵⁶ As the reels of the recording turn forward across the space of decades, student Mary Lou Dietrich describes Sagaris itself as a process, one that required negotiation of power and leadership. That negotiation was indeed messy, marked with conflict poorly handled through non-communication and defensiveness. And its aftershocks traveled outward along with its participants in their lives after the Institute and into my ears via a digitized copy of the magnetic tape that holds their voices.

This is the moment that the portal of Sagaris brings us back to—a moment where several hundred women committed to building a new world on top of the ashes of the old free from the previous one's violence and constraints were still struggling to figure things out. While their utopian vision has perhaps grown fuzzy with age, the knowledge they tucked away, even their knowledge about discomfort and failure, provides vital material documenting the process by which they reached their dissolution, leaving way for future utopia to be staged.

Notes

1. Annotated copy, Gloria Steinem, "Letter to the Feminist Press," August 13, 1975, Papers of Rita Mae Brown, box 163, folder 6, Albert and Shirley Small Special Collections, University of Virginia Libraries.

2. See Redstockings, "Press Release: Redstockings Discloses Gloria Steinem's CIA Cover-Up," May 9, 1975, Women's Liberation Collection, box 12, Sophia Smith Collection, Smith College Special Collections.

3. See *Feminism and Community*, ed. Penny A. Weiss and Marilyn Friedman (Philadelphia: Temple University Press, 1995); Ruth Rosen, *The World Split Open: How the Modern Women's Movement Changed America* (New York: Viking, 2000).

4. This move is widespread but was particularly popularized in Judith Butler's *Gender Trouble* (1990).

5. Elizabeth Freeman, *Time Binds: Queer Temporalities, Queer Histories* (Durham: Duke University Press, 2010).

6. Heather Love, *Feeling Backward: Loss and the Politics of Queer History* (Cambridge: Harvard University Press, 2007).

7. José Esteban Muñoz, *Cruising Utopia: The Then and There of Queer Futurity* (New York: New York University Press, 2010).

8. Alexis Pauline Gumbs, "Two Rivers," *Southern Cultures* 6, no. 4 (winter 2020): 145.

9. This term comes from an essay by Audre Lorde published in *Essence* in 1983; it was also the title of Gumbs's dissertation.

10. Sara Ahmed, *Queer Phenomenology: Orientations, Objects, Others* (Durham: Duke University Press, 2006).

11. SaraEllen Strongman, "The Archaeological Impulse, Black Feminism, and *But Some of Us Were Brave*" *Feminist Studies* 48, no. 1 (2022): 33–52.

12. Strongman, 35.

13. Susan Faludi, "Death of a Revolutionary," *The New Yorker*, April 8, 2013.

14. Janice Raymond, *The Trans-Sexual Empire: The Making of the She-Male* (Boston: Beacon Press, 1979). See also Stone's response to Raymond's attacks: Sandy Stone, "The *Empire* Strikes Back: A Post-Transexual Manifesto," *Camera Obscura* 10, no. 2 (1992): 150–76.

15. Press release announcing Sagaris, June 1974, Mary Daly Papers, box 6, Sophia Smith Collection, Smith College Special Collections. In 2019, I received the Margaret Storrs Grierson Fellowship from Smith College Special Collections, which facilitated my travel there for research. I am thankful for their support of my scholarship.

16. Alice Echols, *Daring to Be Bad: Radical Feminism in America, 1967–1975* (Minneapolis: University of Minnesota Press, 1989).

17. "Feminist College to Open," *Big Mama Rag* 3, no. 1 (1974): 2.

18. "Feminist College to Open," 2.

19. Scholars in critical university studies have spoken extensively of this issue here. For example, see Roderick Ferguson, *The Reorder of Things: The University and Its Pedagogies of Minority Difference* (Minneapolis: University of Minnesota Press, 2012).

20. Marcia Danab, Helene Verna Schiff, Peter Zanger, and David Marx, "Sagaris and the August 7th Survival Community," October 19, 1975, Pacifica Radio Archives. Originally aired on WBAI, https://www.pacificaradioarchives.org/recording/iz1361.

21. $700 in 1975 is equivalent to $5,273.38 at the time of this writing in 2022.

22. Linda Fowler, "High Priced Feminism: Sagaris to Open Doors this Summer," *Big Mama Rag* 3, no. 3 (1975): 1.

23. Fowler, 1.

24. Sagaris Collective, entry in Letters, *Big Mama Rag* 3, no. 5: 17.

25. Cheryl Gould, "New Women's Institute Opens," *The Lesbian Tide* 4, no. 5 (January 1975).

26. Sagaris Collective, "Report on Sagaris," 1975, Mary Daly Papers, box 6, page 20, Sophia Smith Collection, Smith College Special Collections.

27. Redstockings, "Press Release: Redstockings Discloses Gloria Steinem's CIA Cover-Up," May 9, 1975, Women's Liberation Collection, box 12, Sophia Smith Collection, Smith College Special Collections.

28. "Sagaris Schedule," Mary Daly Papers, box 6, Sophia Smith Collection, Smith College Special Collections.

29. Sagaris Collective, "Report on Sagaris," 1975, Mary Daly Papers, box 6, Sophia Smith Collection, Smith College Special Collections.

30. Linda Fowler, "High Priced Feminism: Sagaris to Open Doors this Summer," *Big Mama Rag* 3, no. 3 (1975): 1.

31. Jackie St. Joan, "First Session Sagaris: What Happened," *Big Mama Rag* 3A, no. 7 (1975): 6.

32. Marcia Danab, Helene Verna Schiff, Peter Zanger, and David Marx, "Sagaris and the August 7th Survival Community," October 19, 1975, Pacifica Radio Archives. Originally aired on WBAI, https://www.pacificaradioarchives.org/recording/iz1361.

33. Marilyn Murphy, *Marilyn Revisited* (Serafina, NM: Woman, Earth, and Spirit, 2013), 12–13.

34. Murphy, 12–13.
35. Murphy, 14.
36. Dorothy Allison, *Trash* (New York: Firebrand Books, 1988).
37. Dorothy Allison, interviewed by Kelly Anderson, Voice of Feminism Oral History Project, Sophia Smith Collection, Smith College, November 2007, 15.
38. Allison, 16.
39. Allison, 15.
40. From interview with Ti-Grace Atkinson cited in Ruth Rosen, *The World Split Open: How the Modern Women's Movement Changed America* (2006), 256.
41. Ti-Grace Atkinson et al., "The Battle Lines Are Drawn: Statement by the August 7th Survival Community," *her-self* 4, no. 5 (1975): 7.
42. Atkinson et al., 7.
43. Sagaris Collective, "Report on Sagaris," 16, Mary Daly Papers, box 6, Sophia Smith Collection, Smith College Special Collections.
44. "The Women Activists Found Little Peace at Bucolic School," *New York Times*, August 29, 1975, 32.
45. Sagaris Collective, "Report on Sagaris," Mary Daly Papers, box 6, Sophia Smith Collection, Smith College Special Collections.
46. Sagaris Collective, Pamphlet for Sagaris II, Mary Daly Papers, box 6, Sophia Smith Collection, Smith College Special Collections.
47. For more on this, see Kimberly Springer's brilliant book *Living for the Revolution: Black Feminist Organizations, 1968–1980* (Durham: Duke University Press, 2005).
48. Marilyn Murphy, *Marilyn Revisited* (Serafina, NM: Woman, Earth, and Spirit, 2013), 12–13.
49. Murphy, 14–15. See also Marilyn Frye, "Oppression," in *The Politics of Reality* (New York: Crossing Press, 1983).
50. Murphy quoted in Clark Pomerleau, *Califia Women: Feminist Education Against Sexism, Classism, and Racism* (Austin: University of Texas Press, 2013), 42 (Kindle edition).
51. I use "actress" as opposed to "actor" here in the radical feminist tradition of avoiding defaulting to masculine verbiage.
52. Dorothy Allison interviewed by Kelly Anderson, Voice of Feminism Oral History Project, Sophia Smith Collection, Smith College, November 2007, 28–29.
53. Allison, 28–29.
54. Allison, 30.
55. See INCITE! Women of Color Against Violence, *The Revolution Will Not Be Funded: Beyond the Non-Profit Industrial Complex* (Durham: Duke University Press, 2017).
56. Marcia Danab, Helene Verna Schiff, Peter Zanger, and David Marx, "Sagaris and the August 7th Survival Community," October 19, 1975, Pacifica Radio Archives. Originally aired on WBAI, https://www.pacificaradioarchives.org/recording/iz1361.

Part 2

Toward a Utopian Method

4

Utopian Imaginings

Migration as the Pursuit of the Utopian Society

SECIL E. ERTORER

When the Greek philosopher Plato wrote the first utopian novel, the *Republic*, two thousand years ago, he described the qualities of a perfect city with ideal social, economic, environmental, and scientific conditions.[1] Inspired by Plato, the English philosopher Sir Thomas More detailed the ideal conditions of a utopic island in his book *Utopia*. Seeing it as an unattainable project, he formulated the word *utopia* by combining the Greek words *eu* ("good"), *ou* ("no"), and *topos* ("place").[2] Following them, many philosophers and public servants envisioned different versions of a utopian society (e.g., Bloch, Campanella, Huxley, Zamyatin, Le Guin, and others) with various attributes. To this day, the idea of *utopia* has motivated many people to create or discover a utopian ideal.

Migration is one field that has been habitually motivated by the imagination of a utopian society. While the philosopher-envisioned utopia is an ideal theoretical construct and impeccable governments or social and economic conditions do not exist in the real world, in times of despair, people hope and search for one version of the utopian society. For instance, an asylum seeker escaping a war zone seeks a political *utopia* in which everyone lives in peace and perfect harmony without the fear of getting attacked or killed because of their religious, ethnic, and or political identities. Similarly, a political refugee seeks a utopian haven where the values of self-directed thinking and unrestrained expression are championed, enabling individuals to write, converse, and express themselves without inhibition. Likewise, an economic migrant chases a prosperous economic *utopia* that offers ample opportunities and the egalitarian distribution of jobs, goods, and services.

As a social researcher, I have had the opportunity to meet and work with various migrant and refugee groups in different societies. The convergence of the migration stories I have collected over the years is that the migration journey is always initiated by the imagination of a *utopic* land: a land of freedoms, opportunities, equity, and safety. Then it ends with a shared disappointment in a dystopian land.

According to the 1951 International Refugee Convention, a refugee is "someone unable or unwilling to return to their country of origin owing to a well-founded fear of being persecuted for reasons of race, religion, nationality, membership of a particular social group, or political opinion."[3] Consequently, for a refugee, utopia is a space that is free of the *fear* of oppression and physical harm. Sadly, my first graduate school research project, which examined the experiences of refugees and asylum seekers originating from Turkey and living in England, taught me that *fear* was a constant in a refugee's life, even after escaping from an unsafe country and landing on a safe one.

While I was conducting research for my master's thesis in 2003 in the UK,[4] there were two predominant groups of refugees from Turkey: Kurdish minorities who had faced racism, discrimination, and persecution because of their ethnic and political identities, and white Turks who had met (or had been in fear of) persecution because of their political ideologies, oppositional work, and activities. Initially, being an unseasoned social researcher, I did not realize that an interview delving into the migration stories essentially meant access to the vulnerable and complex realities of these individuals. Naturally, I faced reluctance and, at times, hostility when I asked for an interview. Even some people I had known and socialized with regularly showed signs of discomfort after hearing that I was interviewing people about their migration experiences. Some withdrew themselves from our social circles, ignored my calls, or avoided being in the same space that I was in. While I was not initially able to make sense of their reactions, I ultimately understood that they were acting out of *fear*. In this process, I discovered that asylum seekers might attain physical safety in a destination country but not necessarily a sense of security. To elucidate, these individuals were not granted permanent status in the host society but a conditional temporary position that created precarity and relentless *fear*. They had the sword of Damocles (see Figure 4.1) hanging over their heads constantly.

Figure 4.1. The Sword of Damocles (1812). Richard Westall's oil painting depicts an ancient parable told by the Roman philosopher Cicero dating back to 45 BC. In the painting, Damocles is surrounded by beautiful servants, lavish foods, gold, and riches, all the while concerned about the unsheathed sword above his head. Held at the Ackland Museum, Chapel Hill, NC. *Source*: Public domain.

In other words, even though they would seem safe and secure to outsiders, they were in a vulnerable situation that was in danger of imminent disaster. As asylum seekers awaiting a protected status in the host country, they were under constant surveillance and repeatedly interviewed by migration officers who endeavored to find inconsistencies in their stories. Some suspected I could have been an undercover immigration officer looking for gaps in their stories and collecting evidence that could disqualify them as refugees. Consequently, they tried hiding information about their journey and means of arrival to the "safe utopian" space.

During this research, I learned that when planning to seek asylum in a safe European country, one of the easiest ways to access Fortress Europe is to pay massive amounts of money to criminal organizations that smuggle humans across borders. The journey could take days, even months, with migrants being moved from one place to another in the trailer of commercial trucks and on floating boats until they reach their final destination. Many people I met during this study followed that path, and if exposed, this information would disqualify them as refugees, criminalize them, and even make them potential targets of these criminal organizations. Concurrently, the news about the deportation of asylum seekers in the country fed their *fear*, anxiety, and mistrust of others. Meanwhile, that *fear* of deportation ensured that the newcomers stayed quiet about their personal stories and became rule-abiding, obedient residents. This study helped me realize the connections between the structural forces of immigration, such as immigration and resettlement policies, and the everyday lives of immigrants. Simply put, the residency status, which is intentionally kept precarious for extended periods, and the policy of deportation work as the sword of Damocles, ensuring a docile and submissive migrant population. Ultimately, deportation is a political strategy that maintains control over asylum seekers and discourages others from arriving; it keeps them in *fear* and at bay!

After arriving in Canada as a doctoral student, I conducted research on Karen refugees from Burma (Myanmar) who had fled the prolonged armed ethnic conflict and sought safety in one of the refugee camps along the Thailand border prior to their settlement in London, Ontario. Even though all people escaping persecution are categorized under one sweeping "refugee" label, the asylum conditions of these refugees were dissimilar to those I encountered in England. First, the Karens fled an active war zone. Second, they sought refuge and spent years in a refugee camp sustained by the UN Refugee Agency. Third, they did not choose or plan their journey into the host utopian society. After years (decades for some) of camp residency, with no signs of peace initiatives at home, the UN Refugee Agency referred these individuals to Canada under an international refugee resettlement program. Karens were grateful and appreciative of the people who sponsored their resettlement and gave them an opportunity for a fresh start in London, Ontario. While older members of this group had witnessed civil war, persecution, and the razing of their villages to the ground, the youth were raised in a refugee camp. However, culture shock, as a subjective response to new or unfamiliar situations,[5] was not the only problem members of the group faced. Although they all naturally struggled with learning a new language, culture, values, norms, and ways of life, many successfully adopted integration or assimilation strategies rather than creating ethnic capsules of segregation or choosing to marginalize themselves from society.[6] However, soon after arriving in Canada, the church members who financed their resettlement process started conveying messages that Karens were expected to participate in the religious life at the church. Although it was practical to hold community events and meetings at the church, Karens, who were practicing Buddhists, were persistently invited to the weekly mass and advised to send their children to Sunday School. As the Karen refugees believed that they owed their place in the country to this religious community, they felt obligated to partake. Ultimately, they had no choice but to witness the pulling away of their children from the culture and spirituality of the family. This process demonstrated to them (and to us) that the welcoming Canadian multicultural, interreligious *utopia* (i.e., all forms of religious practice are welcome) was (and is) a myth.

As a professor and more experienced researcher, I have since conducted similar studies with other refugee groups, exposing their dystopias. For instance, while researching Syrian refugees, I found that no country was willing to give them a new home, even though everyone knew they were real (not bogus) refugees (by the UN definition) escaping from the active, deadly war zone in Syria. These refugees crossed borders and roamed countries searching for a safe utopian space but repeatedly encountered hate and expulsion. Many European countries prevented their entry, sometimes activating physical military and police forces at the borders. The European Union went so far as to give billions of euros to the neighboring country Turkey to keep Syrians within its boundaries, to accept Syrians deported from European countries, and to prevent more asylum seekers from entering Europe. The "just keep them outside our borders, we will pay for it" policy (known as the Europe-Turkey deal) demonstrates that Europeans saw Syrians as a virus, an unpleasant encounter that should be avoided at all costs.

Consequently, Syrian refugees were confined in the countries neighboring Syria with temporary permits to reside but not work. As a result of these restricting permits, they were forced to live on the streets or in cramped refugee camps, begging for charity or seeking employment in the informal economy for sub-minimum wages. I discovered that by adopting a temporary protection regime and manufacturing a new status (that is, "not a refugee"), the signatories of the 1951 Refugee Convention are able to deny long-term protections embedded with civil rights to asylum seekers and avoid their legal obligations.[7] Moreover, I learned that this is a fundamental breach of the rights allotted to refugees by the United Nations. The right to apply for asylum is a basic human right, and so is the right to work. However, by crafting and adopting a temporary, *conditional refugee* status, the governments denied Syrians the right to apply for resettlement in third countries. Moreover, Syrians were biometrically registered, their mobility was restricted even within the borders of the country, and they were not granted a right to work. The denial of applying for asylum in safe countries and limiting participation in work activity left these individuals increasingly vulnerable.[8] This research disclosed how migration regimes serve as tools for governments to create a precarious labor pool for the economy. Consequently, while asylum seekers are forced to take any survival-level jobs regardless of the payment and safety conditions, the economies of refugee-hosting countries profit from a flood of both consumers and cheap undocumented labor.

Remarkably, when the Ukrainian war created millions of refugees, neighboring countries showed a significantly different reaction to Ukrainian refugees compared with the Syrian individuals discussed above. These white and presumably Christian refugees were welcomed with open arms. We did not witness human rights violations, rejection of asylum seekers by security forces at external borders, erection of immense refugee camps to contain refugee populations, or dead bodies of asylum seekers washing up on European shores. In the immediate aftermath of the Russian invasion, the same European Union that refused to grant refugee status to Syrians, Afghans, and other non-white asylum seekers agreed to activate the "Temporary Protection Drive" for Ukrainians and to grant them rights to reside; work; live; access education, healthcare, and social assistance; and travel freely in EU countries.[9] As Foucault suggests, by imposing biopolitical policies and biopower, states make decisions about whom they help to live or cast aside,[10] and in that process, religion seems to work as a passport with a visa for the *utopia*.

During one investigation in Canada, I surveyed economic immigrants with diverse backgrounds. For these immigrants, the decision to leave their home country had not been made in an attempt to seek physical safety; instead, it was a pursuit of a utopic space with ample economic, educational, and political opportunities for the family. These individuals were very privileged compared with the refugee groups I studied. They were upper-middle-class professionals in politically safe but economically unstable countries. While their utopic imagining entailed a high status and a comfortable lifestyle ensured by their profession and skill set, the reality met them with a failure in recognition of their earned credentials, degrees, and diplomas. Even though their skills and work experiences made them admissible to Canada, they were told that they must take college/university classes and pass exams to be allowed to practice their profession in their new country. Consequently, many chose to drive taxis and Ubers or start small businesses instead of investing in the same education they had already received in their home country. Those who did pursue additional, albeit repetitive, training faced racial discrimination in hiring and promotion practices and found themselves excluded from social cliques in the workplace. Some highly skilled individuals believed that their ethnic names and religion prevented them from being recruited for professional and managerial positions. Some perceived that their opinions were judged, ignored, or undervalued in the new society.[11] The so-called multicultural and welcoming Canada was neither of these things for these individuals.

Similarly, my current project, which examines the scapegoating of Asian Americans for the spread of COVID-19 throughout the United States, disrupts the "pluralist and welcoming" *utopia* of "post-racial" societies. Individuals perceived as "Asian" were subjected to xenophobia and faced increased rates of harassment and discrimination following the outbreak of the COVID-19 virus. They were physically attacked, called names, spat on, and told to "go back home," even though the United States is their home. When viewed in this light, the utopian ideal of the United States is challenged, as families that have resided in the country for generations still face otherization and exclusion because of their racial identities.

As revealed by the cases shared in this paper, international migration can be motivated by various push factors. At times, political factors such as war or ethnic conflict create refugee situations, as realized in the cases of Syrian and Karen refugees mentioned in this chapter. Sometimes not a destructive war, but political repression or intolerance, repels people, like the Turkish refugees I met in the UK. Sometimes systemic discrimination of racial, ethnic, or religious minorities compels people to leave, similar to the Kurdish refugees living in the UK. It is important to remember that migration is not always political or forced. Frequently it is initiated by economic factors such as stagnation, unemployment, or a lack of opportunities in the home country, which is the case for the economic immigrants I studied in Canada. Indeed, there are some other factors I have not encountered in my studies, such as environmental disasters.[12] The point is that whatever the push factor is, people leave their homes seeking a *utopian* society. For migrants, a *utopian* space is where ethnically diverse groups live in peace and harmony, economic opportunities are vast and accessible, and individual members are neither judged nor persecuted because of their racial, ethnic, religious, sexual, or political identities. These utopian ideals are spaces of safety rather than surveillance and domination. They are places where individuals do not need to be concerned about the survival of their offspring. However, the conversations I partook in with individual members of the groups discussed above demonstrate a different reality. Regardless of how settled and safe such groups may appear to outsiders, refugees and immigrants often find themselves in dystopic spaces under constant surveillance, and they grapple with continuous fear and anxiety.

The dystopia of refugees extends across borders and greets individuals with hate and expulsion. The dystopia of immigrants hits glass barriers in so-called "multicultural and welcoming" workspaces. Moreover, these dystopias extend through time as second- and third-generation immigrants are dehumanized and scapegoated for health and economic disruptions in so-called "post-racial" societies. After years-long research, sharing, and discovery, I can safely conclude that the "x Dream" (American, Canadian, or else) is nothing more than a dream or *imagining of utopia*.

Notes

1. D. Lee and M. Lane, *The Republic by Plato* (New York: Penguin Books, 2007).

2. Thomas More, *Utopia* (New York: Appleton-Century-Crofts, 1949), 1478–1535.

3. UN General Assembly, "Convention Relating to the Status of Refugees," July 28, 1951, United Nations, Treaty Series, vol. 189, 137, https://www.refworld.org/docid/3be01b964.html.

4. Secil Erdogan, "Turkish Refugees in England: The Factors and Challenges of Asylum," master's thesis, Hacettepe University, 2004.

5. Paul Pedersen, *The Five Stages of Culture Shock: Critical Incidents Around the World* (New York: Greenwood Press, 1995), 1.

6. Secil E. Ertorer, "Acculturating into the Canadian Society: A Case of Karen Refugees," *Journal of Ethnic and Migration Studies* 42, no. 11 (2016): 1864–84.

7. Secil E. Ertorer, "Asylum Regimes and Refugee Experiences of Precarity: The Case of Syrian Refugees in Turkey," *Journal of Refugee Studies* 34, no. 3 (2021): 2568–92.

8. Secil E. Ertorer, "Asylum Regimes and Refugee Experiences of Precarity: The Case of Syrian Refugees in Turkey," *Journal of Refugee Studies* 34, no. 3 (2021): 2568–92.

9. Nicholas R. Micinski, "The E.U. Granted Ukrainian Refugees Temporary Protection. Why the Different Response from Past Migrant Crises?," *Washington Post*, March 16, 2022, https://www.washingtonpost.com/politics/2022/03/16/eu-granted-ukrainian-refugees-temporary-protection-why-different-response-past-migrant-crises/.

10. Michel Foucault, *The History of Sexuality Volume 1: An Introduction*, 1st ed. (New York: Pantheon Books, 1976).

11. Secil E. Ertorer, Jennifer Long, Melissa Fellin, and Victoria M. Esses, "Immigrant Perceptions of Integration in the Canadian Workplace," *Equality, Diversity, and Inclusion* 41, no. 7: 1091–11.

12. For push factors of migration, see Hein de Haas, Stephen Castles, and Mark J. Miller, *The Age of Migration, Sixth Edition: International Population Movements in the Modern World* (New York: Guilford Publications, 2020).

5

Public Ritual and Utopia

How Torn Space Theater's Creative Placemaking Strategies Activate the Public Realm

Dan Shanahan

Utopia Is No Place

The core principle of utopia, that the community or society possesses "highly desirable or nearly perfect qualities for its citizens," is a condition that does not exist.[1] The word utopia, originally coined by writer Thomas Moore in 1516, comes from the Greek word ou-topos, meaning "no place." The futurist Kevin Kelly had his own response to the "no place" of utopia and described utopia through a more aspirational prism when referring to what he calls "protopia," an incremental progress toward improvement.[2] Can today be a bit better than yesterday and tomorrow better still than today? Kelly's notion is that if life can improve annually by 1%, it will compound, and when looking at life through the hindsight of a decade, the ideals of an aspirational utopia come into focus. Then we find they have shaped the present moment and things have become a bit better than they were before.[3]

The United States measures 3.6 million square miles and consists of six time zones.[4] The vastness of geography props up the implausibility of a cohesive utopia able to stretch from sea to shining sea. So even if we could design a utopia within the United States, can we imagine a utopia other than within small, isolated enclaves where it would be possible for a shared vision and sense of identity to be communicated, accepted, and reinforced? If utopia is an aspirational state of mind rather than a state of place, where can we introduce playing fields where the ideals of a utopia can at least be exercised?

We likely need to focus on the local because it contains the playing arena where participation and engagement can construct a shared meaning and mythology and, importantly, a trust can be formed; a trust in one another, a trust in mutually constructed meaning, and a trust that not everything is a scam, a sham, where not everything is a business, a racket, a swamp, a zero-sum game. Within the playing arena of the local, aspirations inherent in utopia find tangible outcomes rooted in trust, interest, and empathy for somebody other than the individual.

Public Place as Real Place

As the artistic director of Torn Space Theater for more than twenty years, I have spent the last ten years focused on creating public ritual performance for spaces that are not traditional art spaces to encourage collective engagement with spaces and between peoples. I've developed productions for processing facilities, grain elevators, city lots, factories, and waterways, among other locations. These productions have in large part been funded by economic development grants and foundation dollars with the funding priority to activate the public sphere and transition abandoned or neglected spaces into economically viable and relevant public and private spaces. When the mechanisms of arts-based funding support public ritual, we gain a framework for how an arts organization can activate the aspirational qualities of utopia while providing a tangible roadmap for how to activate the public sphere. The role of the arts organization, in this instance, is to provide an opportunity for the public to connect to their local environment in a new and often compelling way and gain entrance into a real place.

In the article "America Is Having A Moral Convulsion," the political and cultural commentator David Brooks writes, "In America, interpersonal trust is in catastrophic decline. In 2014, according to the General Social Survey conducted by NORC at the University of Chicago, only 30.3 percent of Americans agreed that 'most people can be trusted.'"[5] A vacuum of trust breeds discontent, paranoia, and erosion of agreed-upon truths and norms, and in time we find ourselves at the opposite end of the spectrum, having waded into the territories of a dystopia. Where to turn?

David Brooks continues: "Over the past 60 years, we have given up on the Rotary Club and the American Legion and other civic organizations and replaced them with Twitter and Instagram. Ultimately, our ability to rebuild trust depends on our ability to join and stick to organizations."[6]

The organizations Brooks refers to are not multinational organizations or franchises that populate American commercial districts; instead, these organizations are small, internally stitched together, collectively focused on mission or vision, and clumsily pushing forward with compromise, arguments, eccentricities, and small victories within the confines of frustration and compromise that occur when not everyone is like you or agrees with you.

When Alexis de Tocqueville, the French sociologist and political theorist, traveled to America in 1834 in preparation for his classic work *Democracy in America* (1835), he observed America's unique ability to form "associations" to address social and political objectives.[7] He observed that in a massive country, its citizens separated often by seemingly impenetrable geography would often be left outside a structured federal government or federal response and that they would need to rely on equality and collectivism taking the form of a volunteer firefighter chapter, community center, or health clinic to respond to crises and to form community. The township would not have a performing arts center but instead a vaudeville troupe or amateur theater company to provide entertainment. The local had a function, and it provided a vitality, something to believe in and somewhere to express oneself and show oneself as an individual within a collective cause.

The French philosopher Michel Foucault saw these small organizational structures as "worlds within worlds," and he defined this alternative place as a heterotopia. If utopia means "no place," then heterotopia with the prefix hetero means "other, another, or different" or "other place." Foucault observed that certain cultural, institutional, or organizational spaces were intense, focused, contradictory worlds, mirroring yet subverting, commenting and upsetting what is occurring in the outside world. These other worlds might be a ship with its crew existing within a vessel moving through infinite space, or a boarding school where one must be granted permission to enter and then live out adolescence away from the family and societal structure, or a museum with layers of time folded into a fixed point for the observer to study. These "counter-sites" either impose on or allow the inhabitant to experience the multitudes of existence simultaneously in one space.[8]

If utopias provide us with aspirational perfection of the real, then heterotopias provide us with a landscape to witness and exercise the real; where aspirations can be fought for, challenged, and ultimately negotiated with. Foucault uses six principles to define a heterotopia. The third principle provides context for how an arts-based organization can function as a heterotopia. Foucault stated that a heterotopia "is capable of juxtaposing in a single real place several spaces, several sites that are in themselves incompatible."[9] Foucault uses the analogy of the Persian garden to illustrate this principle. Integrated within a rectangular area of the garden exist four distinct elements that represent four parts of the world. A garden collapses geography and time and allows the inhabitant to view several disparate elements of the natural world within one contained space.

Within the context of Foucault's third principle we can substitute the garden for a performing arts organization; replacing vegetation and soil with performance and image. The notion of *incompatibility* in Foucault's garden is the juggernaut to be resolved by a publicly funded arts organization. An arts organization, functioning as a heterotopia, must work to attract the "incompatible" aspects of the participants who perform the role of creator and spectator. One way to do this is to view the role of the arts organization as a facilitator of public ritual where seemingly incompatible persons coexist in a framed space to create shared meaning through collective engagement. If a utopia cannot be supported because everyone must subscribe to the same vision, then a heterotopia thrives because it is a temporary space carved from "incompatible" beliefs, backgrounds, and skill sets.

Ritual and Performance in a Heterotopia

Torn Space Theater is a nonprofit theater company located in Buffalo, New York, which I founded with Melissa Meola in 2001. In many ways, the organizational structure of Torn Space is that of a traditional arts-based nonprofit operating within the United States. The organization secures government funding, charges admissions, hires staff, provides services to the community, and adheres to a documented mission statement and bylaws. But within the organizational structure, the contours of a heterotopia come into focus. The organization of Torn Space provides a defined entry point for a diverse cross-section of the community to participate and articulate its unique visions in the service of creating a public ritual performance. The relationship between the organization and the participants is reciprocal. The participants shape Torn Space's public ritual productions, impacting both the narrative structure and aesthetics of the work through the participants' individual talents, personas, and histories. The participants come from diverse nations, ethnicities, and socioeconomic backgrounds. As a point of practice, Torn Space often casts performers who have no formal training in the performing arts and who do not identify as artists.

The narrative structure for these performances occurs within the context of the public ritual. To deliver an access point for the audience as well as a narrative perspective, Torn Space has devised a fictitious society consisting of these diverse participants to tell the story within an alternative reality mirroring our own, composed of recycled pop culture, ancient mythologies, machinery, and technology. The society is constructed from traditional and nontraditional performers, ranging from military reenactors, high school marching bands, blacksmiths, horseback riders, boxers, farm animals, gospel singers, and operating engineers, to name a few, providing a unique patchwork of America in the early part of the twenty-first century. A cross-section of the community participates in the creation and execution of the work, and they are engaged in the meaning-making process of the performance.

Torn Space has been conducting these performance rituals since 2013 within the industrial site of Silo City, a campus of grain elevators lining the Buffalo River. The silos are relics of a previous era when Buffalo dominated in the shipping and grain manufacturing industry. These giant industrial remnants combined with the reclaimed natural world that surrounds them is the *sacred* spot where Torn Space's society enacts its late summer rituals.

These rituals at the silos represent what has been metaphorically sown and reaped, familially, locally, and globally. Torn Space provides a gathering space for the local community to return to annually to reflect on the past year and to consider what was gained and what was lost. What has changed and what needs changing? This public forum is both a metaphorical and actual space for the community to prepare for the coming year by reflecting on the recent past.[10]

By incorporating the talents of the community into the public ritual, Torn Space's approach is rooted in the traditions of the ancient Greeks, who believed the "amateur" provided vitality to performance. The conditions for this vitality are more aligned with Foucault's heterotopia than Sir Thomas More's utopia, where the organizing principle of utopic vision is uniformity, conformity, and harmony. The conditions for vitality within the heterotopia require individuals, who on the surface might appear "incompatible," to exist within one time and one place to achieve one goal. The arts organization provides the framework and the entry point for varying biographies, places of origins, and ideologies to create a public work. The arts organization can be the microcosm where the *incompatible* must negotiate to produce something that activates the public realm, carving out an entry point for the public to engage in ritual.

Supporting the Public Ritual through Creative Placemaking

For public ritual to occur, there needs to be a public and an economic system in place to facilitate the participation. When Torn Space began developing work at Silo City, the spaces the company designed lacked basic infrastructure such as power, water, and toilets. Lights, sound, and video projection had to be run off generators, and thousands of feet of cabling had to be snaked throughout the site to power the production design. Audience accommodations had to be brought to the site, security guards contracted to protect rented equipment overnight, and labor hired to build out what would be considered common resources in a traditional arts space. After the performance, all this infrastructure was broken down, removed, and the space returned to its former state. Within this system, economics are supporting a fleeting place in time, much like Foucault's example of the fairgrounds that are momentarily constructed on the outskirts of town.[11] These spaces provide

Figure 5.1. "They Kill Things," Torn Space Theater, Silo City, 2015. *Source*: Photo by Michael W. Thomas, author's private collection.

a gateway to an alternative experience outside the norms of day-to-day life. The infrastructure and events are very real for a moment, but when that moment passes there is nothing left behind to indicate it ever happened. The arts organization in this case is not leaving behind a performance hall, a gallery, or a public sculpture; it is leaving behind a moment that was experienced, and that moment will fade.

For these public rituals at Silo City, Torn Space spends approximately 80 percent of its total production budget to transform a real space into a temporary space. This budget expenditure does not include fees to performers, designers, costumes, set pieces, props, or any other artistic component. On average, earned revenue through ticket sales accounts for 22 percent of the total production budget. The remaining 88 percent of the production budget largely comes from foundations and public funds. Funds from foundations have varying objectives, usually tied to the priorities of the foundation's benefactor or to the trustees who manage the foundation. Public funds, on the other hand, must be used to benefit the public in a measured way, and supporting a heterotopia is not one of them.

The United States' complicated relationship to funding the arts has been well documented, and artworks deemed unfit for public funding have ranged from Andres Serrano's *Piss Christ* to Big Bird. Why should taxpayer dollars be used to fund art people may or may not like, agree with, or even engage with? This point of contention boils over in cycles, often culminating in a call to slash or eliminate the budget of the National Endowment for the Arts (NEA). In 2020 the NEA had a total budget of $162.5 million, or .003 percent of the federal budget. President Biden submitted his 2022 budget to include $201 million in funds for the NEA.[12] Even with Biden's roughly $40 million increase, one would be hard-pressed to argue that eliminating the NEA is being done in the name of fiscal prudence. If art is an idea, it can be offensive or manipulative or persuasive. If art is a public good, it can be difficult to quantify. But if art can be inserted into the language of economics, then there are metrics for measuring its value. These metrics can measure the impact of the arts on job creation or on the local economy or broader initiatives that are more elusive to measure, such as the revitalization of neglected or forgotten spaces. The latter public good falls under the concept of creative placemaking.

Creative placemaking was introduced by economist Ann Markusen and arts consultant Anne Gadwa in a 2010 white paper for the NEA.[13]

Creative placemaking is defined "as a process where community members, artists, arts and culture organizations, community developers, and other stakeholders use arts and cultural strategies to implement community-led change. This approach aims to increase vibrancy, improve economic conditions, and build capacity among residents to take ownership of their communities."[14]

The strategy of creative placemaking is to rejuvenate public places through an acute understanding of place, authentic community engagement, awareness of existing development systems, and an arts-centered approach to that development.[15] The method of creative placemaking has been integrated into regional economic development strategies because it helps support smart growth. "Smart Growth covers a range of development and conservation strategies that help protect the natural environment" through building on existing assets rather than demolishing older buildings and then expanding farther and farther from city centers with new builds.[16]

Torn Space Theater's work at Silo City was funded by economic development grants that supported smart growth and creative placemaking strategies. In Western New York's Regional Economic Development Strategic Plan "A Strategy for Prosperity in Western New York," a guiding principle for strategic investment plans was to support "projects that promote placemaking in other communities and support the general principles of smart growth and sustainable development." The intended outcome of such projects was to assist in "creating infrastructure conducive to sustainable, healthy and attractive development and enhanced quality of life to grow opportunities and bring in new visitors, residents and business to the region."[17]

The infrastructures prioritized for development were those that were a regional asset situated in a strategic location and often consisting of historic buildings and neighborhoods.[18] When historic buildings are on the scale and complexity of those populating Silo City, the principles of smart growth can get sidelined by basic principles of economic development. In the article "The Trouble with Owning a Grain Elevator," which profiles Silo City, Lynn Freehill-May comments that "grain elevators are a stubborn target for urban renewal, because it's so difficult to use them for anything but cleaning and storing grain."[19] Jim Watknis, the site manager for Silo City, explained that grain elevators had been lauded by Bauhaus architects, who "considered them the epitome of form, function, and design."[20] But by the time Rick Smith, a local industrialist, purchased the land and silos in 2006, the buildings were no longer functional, nor were they generally appreciated by the wider public. Commenting about the silos, Rick Smith said; "For my father's generation, Silo City was a symbol of failure and bad decisions, but young people are in awe of its magnificence—their new eyes see its potential."[21]

Activating potential in the early stages of a complex development initiative such as Silo City requires the use of creative placemaking strategies. Creative placemaking provides a tool to reintroduce a location to the public, and through small incremental interventions, a connection to the place emerges. Torn Space's performances at Silo City largely worked within the parameters of creative placemaking; they were developed within the norms of arts-based initiatives to activate place; the work was created by a nonprofit arts organization funded through public dollars earmarked under economic development initiatives, and the work facilitated a connection between the public and the place. The performances built connections between people and the industrial spaces of Silo City by encouraging the public to collaborate in the process and to visualize the structures in new and unexpected ways.[22]

After Rick Smith purchased the grain elevators, Torn Space was invited in 2013 to develop site-based performances within the grain elevators and surrounding sites. The interior and exterior spaces of Silo City were a fundamental component of the production's design and theme. Silo City's website provides an excellent overview of the specifications and history of the varied buildings that make up Silo City. To provide context for the locations of Torn Space's productions, I list the structure's specifications along with corresponding performance titles. The architectural sites included Marine A, a first-of-its-kind grain elevator built in 1925 with an interior corridor of repeating silos measuring 400 feet long by 60 feet wide by 120 feet tall for the productions ("Burden," Torn Space Theater, 2017). The lake and rail elevator was built in four stages from 1927 to 1930 with a total capacity of 4,400,000 bushels with built-in infrastructure for direct train shipment ("Stations," Torn Space Theater, 2019). The American Warehouse was built in 1906 and served as a combination mill and warehouse for the American Malting Corporation. The first floor of the warehouse is a large room with 20-foot ceilings and large concrete columns. The structure is 483 feet long by 150 feet wide by 130 feet tall and is eight stories high ("Storchouse," Torn Space Theater, 2014). The American Grain Elevator was built in 1906 for the American Malting Corporation and used as an elevator for the production of beer. The building is a series of massive white columns that provide a stunning backdrop and video projection surface for productions ("Motion Picture," Torn Space Theater, 2013; and "The Gathering,"

Torn Space Theater, 2016). Perot Malt House is a five-story red brick malt house built in 1907 and is used for malting barley, with malting furnaces located on the ground floor; each floor contains expansive machinery used for transporting grain ("They Kill Things," Torn Space, 2015).[23]

While Torn Space's work at Silo City was rooted in creative placemaking strategies, it only was able to take on the contours of a heterotopia because the work was encouraged by Rick Smith, the property owner, and Jim Watkins, the property steward. Both Watkins and Smith were uniquely positioned to usher in a "world within a world."[24] They rejected more traditional methods of revitalization that seek out broad appeal for tourism and instead encouraged experimental works grounded in the mythology and history of the site.

Creative placemaking is a strategy that shifts in meaning depending on which stakeholder is advocating for it. A property developer might consider creative placemaking a useful tool to activate a space in the short term in hopes of attracting significant future investment. A political leader might employ creative placemaking to rebrand a post-industrial section of the city to raise property values and attract businesses. Torn Space's work in creative placemaking at Silo City was funded by public dollars to increase the public's awareness of a strategically located space that was architecturally and historically significant and to strengthen the relationship between public and the place. Under this fairly broad mandate, and with the support of Rick Smith and Jim Watkins, Torn Space set out to design a public ritual anchored in community-wide participation providing a model for arts-based civic engagement. It is here that the heterotopia appears and where it can merge with the established arts-based funding priorities of creative placemaking.

People in Space

When the public enters the physical spaces of Silo City for a Torn Space production, the space has been overlaid with a temporary set of design principles that facilitate engagement between the public and the location. Silo City's interiors are not spaces most people move in and out of throughout their routines. They are not entirely recreational public spaces like a park, and they are not transactional public spaces like a shopping mall. They are spaces transitioning from a utilitarian producer and exporter of grain to one of cultural activity supported by creative placemaking initiatives. Should Silo

Figure 5.2. "FEAST," Torn Space Theater, Silo City, 2019. *Source*: Photo by Michael W. Thomas, author's private collection.

City act as a passive, albeit impressive, backdrop for cultural activities, the space would remain a dead space devoid of its utilitarian origin, interesting to look at but nothing more than a movie set. The vitality of space occurs when it moves into the realm of the public sphere where the public is impacted by space through means of their relationship to that space and to others who occupy the space with them.

To activate the space, the performances of Torn Space use the architecture, machinery, and landscape of Silo City as character. The physical space provides the throughline for the narrative, connecting the psyche of the space to the psyche of the performance. The public is accessing the relationship between space and performance, and it is here that the performance becomes the event that triggers human togetherness while opening up the space to the public sphere.[25] Engagement in the public sphere is a concept discussed by the political philosopher Hannah Arendt, who argued "that freedom needs a public realm to make its appearance."[26] We cannot act in isolation because action needs someone to respond to it and then pick up that action and move it further into the world, resulting in impact. This impact is the exercise of democratic freedom, providing us with continuous beginnings and opportunities for action.[27] For this action to occur in the public sphere, it requires Arendt's conditions of plurality.[28] Should a space become homogeneous and "pure" through means of policing what can and can't be done, by enacting what is proper and what is deviant, we erase the conditions where action is possible and freedom can occur.[29] The conditions outlined by Arendt are at odds with the harmonious qualities of a utopia but are aligned with the disparate elements of a heterotopia, and it is within this concept of heterotopia that the public ritual performances of Torn Space occur.

The work developed by Torn Space for the grain elevators are not plays. They don't necessarily rely on text or performers learning their roles and then performing them. They are public rituals that, when positioned within a creative placemaking framework, provide a model for arts-based civic engagement. They promote engagement rooted in shared meaning and shared experience occurring outside the bounds of more traditional civic infrastructure such as a mall, town square, or public park. Existing on the outside, these spaces become temporary heterotopias supported by the economics of creative placemaking strategies and constructed by a cross-section of the community.

For the concept of performance as a public ritual, Torn Space draws on the work of Antonin Artaud (1896–1948). One of the most influential theater theorists of the twentieth century, Artaud developed a concept of performance known as Theatre of Cruelty. The Theatre of Cruelty is both a philosophy and an artistic discipline. Artaud wanted to disrupt the relationship between the audience and performer. He was looking for a total collapse of the fourth wall or the proscenium relationship that separated the audience from the action on the stage.

His "cruelty" was centered around sensory disruption, and the performance was formulated through "organized anarchy." The need for this anarchy, according to Artaud, is driven by a lack of ritual and ceremony in most of our everyday lives that are often orderly and scripted.[30]

Another example of arts-enacting ritual is found in Hermann Nitsch, an Austrian artist known for his visceral performance art practice, often based on the ritualistic practice of sacrifice that occurs within fairly contained spaces such as a gallery, that amplifies the aesthetics and sensory qualities of the act. Nitsch was the creator of *Das Orgien Mysterien Theater* (The Orgiastic Mystery Theater), a long-running series of ritualistic performances that involved slaughter, religious sacrifices, music, dancing, and audience participation.[31] Artuad and Nitsch valued the act over the representation or depiction of the act, where the creator of the performance designs conditions for the participant to engage with the *actual* as opposed to the illusion. This approach contrasts with Konstantin Stanislavski's concept of method acting, where a trained actor assumes the physiological underpinning of a character so as to play that character in a truthful and responsive way on stage.[32] The illusion that Marlon Brando is Stanley Kowalski, a fictional character in Tennessee Williams's play *A Streetcar Named Desire*, is so compelling that Brando and Kowalski become indistinguishable. The seductive quality of illusion hides the truth, whereas the *cruelty* of ritual is intended to expose the truth by disrupting illusion and bring the public into the process of engagement.[33] In an arts-based ritual, the public is entering into a relationship with the performance, and the performance is being directly impacted by the public. This symbiotic relationship can only occur when the curtain is pulled back to reveal the mechanics used to construct an illusion, preventing the spectator from being a passive observer.

This engagement allows the artists and participants to gain a better understanding of how skill sets and professions impact the way society is constructed by providing a viewing space to confront the process for how *things get done*. To make visible the process for how things get done, Torn Space has made the purposeful decision to work with a range of tradespeople, athletes, and professionals outside of traditional arts-based disciplines to simultaneously showcase the final outcome of labor and the act of labor itself. To illustrate this point, I have provided three examples for productions by Torn Space.

The Cow

In 2019 Torn Space partnered with Michael Parkot, owner of Always Something Farm, whose aim is to create a sustainable local food system. One aspect of Parkot's approach was facilitating participation between the consumer and the food system. Torn Space designed a moment in the production where a cow was brought into the performance space and audience members were selected to approach the cow and begin milking it. In this instance, time is not dependent on beats of action or units of suspense, but rather on the reality of how long it takes to milk a cow. The public is both participating in the construction of the performance while viewing the labor required to produce a glass of milk.

Figure 5.3. *FEAST*, Torn Space Theater, Silo City, 2019. *Source*: Photo by Michael W. Thomas, author's private collection.

The Machine

Torn Space hired union machine operators at their standard pay rate to perform a choreographed routine with excavators. The sequence was choreographed and lit by frequent Torn Space collaborators Electric Light and Oil. This performance sequence existed within several instances of engagement. The public were able to view a series of events as a large-scale spectacle where heavy machines engage in a ballet while also being acutely aware of the skill and mechanics being employed to move the machines in such a way. The operators were able to transfer their trained skill into a different context and participate in the construction of a live art event. The performance directors had to navigate the labor laws of the construction industry, work with shipping companies to transport the excavators to the site, and communicate a language based in the arts to one based in the logistics of construction and operation.

Figure 5.4. "The Gathering," Torn Space Theater, Silo City, 2017. *Source*: Photo by Michael W. Thomas, author's private collection.

The Boxer

Torn Space hired boxers to participate in a boxing match held within the American Warehouse, an industrial processing facility for grain. The boxers trained at a local gym, and before agreeing to participate in the performance, I had to visit the gym and spar with their head trainer. The trainer set out rules: whenever I landed a hit he would do a squat, and when he landed a hit I would do a squat. In the end I did several squats and he did none. The objective of this exercise was to provide me with a deeper appreciation of the skills needed to box. If I was going to integrate their talents into a production, I had better understand the labor and physicality required to box. When the boxers performed in the production, they were not performing the role of the boxer, they were boxing, and therefore providing the public an opportunity to view the act and the construction of the act simultaneously.

These examples demonstrate the ways that community members who do

Figure 5.5. "Storehouse," Torn Space Theater, Silo City, 2015. *Source*: Photo by Michael W. Thomas, author's private collection.

not identify as artists participate in the construction of an arts-based public ritual. The ritual collapses the fourth wall and dismantles the separation of public and performance, artist and "non-artist." The result is to bring the public closer to the construction of the act. Without engagement with the construction of image, the public can become either increasingly alienated and distrustful of the illusion or seduced and manipulated by illusion because they no longer know how the illusion was built. The public ritual of performance is akin to attending the local common council meeting where the public gains access to the slow, methodical workings of government rather than viewing the workings of government through sensational headlines.

Jean Baudrillard, the French sociologist, philosopher, and cultural theorist, coined the phrase "simulacrum," which is something that replaces reality with its representation.[34] Utopian visions often are facsimiles of the past, artificial stand-ins for what we think a perfect reality ought to be. Consider Disneyland as a utopia of childhood and the height of the family bond, making memories that will "last a lifetime." Consider Applebee's as the simulacrum of the neighborhood watering hole supported by marketing slogans to include "There's no place like the neighborhood" or "Eatin' Good in the Neighborhood."[35]

These are relatively benign examples, but Baudrillard focuses on the first Gulf War, where the battle became for many Americans a mediated experience where Scuds and the Scud Stud were players in a distant, video game–like reality.[36]

Within an era of globalization, the small clan networks of local life—main streets, lawn fetes, softball leagues, and social clubs—create tangible anchors that facilitate belief in institutions with a small *I* and reinforce the REAL. But if the line between reality and virtual reality continues to be erased to the point where bold actions can be done impassively and anonymously behind the shield of social media accounts or drones, where do we go to feel authentic, visceral, tangible experiences; where do we go to feel trust, and where is the "public sphere?"

In the same article referenced prior, David Brooks's "America Is Having a Moral Convulsion," he looks at history for some parallel to a time similar to our own and zeros in on the 1870s, when trust in everything was also at an all-time low; the industrial revolution was creating mass displacement, and economic divide and corruption were perceived to be everywhere.[37]

In reaction, Brooks notes, "people built organizations at a dazzling pace," and the civic revival began. The United Way, the NAACP, Boy Scouts, American Legion, American Bar Association, and so many other civic organizations were formed during this period and helped usher in the Progressive movement. The local organization was providing an anchor between the people and the communities where they resided.[38]

Creative placemaking strategies that support public ritual performance provide a similar vitality and a similar connective force between people and place. The public ritual of performance contains an element of utopia; not a utopia of simulation or perfection, but of real, person-to-person participation where incremental one-percent improvements can occur.[39]

The utopia of our existence is the experiment in which we are all living. It takes shape and is expressed not through perfection but through aspirations for perfection crafted through messy negotiated participation in the public realm. Creative placemaking supports a temporary space of ritual where the public can enter a heterotopia to exercise their ideals that both mirrors and subverts the outside world.

Notes

1. Thomas More, *Utopia* (Portland: Mint Editions, 2022).

2. Kevin Kelly, *The Inevitable: Understanding the 12 Technological Forces That Will Shape Our Future* (New York: Penguin Books, 2017).

3. Diana Budds, "What I Learned from a Year in Utopias," Curbed, December 23, 2019, https://archive.curbed.com/2019/12/23/21032132/failed-utopias-2019-nice-try.

4. "United States of America," *Encyclopedia of the Nations*, https://www.nationsencyclopedia.com/economies/Americas/United-States-of-America.html.

5. David Brooks, "America Is Having a Moral Convulsion," The Hundreds, https://thehundreds.com/blogs/monologue/america-is-having-a-moral-convulsion-david-brooks.

6. Brooks, "America Is Having a Moral Convulsion."

7. Alexis de Tocqueville, *Democracy in America* (New York: Knopf, 1994), 596.

8. Michel Foucault, "Of Other Spaces: Utopias and Heterotopias," October 1984, https://web.mit.edu/allanmc/www/foucault1.pdf.

9. Foucault, "Of Other Spaces," 6.

10. Melissa Meola, "Artist Talk," Torn Space Theater, given over Zoom, April 28, 2021.

11. Foucault, "Of Other Spaces," 7.

12. "National Endowment for the Arts Appropriations History," Appropriations History, https://www.arts.gov/about/appropriations-history; "President's Fiscal Year 2022 Budget Proposes $201 Million for the National Endowment for the Arts," https://www.arts.gov/news/press-releases/2021/presidents-fiscal-year-2022-budget-proposes-201-million-national-endowment-arts.

13. Ann Markusen and Anne Gadwa, "Creative Placemaking," National Endowment for the Arts, https://www.arts.gov/impact/creative-placemaking.

14. "Creative Placemaking," American Planning Association, https://www.planning.org/knowledgebase/creativeplacemaking/.

15. Markusen and Gadwa, "Creative Placemaking."

16. Environmental Protection Agency. "About Smart Growth," September 22, 2022, https://www.epa.gov/smartgrowth/about-smart-growth.

17. Western New York Regional Economic Development Council, *A Strategy for Prosperity in Western New York*, WNY Regional Economic Development Strategic Plan, November 2011, 22, https://regionalcouncils.ny.gov/sites/default/files/2017-11/A_Strategy_for_Prosperity_in_Western_New_York_November_2011.pdf.

18. Western New York Regional Economic Development Council, *A Strategy for Prosperity in Western New York*.

19. Lynn Freehill-Maye, "The Trouble with Owning a Grain Elevator," *The New Yorker*, July 31, 2016, https://www.newyorker.com/business/currency/the-trouble-with-owning-a-grain-elevator.

20. Freehill-Maye, "The Trouble with Owning a Grain Elevator."

21. "The Transformation of Silo City Signals a New Future for Buffalo," Metropolis, August 20, 2021, https://metropolismag.com/projects/silo-city-buffalo-adaptive-reuse/.

22. "Creative Placemaking."

23. "History," Silo City, https://www.silo.city/history.

24. Mozhdeh Bashiran, Yani Kong, and Tamara Lee, "Heterotopias (Worlds Within Worlds)," The Comparative Media Arts Journal, https://www.sfu.ca/cmajournal/issues/issue-eleven--heterotopias--worlds-within-worlds-.html.

25. Gert Biesta, "Becoming Public: Public Pedagogy, Citizenship and the Public Sphere," *Social & Cultural Geography* 13, no. 7 (2012): 683–97.

26. Biesta, "Becoming Public," 687.

27. Hannah Arendt and Anne Applebaum, *The Origins of Totalitarianism* (London: The Folio Society Ltd., 2022).

28. Biesta, "Becoming Public," 684.

29. Biesta, "Becoming Public," 689.

30. Antonin Artaud, *The Theater and Its Double* (New York: Grove Press, 2004).

31. "Hermann Nitsch (1938–2022)." Online edition of *Artforum* International Magazine, April 19, 2022, https://www.artforum.com/news/hermann-nitsch-1938-2022-88395.

32. Konstantin Stanislavsky, *Actor Prepares* (New York: Routledge, 1989).

33. Artaud, *The Theater and Its Double*.

34. Jean Baudrillard and Sheila Faria Glaser, *Simulacra and Simulation* (Ann Arbor: University of Michigan Press, 2020).

35. "Applebees Slogans," Slogan List, https://www.sloganlist.com/restaurant-slogans/applebees-.html.

36. "The Gulf War Did Not Take Place," in *Jean Baudrillard: Selected Writings*, ed. and intro. Mark Poster (Stanford: Stanford University Press, 2002), 231–53.

37. Brooks, "America Is Having a Moral Convulsion."

38. Brooks, "America Is Having a Moral Convulsion."

39. Kelly, *The Inevitable*.

Part 3

Toward a Troubled Utopia

6

Repossessing Utopia from Below

Black/Feminist/Queer Utopianism in
American Political Thought

ALIX OLSON AND ALEX ZAMALIN

Over the past few decades, utopia has been increasingly abandoned as a conceptual resource for left-political critique and activism. Loss of faith in universal rationality, skepticism surrounding totalizing knowledge, and the erosion of grand narratives have led to the contention that utopia be replaced with less transcendent and more pragmatic ideas. In the early twentieth century, revolutionary dreams of socialism and communism united citizens across the world with the radical hope that a foundational transformation of the world might be possible—that capitalism could be toppled, global solidarity was within reach, and peace could prevail. But by the beginning of the twentieth-first century, if utopianism was not conflated with the failures of Soviet Russia, the horrors of Nazi Germany, and its dreams of perfection linked to totalitarianism, then it was viewed as a naive and flimsy ground on which to build a new society. The intellectual historian Russell Jacoby writes, "A utopian spirit—a sense that the future could transcend the present—has vanished . . . This is the wisdom of our times, an age of political exhaustion and retreat."[1]

Utopian skepticism is not new. Since its ancient formulation in Plato's *Republic*, which imagines rule by philosopher kings committed to justice, to its modern manifestation in Thomas More's *Utopia*, which envisages a socialist society of riches and happiness, utopia has been subject to countless critiques: the ideal of perfection leaves little room for flexibility; idealism squashes realism; messianic hope glosses over hierarchy. In the words of political theorist Judith Shklar, utopia is something of a "moralist's artifact" and defined by a "changeless harmonious whole . . . In utopia, there cannot, by definition, be any room for eccentricity."[2] If these criticisms are accurate, then it would be understandable why utopia has not been part of the armor of contemporary left-politics, which tend to champion diversity, non-hierarchical distributions of power, direct democracy, and positive freedom. But is utopian thinking synonymous with these aforementioned problems? Can utopia be liberated from some of its most reactionary proclivities? Our answer is yes.

There is, in fact, much to be said about the ways in which utopia can energize contemporary political thought and praxis, but this endeavor hinges on the following question: which utopian imaginings ought we to prioritize? We argue that while all utopian thought is organized around an aspirational horizon, in which pain and suffering are minimized, there is a marked difference in those visions that emanate from below: from the dispossessed, discounted, and disenfranchised. This chapter considers the experimental insights of political thinkers whose vital reflections have been long marginalized by the mainstream—the white, heteronormative, masculinist, Euro-modern utopian tradition, broadly construed. Drawing on select exemplars of Black/queer/feminist political theorists, novelists and activists who have *repossessed* utopian analysis by grounding it in concepts of liberation in/as/through struggle, disjointed temporality, and reflexive critique, we argue for its continued relevance in confronting contemporary dystopic times.

Black Utopia: Rising Above/Within a Cruel Planet

Liberation is a concept that is a hallmark of contemporary left politics, and of utopia. To be free from domination, to have radical autonomy over your desires, is crucial for political sovereignty. But the struggle for liberation takes different shape in Black utopian thought: desires for perfection, social harmony, and absolute knowledge are replaced with privileging radically transformative accounts of/for the dispossessed. Take for instance the first modern Black utopian text, Martin Delany's Afrofuturist work of fiction *Blake* (1859), which imagines a global antiracist, abolitionist uprising against white supremacy, led by an ex-slave Henry Blake. *Blake* is written in a moment when nineteenth-century utopianism was at its height: Robert Owen's socialist commune in New Harmony, Indiana; George Ripley's Brook Farm in Massachusetts; and dozens of Fourier-inspired associationist or "phalanx" colonies springing up throughout the United States. But whereas these experiments imagined utopianism as creating a decisive outline of social harmony, including division of labor, established social roles, provision of basic resources, and leisure for all, *Blake*'s critical utopianism centralizes the active examination and excising of reactionary ideas. In particular, Blake questions Eurocentric wisdom about political development as he works to imagine a movement for a global pan-African community. To the Cuban poet Placido, who claims that enslaved Africans "have much yet to learn to fit us for freedom," Blake responds, "we know enough now." Later in the novel, Madame Cordora, a revolutionary councilwoman, issues a demand to Blake that simultaneously reverses patriarchal expectations about women's political inferiority: "why have we so long submitted to [racist] laws?"[3]

A similar line of critical utopian examination is reflected a century later in another Black utopian meditation on freedom. The novelist Richard Wright's *Black Power* (1954)—a travelogue of his visit to Ghana in the midst of its overthrow of British colonialism under the leadership of Kwame Nkrumah—considers how the future (in Black) might be built and sustained. For Wright, essential to this project is a sense of ambiguity: "I refuse to make a religion out of that which I do not know. I too can feel the limit of my reactions, can feel where my puny self ends, can savor the terror of it [. . .] I don't know. *Must* I know that?"[4] Later, on the question of linear political development, Wright asks: "Was Africa 'primitive?' But what did being 'primitive' mean? [. . .] I was dismayed to discover that I didn't know how to react to it."[5] Contrary to the self-certainty and moral absoluteness that often characterizes Euro-modern utopian meditations, Wright (like Delany before him) interjects a productive ambivalence into theorizing liberation. Utopia, in this sense, is a problem to be worked out and worked through—with an examination of all the contradictions, obfuscations, and inconsistencies—rather than a preexisting ideal to be mapped onto reality. This is the theme of *Black Power*: Wright questioning his Marxism, asking whether it fits into a postcolonial vision of pan-African solidarity, interrogating the patriarchic milieu in which he exists, and becoming more attentive to intersectionality. More generally, in *Black Power*, Wright is decentering the meaning of freedom away from a simplified notion of

Western liberalism and toward a more expansive vision of autonomy: "But here in Africa "freedom" was more than a word . . . It meant the right to public assembly, the right to physical movement, the right to make known his views, the right to elect men of his choice to public office, and the right to recall them if they failed in their promises. At a time when the Western world grew embarrassed at the sound of the word "freedom," these people knew that it meant the right to shape their own destiny as they wished."[6]

Black utopian thought questions not only the end(s) of liberation, but also its temporality; there is not a smooth progression from exclusion to inclusion, from domination to freedom, but instead a disjointed rhythm. Unlike in Euro-modern utopianism, where a perfect world is revealed in its beauty—think of Plato's image of philosopher king rule, Charlotte Perkins Gilman's all-women society, Fourier's utopian socialism of classless society—in Black utopia history resurfaces, and the future is revealed as opaque, uncertain, and often bleak. If the allure of Euro-modern utopianism is immaculate ideal, the animating impulse behind Black utopias is critical analysis. One of the most notable examples of this is George Schuyler's Afrofuturist, Harlem-Renaissance novel *Black No More* (1931). A satire addressing liberal fantasies of colorblindness, *Black No More* considers the question of post-racialism through its fictionalized account of a future in which Black citizens can, through a painful scientific procedure called "Black No More," become white. Far from creating a world of harmony and opportunity, the procedure becomes a way to advance elite interests. A Black man (Max Disher) undergoes the procedure and, recognizing white supremacy as a lucrative discourse, becomes a leading spokesperson for a white supremacist organization. The inventor of the procedure (Junius Crookman) charges exorbitant fees and recruits a small security force to protect his newfound wealth. Outside his offices, Crookman employs "a riot squad armed with rifles, machine guns and tear gas bombs [to maintain] some semblance of order."[7]

In the novel, the number of people with Black skin become negligible, and anxiety among white people (no longer able to use their skin as social status) becomes widespread. As universal whiteness is the norm, new attempts to create racial distinctions arise—those who have paler skin are considered inferior to those who don't. To add to the farce, the "new Caucasians," who ostensibly have more pinkish skin, are segregated, paid less, and, as a result, form a down-with-white prejudice league. Those with "stained skin," as the narrator puts it, become part of a new elite class. In Schuyler's estimate, then, post-racial utopianism is a fantasy in part because of underlying cultural dynamics in US society—acquisitive individualism, sexism, classism—which universal whiteness will not eradicate. If anything, these dynamics will replace the role of racism, while racism will find new ways to amplify its reach. The lesson from *Black No More* is clear for utopian political analysis: purity is a fantasy, and the time of liberation is always disjointed and asynchronous. The call to action, however, is not to abandon the quest for liberation but to treat it with irreverence, to understand how it gets undermined and sabotaged, and to recognize the remainders.

Black utopian thought undoes the romantic investment in easy progress and untroubled resolution. It substitutes the idea of perfection with an idea of perfectibility within contradiction. And yet it nonetheless envisions a horizon for radical transformation and locates moments of solidarity for that horizon to be nearer to the present. The best case in point, perhaps, is W. E. B. DuBois's short story "The Comet" (1920), part of his collection *Darkwater*. Set in a post-apocalyptic New York City that has just been destroyed by a comet, DuBois investigates possible futures for Black autonomy and the abolition of white supremacy. In the course of the narrative, which chronicles an encounter between the two lone survivors of the comet—Jim (a Black man) and Julia (a white woman)—DuBois merges critique with hope. The conclusion, which features Julia's husband (alive, as it turns out) accusing Jim of sexual violence, dislodges the social aspiration of vanquishing racism and suggests that history will interject; this, at a historical moment in the 1920s when lynching is on the rise and the Klan is ascendant. And yet, throughout their brief encounter, Jim and Julia model a space of utopian ethical engagement, mutual aid, and reciprocity, responding to each other's needs and desires without impulse for monopolization or domination. As DuBois writes, "Yet as the two, flying and alone, looked upon the horror of the world, slowly, gradually, the sense of all-enveloping death deserted them. They seemed to move in a world silent and asleep,—not dead. They moved in quiet reverence, lest somehow they wake these sleeping forms who had, at last, found peace."[8]

DuBois's voicing of this possibility anticipates the poetic musings of a later Black utopian, the avant-garde jazz musician Sun Ra, who (in 1972) wrote: "And the Greater love has no god than I / For I like my greater love / Am Immeasurable."[9] A vibrant member of the Black Arts Movement, Ra lived through the optimism that characterized the Black freedom struggle of the 1960s, but also saw the right-wing assault on all its gains. As an artist, Ra saw it as his obligation to make music for a "humanitarian purpose." He once proposed to create a concert of 144,000 musicians, whose collaboration could destroy all the atomic bombs in the world. In Ra's view, the greatest threat facing the world was ruthless acquisitive individualism and thoughtlessness—the antidote to which was solidarity rooted in unconditional generosity, mutual respect, and socioeconomic equality—which might allow citizens "the freedom to rise above a cruel planet."[10]

Like Ra and DuBois, the Black feminist science fiction writer Octavia Butler reinvents utopianism as the mobilization of continual emergence in service of political struggle. She also alerts us to the ways in which turbulence, as the dominant logic of the world around her/us, might provoke attachments to escapist utopian fantasies—whether through the cruelly optimistic longings for a past world or for a world purified of power relations. Butler's novel *Parable of the Sower* (1993) plunges us into a post-apocalyptic portrait of the United States in the mid-2020s where chaos is the central characteristic: right-wing fascism, racist violence, homelessness, drought, environmental catastrophe, debt peonage, and an eviscerated public sphere populate the terrain, presided over by corporations backed by a militarized state. For Butler, this is the trajectory of the latent tendencies of our current order. The protagonist, an African American teenager named Lauren Olamina, lives in a fictional Los Angeles privatopia where her "walled-in" neighbors struggle to face a socio-corporate order that has abandoned all "illusions of security."[11] Refusing to relinquish cruel optimism, these "dying, denying, backward looking peoples" cling to return narratives in which twentieth-century growth and progress—marked by gas-fueled vehicles, national borders, blazing city lights, and big-screen televisions—will soon be restored. This older generation "hasn't been wiped out by a plague so they're still anchored in the past, waiting for the good old days to come back," Lauren observes, "But things have changed a lot, and they'll change more. Things are always changing."[12] In an effort to combat the fear and political paralysis that surround her, Lauren develops a novel life/political philosophy, Earthseed, that sacralizes impermanence itself as a permanent feature of the world. Rather than centering around dogma, ideology, or a panacea, Earthseed promotes adaption to change as key to the pragmatic (and always emergent) work of utopian world-building. The essence of this strategic framework is found in Earthseed's (and the novel's) central tenet: "All that you touch You Change/All that you Change Changes you/The only lasting truth Is Change/God Is Change."[13] While Power/God cannot be permanently "stopped," power relations can be immanently tweaked through ceaseless and creative struggle; it is possible to "rig the game in our favor."[14] The point of Earthseed is explicitly not to reify a canon of ideas but instead to maintain an alert openness toward the world. It is the spurning of a blueprint for a future social order in favor of *transformative utopia in emancipatory action.*

Notably, Butler does not portray the exchange of cruel optimism (historically escapist longings for stability) or fatalism—for a utopian orientation toward contingency as painless surrender. Wrestling with her own anxiety, Lauren scribbles furiously, "God is Change. I hate God."[15] But as her individual journey transfigures into an emerging coalition of refugees, accruing a "mixed group" of multiracial, intergenerational, gender-diverse survivors of neoliberal crisis, Lauren "learns to be an activist."[16] Lauren's radical sensibility is centrally shaped by being a "sharer," someone whose being is phenomenologically bound up with the humanity of the other. While this capacity for "hyper-empathy" is stigmatized as a disability by the corporate-medico establishment, Butler establishes empathy as a symbolic negation of Lauren's avaricious surroundings and core utopian political value. Earthseed is a practical ethics of being as "being-with-others" to shape change toward a "future that makes sense."[17] Ultimately, Lauren and her "harvest of survivors" seed an "Acorn" community in the wilderness of the apocalyptic world. Acorn is not anarchist, nor does it represent idyllic retreat, immunity from the social/economic violence of the corporate order that surrounds it: "if people threaten us or our crops, Lauren affirms unequivocally, "we kill them . . . we kill them or they kill us."[18] Instead, Acorn is a hopeful experiment in communalist survival and a statement of faith in conscious solidarity as adaptive response to a heart-rending terrain.

In this way, Butler demonstrates the ways in which the omnipresent possibility of change provides a reason for staying with the trouble of the world. While this position reduces the salvific potential of human agency, it implores us to find utopian impulse laced through the social and material realities of the present. Lauren writes: "The world is full of painful stories. Sometimes it seems as though there aren't any other kind and yet I found myself thinking how beautiful that glint of water was through the trees."[19] As time passes, Lauren begins to articulate the movement's ultimate "Destiny" as an extra-solar Promised Land without a "long expensive umbilical cord" to Earth and cleansed of ecological, economic, and political troubles. This nostalgia for another time and place, perhaps illustrating the pull of emancipatory exodus, provides a horizon for Lauren's work on Earth.

Despite the temptation to treat Earthseed with deference, or to imagine that Acorn's credo of resilient living within immanence would somehow be sufficient for overcoming disaster, Butler complicates our expectations about the requirements of utopian solidarity and community. Acorn is sustained through an ethos of shared responsibility. Butler writes, "Its promise is not of mansions to live in, milk and honey to drink, or eternal oblivion in some vast whole of nirvana. Its promise is of hard-work and brand-new possibilities, problems, challenges, and changes." But this sense of shared responsibility creates a community that is, at times, self-policing. "Serious misbehavior is harder to get away with, harder even to begin when everyone who sees you knows who you are, where you live, who your family is, and whether you have any business doing what you're doing."[20] The idea of horizon keeps Acorn members struggling to survive, but also creates a sense of self-preservation and isolation—where there is an ever-present fear of infiltration and subversion. Acorn creates schools and scholarships for its believers, but to sustain this intentional community, Acorn's leaders prioritize vocational training—building a generation of engineers, doctors, and lawyers. In Butler's formulation, then, utopian projects based in transcendence are haunted by a sense of history—the return of exclusionary impulses and anxieties that are never far from the surface. Like *Black No More*, the *Parable* books treat history as formative and inescapable. The goal is not to repress its recurrence, but to be mindful of it.

The Hugo Award–winning novelist N. K. Jemisin, representing a new frontier of eco-critical Black feminist speculative fiction, takes up Butler's call to reburden utopian analysis with the painful historical present. Jemisin's Broken Earth trilogy describes the dystopic effects of (ecological and social) extractivism and explodes post-racial and technological utopian narratives (like the neoliberal saviorism of sustainable development) as cruelly optimistic fantasy. The first novel, *The Fifth Season*, takes place forty thousand years from now (or before) on a sprawling Pangean continent called the Stillness, an ironic name because it is subject to unceasing apocalypse. Written through the concept of deep time, every several decades (or centuries) communities must struggle to survive and rebuild society through a menacing "Fifth Season" unleashed by an agential and vengeful Father Earth. Life in Sanze, the dominant human society, is a socioeconomic caste-based system built around the systematic subjugation of the magical orogenes—people born with the genetic ability to "sess" (sense and manipulate) the geological catastrophes; environmental dystopia is at once a slave dystopia, in which those who can understand the earth (and potentially overthrow the social order) are exploited as a docile (and subhuman) labor force. If not murdered, orogenes are funneled into an institution called the Fulcrum, where they are trained by state-assigned Guardians to use their powers to stabilize existing civilization and provide seismic stillness for the rich. Citizens live a perfunctory historical existence; dubious objects of dead civilizations float in the sky, and folklore furnishes an account of geopolitical origins. According to these myths, the earth was destroyed through human efforts (primarily the orogenes') to harness unlimited energy from its core: they "poisoned waters beyond even his ability to cleanse, and killed much of the other life that lived on his surface. They drilled through the crust of his skin, past the blood of his mantle, to get at the sweet marrow of his bones." Scripture-like "commandments" for surviving the Fifth Seasons are chiseled in stone, but even these fluctuate to naturalize imperialism and reinscribe power relations. As Alabaster, the most powerful (and secretly revolutionary) orogene, explains bitterly, "every civilization adds to it; parts that don't matter to the people of the time are forgotten."[21]

In The Broken Earth series, Jemisin writes back to the utopia/dystopia genre of "power fantasies," which feature rugged individualists (white men) fashioning a post-apocalyptic world in their image.[22] Instead, she recasts as protagonist a "Black 40-something, overweight, dreadlocked hero" named Essun, an orogenetic schoolteacher. As Jemisin asserts in a recent interview, "I wanted to see someone else change the world."[23] The book opens with twin world-ending moments (personal and global) that operate at interacting levels: Essun's discovery of her murdered (orogene) son and missing daughter is mirrored by an apocalyptic disaster that has broken the earth. Jemisin follows Essun's multitemporal journey (alongside Alabaster, her orogene mentor) across perilous terrain as she searches for her daughter and absorbs agonizing truths about orogene oppression. The pervasiveness of dystopic injustice is dramatized when Essun and Alabaster escape to a secret island enclave called Meov where, to protect itself from the Sanze empire, orogenes have been put in charge. Even here, Essun and Alabaster are tracked down by the authorities and forced to continue their journey in hiding. Utopia, Jemisin reminds us, can never exist outside of real-world power relations.

Toward the end of the novel, we learn that it is Alabaster who has cleaved the latest rift through the continent, imploding existing civilization to clear ground for the utopian promise of the unknown. As Alabaster explains, couching Afro-utopianism within Afro-pessimism, "the world is what it is. Unless you destroy it and start all over again, there's no changing it."[24] His suggestion is that the propagation of systematic injustice has been so deeply naturalized that it cannot be reformed from within. The first novel concludes with Essun's predicament: seal the earth's fissure, working to redeem humanity, or finish off Alabaster's world-ending destruction.

In an interview in The Paris Review, Jemisin argues: "We don't have good fairytales for the justice system that we're currently living in," so "on some level, fantasy writers [. . .] tend to be trying to create the fairy tales that we need to survive."[25] *The Fifth Season* consciously destabilizes neoliberal fairytales that rely on cruelly optimistic progress narratives: that respectability politics and assimilationism will provide safety and justice for the racially marginalized, that scientific and technological innovation will save humanity, that racial and ecological justice can be pursued as separable destinies, and, fundamentally, that we can transition to a better world without humble recognition of its profound broken-ness. In other words, for Jemisin, apocalypse is not a singular occurrence but an ongoing condition—and one that exists for much of the world's population. "When you look at human history," Jemisin explains, "it's full of fifth seasons."[26] In this way, Jemisin makes it clear that the social dreaming of Black feminist speculative literature is not simply abstract thought experimentation but might also ignite struggles for radical restructuring—and, as such, utopian thought is an acutely pragmatic instrument for liberatory politics. While she refuses to undertake this toil of dreaming for us, Jemisin invites our entry into questioning the stakes of defending a colonized future built on anti-Black oppression and economic/ ecological exploitation, and what is at stake in ending it. As the narrator of the final book in the series warns: "Don't lament when those worlds fall. Rage that they were built doomed in the first place."[27]

This conjunction of dystopian admonition and (tenuous but) inexorable utopian hope that drives Jemisin's series is at once its political orientation. The refusal to submit to fatalism—even amid the relentless fatigue of our "broken earth" times—serves as a rejoinder to Frederic Jameson's assertion that "it is easier to imagine the end of the world than to imagine the end of capitalism."[28] While *The Fifth Season* keeps us in suspense about whether the world is too broken for rebirth, in the tradition of Black feminist abolitionism, it offers utopian possibility in its destruction—with all of the suffering that inevitably entails. Jemisin acknowledges this radical puncture of "handwaving [toward] shiny, happy, utopian futures," avowing that "sometimes a revolution is necessary; sometimes you do have to burn it all down. I want to depict realistically what that'd be like. If you burn it all down, a whole lot of people get hurt."[29]

Feminist Utopia: Imploding Radiant Sandcastles

While Octavia Butler and N. K. Jemisin are integral to the Black utopian tradition, their work also extends and deepens earlier feminist utopian thought of the 1960s and 1970s—a political project ushered in by second-wave feminist novelists invested in reclaiming temporal/spatial landscapes otherwise denied women and minoritized subjects, but deeply suspicious of dominant utopian narratives: static Platonic ideals (located outside history and isolated in space) or "rationalist utopias" (rooted in Enlightenment ideas of linear progress). In Ursula Le Guin's 1983 essay "A Non-Euclidean View of California as a Cold Place to Be," she characterizes the masculinist utopia of the Grand Inquisitor as a power trip, "obsessed by the idea of regulating all life by reason and bringing happiness to man whatever the cost." These "radiant sandcastles," Le Guin contends, having arrived in their final form and devoid of processes that might trouble them, are mechanistic, inhabitable, and of little political value for feminist/revolutionary thinking.[30]

While feminist engagements with futurity rejected utopia as map or blueprint, they refined it as a critical method for opening up the future as indeterminate, or something other than a monotonous repetition of the present. Through these feminist utopias, the past [as present] is transformed into disputed domains, demonstrating the future is imperiled and in dire need of feminist struggle. Among these were Joanna Russ's *The Female Man* (1970), James Tiptree Jr.'s *Houston, Houston Do You Read?* (1976), Elisabeth Mann Borgese's "My Own Utopia" from *The Ascent of Woman* (1963), Sally Miller Gearhart's *The Wanderground* (1978), Marge Piercy's *Woman on the Edge of Time* (1976), and Ursula K. Le Guin's *The Dispossessed: An Ambiguous Utopia* (1974). Collectively, these feminist writers further liberated the utopian imagination from didactic tutorial, reshaping utopia as a discursive practice of challenging the patriarchal order. Their speculative worlds offered actionable space to play out heretofore unthinkable tenets and theories of power being forwarded by feminist theorists: decentralized decision-making and conflict resolution; banishing the nuclear family in favor of collective care; contesting normative practices of sex, birth, child-rearing, and dying; undoing biological essentialism/gender roles and racialized hierarchies; and ultimately disrupting the neoliberal conviction that "no alternative is possible." In this sense, feminist utopian literature issued a warning call, inspiration, and guide for action, defamiliarizing the present as a site for pre-figuring (out) alternative futures.

Le Guin's *The Dispossessed: An Ambiguous Utopia* (1974) wrestles with the viability of embodied anarchy, a society organized around the seductive principles of horizontally shared power, knowledge, and labor—in service of freedom-in-common. In the novel, revolutionaries have fled their capitalist planet, Urras, and (inspired by the socialist writing of a woman named

Laia Asieo Odo) founded an anarcho-syndicalist community on an almost inhabitable desert moon called Annares. One of its residents, the brilliant physicist Shevek, transgresses the (physical and ideological) wall that limits contact with Urras to share his developing philosophy of time that is unpopular on Annares. As the narrative spirals through Shevek's disparate experiences of these worlds, he reckons with tensions between individual freedom and community responsibility, personal autonomy and solidarity of the "social organism," the free pursuit of knowledge and its use and/or commodification, and ultimately how these conciliations might be forged—but never fully satisfied.

As evidenced by its (oxymoronic) subtitle "An Ambiguous Utopia," Le Guin's project is a thought experiment in which social dissidence, disciplining, and ostracism persevere on a planet freed from the repressive forces of the state, organized religion, and private property. As Shavek's friend Bedap avers: "the will to dominance is as central to human beings as the impulse to mutual aid."[31] This political reality (highlighted by Anarres's slow slippage into centralized power, bureaucratic regulation, and ossifying social norms) emphasizes revolution as ongoing struggle and nonlinear journey. This caution is echoed by Shevek when he reminds his fellow anarchists that (in Odo's words), "if [Revolution] is seen as having any end, it will never truly begin."[32]

This "subversive" approach to utopia-as-dynamic (and ambiguous) foregrounds a temporality of continual return. Annares utopia exists in dialectical relationship with—rather than in binary opposition to—hyper-capitalist dystopian reality on Urras. While it is the class and gender-based exploitation on Urras that prompted the uprising, its ongoing oppression offers a cautionary tutorial about anti-authoritarian vigilance; namely, to reflect on and adjust revolutionary "promises" (under changing conditions) so as to shield them from calcifying into reactionary dogma. Instead, utopian aspirations are an omnipresent home to which activists can continually return, people and social dreams transfigured in unpredictable ways by journeys out and beyond. As Shevek is instructed, "you *can* go home again . . . so long as you understand that home is a place where you have never been."[33] Through this utopian ambiguity, Le Guin offers an innovative method for social analysis and a guide for political action that emphasizes (in Donna Haraway's words) staying with the trouble of the world. Utopia is not elsewhere (another planet), but can be glimpsed in existing (post-capitalist) practices and relations—past and present. For Le Guin, an ahistorical model rationally constructed to control human behavior obscures these prefigurative possibilities for *more* just and cooperative ways of life—their potential for generating disquiet and ambiguity, and their open promise.

This commitment to utopia as heuristic for inspecting power relations in the present, while mobilizing critical feminist aspirations for freedom, is also adopted by Marge Piercy's *Woman on the Edge of Time* (1976). Like her contemporaries, Piercy claims being "weary of affluent white males hogging the genre [of utopian time travel]" and of few (always mythological) historical pasts "leading to [people like] me."[34] The novel's protagonist, Connie Ramos (a poor, middle-aged Chicana woman), is incarcerated in a mental institution—where she is subject to involuntary brain experimentation. She is approached by an emissary (Luciente) from the year 2137, who introduces her to a future communitarian society, Mattapoisett. Revolution has eliminated economic, racial, and gender power relations in favor of an eco-feminist anarchist way of life that revolves around collective care and spiritual "in-knowing." While Connie's life has been one of unbearable precarity and loss, it is precisely this failure in the face of an oppressive world that renders her mentally receptive to crossing temporal borders. Designated as mad, she is available as a "catcher" for utopian consciousness-raising and enlisted in the battle for the future.

As utopian impulse, Mattapoisett does not signify Connie's wish fulfillment, and, in fact, she is unnerved, even revulsed, by aspects of Mattapoisett as utopian model: the severed signification between biology and formations of gender identity/racialization; the supplanting of biological birth with artificial gestation and genetically unrelated (and communal) motherhood; an agricultural lifestyle that contradicts her expectations of "rocket ships, skyscrapers into the stratosphere [. . .] glass domes over everything." Connie exclaims: "You sure we went in the right direction? Into the future"? In response, Luciente emphasizes her utopia's lack of progress narrative: "it has taken a long time to put the old good with the new good into a greater good." Over time, and through radical consciousness-raising, Connie comes to understand her own time as a patriarchal "Age of Greed and Waste" and to see her shame over being "second class goods" (poverty, the loss of her child, mental illness, and sexual violence) as the structural effect of that dehumanizing world.[35]

At the same time, as in Le Guin's depiction of Annarres, Mattapoisett's vision for justice is not invested in final arrival, but in omnipresent responsivity and innovation. This radical open-ness is bolstered by the noticeable absence of founding visionary, revolutionary hero, or even a coherent history of its own radical transformation. When Connie disparages Mattapoisett,

Luciente rebuts, "We'd change it if we didn't like it, how not? We're always changing things around. As they say, what isn't living dies." It also is not a utopian space safeguarded from conflict or violence, as a war (over the question of genetically modifying embryos) rages just outside its borders and requires citizen military service. Piercy presents neither history nor utopia as fait accompli but as demanding continual grassroots struggle. As one Mattapoisett explains, people "had myths that a revolution was inevitable. But nothing is! All things interlock . . . Alternate universes coexist. Probabilities clash and possibilities wink out forever." Countering Connie's retort that she is powerless to enact change, Mattapoisetts explain that it is not the "powerful who make change," but those "who worked out the labor-and-land intensive farming [. . .] who changed how people bought food, raised children, went to school [. . .] who made new unions, withheld rent, refused to go to wars, wrote and educated and made speeches."[36] In other words, through Piercy's temporal web, we see that how (and by whom) the future gets shaped determines how it gets used in contemporary political life. For Connie, utopian dreaming is an aspirational demand from the future that distances her from, and presses on, her suffocating present, "that thing that lets us feel that this world is not enough,"; it is this "anti-anti-utopian" orientation named by Jameson (2004) that ultimately radicalizes Connie to act, committing violence to resist the mental health system and the tyrannical future it represents.[37]

Queer/Trans Utopia: Impossibility Now!

More recently, feminist utopian theorizing has given rise to queer utopianism, which is marked by queer theory's engagement with temporality and the need to interrogate and work in opposition to what Judith Halberstam coined "straight (or "repo") time."[38] Halberstam argued that queer time intervenes in heterocentric and linear notions of past and future to resist the tyrannical normativity of the present. This epistemic moment within queer studies also included what is characterized as the "anti-relational" (and implicitly anti-utopian) thesis and its emphasis on "negative affect." Lee Edelman's polemic *No Future: Queer Theory and the Death Drive* contended that a structural logic of hope implicates queer politics in a repro-normative impulse. Famously railing against the concept of futurity as "kid stuff," Edelman pronounced that queer resistance entailed abandoning the future (which was never made for queers) altogether.[39]

In his seminal *Cruising Utopia: The Then and There of Queer Futurity* (2009), Jose Muñoz mobilizes a queer critique of time to contest Edelman's "logic of negativity," drawing attention to its foreclosure of intersectionality: racialized and queer kids, he interjects, "are not the sovereign princes of futurity." Instead, Muñoz insists that the future must be reimagined as queer. This reparative promise of queer utopianism is also directed toward dominant contemporary North American LGBT politics, and in particular the assimilationist agendas of lobbying groups like the Human Rights Campaign. For Muñoz, both homonormativity's "stultifying regime of pragmatism" (future as reproductive/assimilationist) and the antisocial critique's "various romances of negativity" (withdrawal from the future) represent failures of the queer imagination that queer politics could not afford. A utopian turn to "queer idealism," Muñoz posits, "may be the only way to usher in a new mode of radicalism that can perhaps release queer politics from its current death grip."[40]

Muñoz argues not only that queer critique must be invested with utopia but that queerness itself can only be gleaned through an apprehension of utopia. Put differently, queerness is "not yet here" but exists as a mode of critical ideality and "warm [anticipatory] illumination" that can inform our relations in the present.[41] Queer utopianism is ultimately dedicated to restructuring time in the interest of queer liberation within the present, as well as realizing its transformative political and aesthetic power in/for the future.

In her essay "'68, or Something," queer theorist Lauren Berlant acknowledges the intense anxiety and dismissal that associations with utopia discharge for queer thinkers. Marked by a move from "tragedy to farce," she posits, the concept of utopia is synonymous with a history of failed experiments and vulnerable to accusations of naive hope rooted in cruel optimism.[42] Still, Muñoz insists, "shouting down utopia is an easy move."[43] To reactivate the poignancy of utopian thinking for queer politics, he turns to Marxist Utopian Ernst Bloch's notion of concrete utopia as collective longing situated in material struggle. This is the praxis function of utopia, the immanent labor of world-making in the present, from which subaltern knowledges and alternative socialities emerge.

For Muñoz, queer utopianism is not prescriptive, nor does it hold out a fixed vision. Instead, it organizes a "great refusal" of the ontological seizure of contemporary ways of being in the world by holding out tantalizing prospects for how things could be otherwise. Permitting affective attachment to the "not-here-yet," critical utopianism's unsettling temporal rhythm "educates" our hopes beyond the grid of naturalized logics and biopolitical control of neoliberal life—acuminating and revivifying the queer imagination. Feeling Revolutionary is a feeling that "what stands for the world" is profoundly lacking, and opens up space to imagine "going-off script" together, a collective "exodus." It is through this new structure of (revolutionary) longing that the relationship between queerness and utopia becomes explicit: both contain "the desire for a new world despite an emotional/world situation that attempts to render such desiring impossible."[44]

Beyond explicating this critique function in/for the present, Muñoz calls on utopia as a lens through which to view subaltern queer of color aesthetic practices (of the recent past) as prefiguring more liberatory worlds. Relying on Bloch's terminology, Muñoz advocates for looking back on that which is "no-longer-conscious" to engender that which is "not-yet-here."[45] This is not escapist disavowal or romanticism, but an attunement to utopia's multidirectional pull. Muñoz "cruises" through a promiscuous archive: drag performances, scenes of punk nightlife and gay burlesque, visual art, activist mission statements and stickering campaigns, sites of public sex, and political vigils. In these flamboyant sites of connectivity and belonging, Muñoz recovers revolutionary gestures, glimpses, and energies that have been lost or annulled by a violently atomizing neoliberalism and assimilationist homonormative agenda.

For instance, Samuel Delany's memoirs (1988, 1999) bear witness to a pornotopic New York City subculture of ecstatic cruising and anonymous public sex—under the constant police raids and surveillance of the Giuliani and Bloomberg administrations. For Delany, these were zones of interracial and cross-class intimacy in which conventional hierarchies and power relations were transformed. Muñoz's turn to Delany reveals the "what is" of contemporary gay pragmatism as the historical limit beyond which utopian futurity might be gleaned. The labor of recovering these glimmers from the past (relegated to the margins of pre-Stonewall LGBT history) denaturalize the "coercive choreography" of heteronormative-capitalist renderings of the world, presented as ahistorical. Rather than reveling in nostalgia, Muñoz asks his readers to put these ecstatic impulses to work, both in critically accessing the unerotic and rigidly structured present and in rehearsing for more just futures. In this, Muñoz advances a rejoinder to critical utopianisms (like Jameson 2001) in which sexual politics and desire are not only inadvertently disavowed but appraised as apolitical in their world-making capacity. Queer futurity, argues Muñoz, "does not underplay desire. In fact, it is all about desire."[46]

Despite its reputation, theorists of critical queer utopianism are profoundly realistic about pain, trauma, grief, depression, fear, bitterness, despair, and above all loss. Indeed, this affective arsenal is inseparable from "Feeling Revolutionary" since, as queer refusals of "what stands for the world," these negative but vitalizing forces provide the prompt toward educated hope. In this way, negation itself becomes "an important resource" for critical queer utopianism, rather than a hindrance. As Joshua Chambers-Letson, Tavia Nyong'o, and Ann Pellegrini assert in their foreword to the 2019 edition of *Cruising Utopia*, "Queer utopia is the impossible performance of the negation of the negation."[47]

The expanding field of critical trans studies begins with this embrace of negativity as a starting point for utopian analysis. Coherence around a "failure"—or unwillingness—to be normal need not lead to nihilistic resignation but instead to disidentification from a stultifying neoliberal present that willfully *fails* (most of) *us*. Dean Spade takes up the way in which trans-ness—embodying this ontological failure—can inform a critical trans utopian praxis that radically opens up the future. Like trans subjectivity, utopia challenges us to imagine the impossible. In the manifesto *Impossibility Now!* Spade avers, "we are impossible people . . . We're being told that we're politically unviable and impossible, we're told that constantly, and yet I think there's a space of possibility that exists in part because we are not yet included or recognized." This is a productive paradox (affirming viability through acknowledging impossibility) that summons the inspirational mandate of the May '68 Situationists: "Be realistic, demand the impossible." Rather than ushering in aporia, the slogan indicts so-called "pragmatic" political action as failure. Likewise, Spade advances a trans-abolitionist vision as a "matter of life and death" against our "deadly and monstrous" contemporary world. The impossible demands that will bring about justice—"an end to prisons and borders and poverty"—cannot be made within the confining framework of legal rights and "social work style paternalism." Practicing utopianism in the present means passing on entreaties to participate in the violent logics and institutions of the "real world," Spade announces, and enacting the "democratic, collaborative, horizontal, care-based" world we desire.[48]

Catarina Nirta's *Marginal Bodies, Trans Utopias* builds on this paradox of trans ontological "impossibility" to potentialize queer utopianism as a radical trans ethics of/for trans folks—a weapon against the matrix of neoliberal subjectivization. Here, Nirta challenges Muñoz's persistent association of queer utopia with the anticipatory "not yet" of futurity, claiming queer utopia as empirically manifest in minoritized trans embodiment. Trans bodies are a utopia of the now, Nirta insists, that do not depend on the privileged position of the future for authorization of authenticity. These "impossible" subjectivities—as territories of disobedience to mind-body dualism and gender essentialism—actualize and immerse utopian futurity in the "here and now." Understanding trans embodiment in relation to a future "then and there" abandons their present *being-ness*, Nirta insists. Instead, we should understand trans subjectivity as a revolutionary site of contradictions that embodies the "motion of perpetual becoming" (like utopia itself) that never fully arrives. This interpretation brings the virtual into the actual, the present and the real: "going there" does not belong to the past," nor does it lend itself to "projections of the future." At the same time, Nirta proposes that such a trans utopian ethic can foster resistance against the disciplinary legal/medical frameworks that sustain an unyielding gender binary and govern trans bodies/subjectivities, often denying them ontological recognition. It is the very "dramatic corporeality" of transgender subjectivity (at once unified, multiple, and self-transforming) that provides its disruptive (utopian) force for biopolitical institutional discourses.[49]

Conclusion: Toward the Counter-Fairy Tales

As humanity confronts intersecting political, ecological, and economic crises; and the existential ultimatum of the collapse of the biosphere, vital concepts like utopia—often discarded as anachronistic and unserviceable—continue to inform Black, queer, and (often queer of color) feminist critical theory, philosophy, and literature. Against the derisive notion that utopias are impossible, these thinkers remind us that the utopian tradition (like all tradition and like a critical utopian formation itself) is dynamic, available for radical reinscription, and an imitable part of the political imagination. Collectively, their work makes clear that our survival as a species depends on rebuffing the chimera of progress and neoliberalism's cheerful admonishment that there "is no alternative." The latter are normative (utopian) fairytales that render the existing social order natural, static, and impermeable and in turn produce (and ensnare us in) the future as reproductive extension of the here and now. As counter-fairy tales, critical utopian thought pries open the historical process to contingency by conjoining past and future in the transformative lived experience of the present, and coaxes us toward material possibilities for collective human action; reimagining/revisiting time and reinhabiting space coalesce. As Muñoz reminds us, "hope is spawned of a critical investment in utopia, which is nothing like naïve but, instead, profoundly resistant to the stultifying temporal logic of a broken-down present."[50] As opposed to being "nowhere," critical utopianism remains an inimitable resource for those dispossessed subjects working from below to create and *repossess* livable spaces and practices of freedom—without guarantee of a wholly different world. In this regard, we might allow the words of Piercy's utopians to reach us from the year 2137: "you of your time may fail to struggle together . . . We must fight to come to exist, to remain in existence, to be the future that happens. That's why we reached you."[51]

Notes

1. Russell Jacoby, *The End of Utopia: Politics and Culture in an Age of Apathy* (New York: Basic, 2000), xii.

2. Judith Shklar, "The Political Theory of Utopia: From Melancholy to Nostalgia," in *Utopias and Utopian Thought*," ed. Frank E. Manuel (Boston: Beacon, 1967), 105.

3. Martin Delany, *Blake; or the Huts of America* (Cambridge, MA: Harvard University Press, 2017), 264.

4. Richard Wright, *Black Power*, rev. ed. (New York: HarperCollins, 2008), 38.

5. Wright, *Black Power*, 19.

6. Wright, *Black Power*, 76.

7. George S. Schuyler, *Black No More: Being an Account of Strange and Wonderful Workings of Science in the Land of the Free, A.D. 1933–1940* (New York: Modern Library, 1999), 26.

8. W. E. B. DuBois, *Darkwater: Voices from Within the Well* (New York: Dover, 2009), 157.

9. Sun Ra, *Collected Works*, vol. 1, *Immeasurable Equation*, ed. Adam Abraham (Chandler, AZ: Phaelos, 2005), 116.

10. Ra, *Collected Works*, 118.

11. Octavia Butler, *Parable of the Sower* (New York: Four Walls Eight Windows, 1993), 133.

12. Butler, *Parable*, 20–21.

13. Butler, *Parable*, 131.

14. Butler, *Parable*, 25.

15. Butler, *Parable*, 158.

16. Butler, *Parable*, 334.

17. Butler, *Parable*, 79.

18. Butler, *Parable*, 93, 228.

19. Butler, *Parable*, 235–36.

20. Butler, *Parable*, 169.

21. N. K. Jemisin, *The Fifth Season* (New York: Orbit Books, 2015), 379, 125.

22. Jessica Hurley and N. K. Jemisin, "An Apocalypse Is a Relative Thing: An Interview with N. K. Jemisin," *ASAP/Journal* 3, no. 3 (2018): 469.

23. Elizabeth Flock, *The Fifth Season Author N.K. Jemisin Answers Your Questions*, PBS, June 27, 2019, https://www.pbs.org/newshour/show/the-fifth-season-author-n-k-jemisin-answers-your-questions.

24. Jemisin, *The Fifth Season*, 371.

25. Abigail Bereola, "A True Utopia: An Interview with N.K. Jemisin," *The Paris Review*, December 3, 2018, https://www.theparisreview.org/blog/2018/12/03/a-true-utopia-an-interview-with-n-k-jemisin/.

26. Bereola, "A True Utopia."

27. N. K. Jemisin, *The Stone Sky* (New York: Orbit Books, 2017), 7.

28. See Fredric Jameson, *The Seeds of Time* (New York: Columbia University Press, 1994), xii.

29. Hurley and Jemisin, "An Apocalypse Is a Relative Thing," 473.

30. Ursula K. Le Guin, "A Non-Euclidean View of California as a Cold Place to Be," *The Yale Review* 72, no. 2 (1983): 161.

31. Ursula K. Le Guin, *The Dispossessed: An Ambiguous Utopia* (New York: Harper Voyage, 1974), 168.

32. Le Guin, *The Dispossessed*, 76.

33. Le Guin, *The Dispossessed*, 55.

34. Marge Piercy, "Telling Stories About Stories," *Utopian Studies* 5, no. 1 (1994): 1.

35. Marge Piercy, *Woman on the Edge of Time* (New York: Knopf, 1976), 68, 62–63, 24.

36. Piercy, *Woman on the Edge of Time*, 62, 169–70, 214.

37. J. E. Muñoz, *Cruising Utopia: The Then and There of Queer Futurity* (New York: New York University Press, 2009), 1; Frederic Jameson, *Archeologies of the Future: The Desire Called Utopia and Other Science Fictions* (New York: Verso, 2005).

38. Judith Halberstam, *In a Queer Time and Place: Transgender Bodies, Subcultural Lives* (New York: New York University Press, 2005).

39. Lee Edelman, *No Future: Queer Theory and the Death Drive* (Durham, NC: Duke University Press, 2004).

40. Muñoz, *Cruising Utopia*, 95, 1–2, 172.

41. Muñoz, *Cruising Utopia*, 1.

42. Lauren Berlant, "'68, or Something," *Critical Inquiry* 21, no. 1 (autumn 1994): 125.

43. Muñoz, *Cruising Utopia*, 10.

44. Lisa Duggan and J. E. Muñoz, "Hope and Hopelessness: A Dialogue," *Women and Performance: A Journal of Feminist Theory* 19, no. 2 (2009): 278.

45. Muñoz, *Cruising Utopia*, 12.

46. Muñoz, *Cruising Utopia*, 118, 30.

47. Muñoz, *Cruising Utopia*, 13, xii.

48. Dean Spade, *Impossibility Now*, New York, Barnard Center for Research on Women, August 12, 2013, https://www.youtube.com/watch?v=OU8D343qpdE.
49. Caterina Nirta, *Marginal Bodies, Trans Utopias* (London: Rutledge, 2018), 10.
50. Muñoz, *Cruising Utopia*, 12.
51. Piercy, *Woman on the Edge of Time*, 190.

7

"If you don't love children, you don't understand socialism"

The Children of Peoples Temple

ALEXANDRA LEAH PRINCE

> You goddamn miserable Christian. You wouldn't say fuck but you'd stand by and let the Nazis kill children.
>
> —Jim Jones, Sermon, November 1978

> What a beautiful place this was. The children loved the jungle, learned about animals and plants. There were no cars to run over them; no child-molesters to molest them; nobody to hurt them. They were the freest, most intelligent children I had ever known.
>
> —Annie Moore, member of Peoples Temple, from a letter she wrote on the last day at Jonestown

Children are everywhere and nowhere in the histories of Peoples Temple.[1] Children occupied the church pews in Indianapolis and swam in the community pool in Redwood Valley. Children attended Peoples Temple schools and distributed newspapers to expand the reach of Peoples Temple in San Francisco. They sang in the Temple's youth choirs and packed onto the community's Greyhound buses for weeks-long missionary journeys across the country. Their small faces graced Peoples Temple publications, promotional materials, and the group's music album in 1973. Infants, children, and teens comprised around a quarter of Peoples Temple members over its nearly two-decade-long history.[2] And when Peoples Temple came to its tragic end on November 18, 1978, in Jonestown—the Peoples Temple agricultural settlement in Guyana—304 individuals under the age of eighteen were murdered.[3]

Peoples Temple was one of the largest-scale and most enduring interracial utopian movements in the United States. The community succeeded Father Divine's Peace Mission Movement as the twentieth century's greatest effort to reimagine the boundaries of American race and class. From 1956 to 1978, Peoples Temples functioned as a Black-majority interracial church and communalistic political body dedicated to ending racial segregation, poverty, and the manifold social inequities the group believed was perpetuated by American capitalism and global imperialism.[4] Its socialist ethic fostered housing and medical services for hundreds of seniors, free education and college, free healthcare, foster homes for children, and job training and rehabilitation for drug users, criminal offenders, and others who had fallen through the expanding cracks of the American welfare system and President Lyndon Johnson's war on poverty.

Since the tragedy in Jonestown that claimed 918 lives, Peoples Temple members have been dismissed as the "brainwashed" followers of Jim Jones. In turn, Jones has been depicted by critics as a megalomaniac whose role in Peoples Temple was nothing more than a ruse to gain power and inflict abuse. A 1978 *Time* magazine cover published after the devastation at Jonestown referred to the group as the "Cult of Death," cementing public understanding of Peoples Temple as a "dangerous, murderous cult."[5] "Jonestown became the most powerful negative metaphor in 20th century religious history," observed author and minister Lowell D. Streiker in 1989.[6] For decades, former members, relatives, and scholars of Peoples Temple have called for more nuanced historical considerations that push beyond pathological profiles of Jones and the sensationalist and reductionistic frameworks perpetuated by popular media. In the process, the *people* of Peoples Temple, with their diverse identities, backgrounds, experiences, and motivations, have been brought to the forefront.

A growing number of voices, such as religious studies scholars Rebecca Moore and Mary McCormick Maaga, historian James Lance Taylor, and writers like Sikivu Hutchinson, have offered more inclusive and complex lenses to consider Peoples Temple. Their examinations have advanced popular and scholarly consideration of the groups' Black majority, forefronted Black women's roles and experiences, explored how Peoples Temple represented one of the largest and most significant Black movements of the twentieth century, and analyzed the dimensionality of women's leadership.[7] Such treatments of Peoples Temple fully acknowledge the multiple abuses and systems of power that deteriorated the vision of the community, and the paradox of Peoples Temple as both a utopian success and tragic failure.

Yet, despite repeated calls from scholars, former members, and relatives to reconsider, reexamine, and "take a second look" at Peoples Temple, the role of children and the youth within the movement—numerically, practically, and ideologically—has yet to be investigated. Children, including babies and teenagers, made up 36 percent of the Jonestown community in November 1978, the month of the tragedy.[8] A total of 304 individuals aged seventeen and younger died; the majority of them were Black. Of that total, 190 were under the age of twelve.[9] Many of the teens were Black urban youth.[10] When children are mentioned or considered, the horror and sadness surrounding their untimely deaths has largely defined the scope of consideration. Frameworks of victimization and abuse continue to dominate accounts of children within Peoples Temple in keeping with trends within studies of children in new religious movements.[11] An attendant preoccupation with threats to child safety have historically been foundational to anti-cult efforts more broadly.[12] To be sure, the hundreds of children who were killed at Jonestown *were* victims, but their lives, and their influence on the broader movement of Peoples Temple, like those of the adult and senior members, cannot be fully understood or appreciated within a victimization or abuse framework.[13]

The definition of childhood is a shifting and culturally informed category. In the following, I examine the place and role of individuals from infancy to the age of eighteen with an emphasis on the pre-Jonestown era. I assume a child-centered lens in the methodology of childhood studies, which situates children at the center, to recognize how children, as both literal and figurative beings, shaped Peoples Temple. This lens enables children to be viewed as relational co-creators of Peoples Temple rather than the passive repositories of their parents and elders' ambitions. However, unlike social scientific studies of children, I am not so much concerned with children's views of the community and their religion, but rather with what we can further uncover about the daily dynamics, politics, and philosophy of Peoples Temple by examining how its vision of child welfare occupied a central role in the effort to build a more just society. To a lesser extent, I examine the education of teens to analyze the socialist models within which children were educated.

Speaking of the role of children in studies of religion, scholars Bonnie J. Miller-McLemore and Don S. Browning have remarked that "the neglect of children in the academic study of religion has not only robbed us of a deeper understanding of them, it has deprived us of an important angle of vision on understanding these diverse religions themselves."[14] While Peoples Temple was officially affiliated with the Disciples of Christ, and before that the International Assemblies of God, and many members were devout Christians, Jones and the movement more broadly had a complex relationship with Christianity and organized religion, with a large contingent of members avowing Communist, socialist, and atheist sensibilities. Nonetheless, McLemore and Browning's sentiment conveys the utility of applying the lens of childhood to better understand the whole of a community. By examining how a community or religion understands and is influenced by children, we can access a critical dimension of their theology or what a group "truly cares about."[15] I explore the role and meaning of children and the youth ideologically, practically, as tools for Peoples Temple publicity and monetary solicitation, and finally as political battlegrounds. Through examination of remembrances by former members and relatives, newspaper articles, Peoples Temple publications, sermons, journal entries, poetry, and government documents, I demonstrate that children's welfare was a core principle of the interracial socialist utopian vision of Peoples Temple, a critical foundation of the community that cannot be overlooked.[16]

Human Family

Throughout Peoples Temple history, Jones's formation of a multiracial "rainbow" family, or adoption of children from different racial backgrounds, became a popular means of allegorically relating Jones's—and by extension Peoples Temple's—commitment to racial integration. "Show us a man other than Jim Jones who has adopted children of all races," proclaimed the August 1970 Peoples Temple newsletter.[17] In the early 1950s, Jim and his wife Marceline were living in Indianapolis and working toward finding a home for the integrated church that would become Peoples Temple. They started their family by adopting Agnes, a child around the age of ten with Native American ancestry.[18] In 1959, the Jones adopted three orphaned

Korean children: Kun Eun Soon, Eun Ok Kyung, and Pac Chi Oak, who were renamed Stephanie, Lew Eric, and Suzanne, respectively. The children's adoptions were the first phase of a larger Peoples Temple project that sought homes for orphaned children fathered by American servicemen stationed in Korea, an effort members financed through dinners and profits from the church's restaurant and cleaning business.[19]

Just a year after the adoption, Stephanie died at the age of five in a car crash along with four other members of Peoples Temple on the way home from a church trip to Cincinnati. Stephanie's death prompted the question of where members of Peoples Temple, as an extended interracial family, would or could be buried during a time when cemeteries in Indianapolis, like much of the United States, remained racially segregated. Funeral directors in the city denied Stephanie burial in the white section of the cemetery because of her Asian race. The headline "Segregation Pursues Crash Victims into Grave" announced the decision on the front page of *The Indianapolis Recorder*, the city's African American newspaper.[20] In response to the funeral director's decision, Jones commented, "I decided to stay with my people, and arranged to bury her in a 'colored' location." Jones's reference to "my people" referred to all Blacks and people of color, a statement meant to both show loyalty to his Black-majority church community and his attendant disdain for racist segregationist White culture. More than a decade later, Jones would reference Stephanie's burial in a waterlogged area of the segregated section of the cemetery in his sermons, an interment that reflected the larger structures of racism that subverted the lives of nonwhite children. Her gravestone was inscribed with "Our Korean Daughter," a dedication that set Stephanie's adoption by white parents in stone.[21]

Three weeks after Stephanie's death, the Jones's only biological child, Stephan, was born, his name a tribute to Stephanie's memory.[22] A year later, Jim and Marceline expanded their rainbow family further by adopting a Black child whom they renamed James Warren Jones Jr., or Jim Jr. for short, a choice that boldly signaled the couple's pride in their nonwhite child.[23] In doing so, Jim and Marceline Jones reportedly became the first white couple in the state of Indiana to adopt a Black child. Jim Jr.'s adoption was intended as a public challenge to a racist system that denied parental love and care to children on the basis of race. The couple's decision to raise a Black son became a milestone regularly referenced by Peoples Temple members and sympathizers to symbolize Jim and Marceline's heartfelt conquering of racism. To their followers in Indianapolis, the Jones's rainbow family was the living metaphor of their dedication to dismantling racism. To critics, the public multiracial family signaled Jones's status as a dangerous maverick who subverted America's racial caste system.

Jones's communal vision for Peoples Temple was modeled on his immediate rainbow family, with Jones as Father and Marceline as Mother. This living paradigm of extended interracial familiarity was displayed on the front page of *The Indianapolis Recorder* in April 1961, with a photograph captioned "Human Family." The image shows Jim and Marceline reading a story out loud to their children, who are gathered around them staring

HUMAN FAMILY: Rev. James W. Jones, director of the city's Commission on Human Rights, is at home in his job because he has a good sampling of the human family at home. Here Rev. and Mrs. Jones are shown with their international, interracial family: left to right, Lew Eric, 4; Jimmy (James W. Jones, Jr.), 8 months; Rev. Jones; Agnes, 18; Mrs. Marceline Jones, a native of Richmond, Ind.; Stephan Gandhi, 22 months, and Suzanne, 8. Only one of the children is a natural offspring of the Joneses, and all the others are adopted. (Recorder photo by Houston Dickie)

Figure 7.1. From *The Indianapolis Recorder*, April 1, 1961. Photograph caption reads: "Human Family: Rev. James W. Jones, director of the city's Commission on Human Rights, is at home in his job because he has a good sampling of the human family at home. Here Rev. and Mrs. Jones are shown with their international, interracial family." *Source*: Courtesy of *The Indianapolis Recorder*.

intently at the pages. Jones had recently been appointed as director of the city's Commission on Human Rights, and the photo's caption—"he has a good sampling of the human family at home . . . with their international, interracial family"—suggested that his new political duties were a natural extension of his fatherly position.[24] Nearly three years later, the same photograph of the family reading together was published to highlight the injustices Jones faced as a civil rights activist in Indianapolis. During his tenure as the director of Indianapolis's Human Rights Commission, Jones faced backlash from the city's white residents for forcing the integration of the city's hospital wards. His integration of Peoples Temple's church services similarly incensed many neighbors.

Peoples Temple and Jones's challenges to Jim Crow in Indianapolis were meted out on the Jones family. While waiting for the bus one day, a middle-aged white woman walked up to Marceline and spit on her while she was holding Jim Jr. As Marceline began to cry, the woman spat on Jim Jr. out of apparent disgust at the sight of a white woman holding a Black child and the presumption of miscegenation. Not long after, an anonymous phone call to the Joneses' housekeeper threatened the safety of the Jones children if they continued to visit the neighborhood playground. "Lay off civil rights," said the voice. Another critic of the Joneses' race politics was more blunt with their phone message: "Nigger lover get out of town."[25] In 1965, Jones moved along with around 140 followers to "greener and safer pastures" in Northern California.[26] The children went with them.

Noah's Ark in a Time of Storm

"One of things that first impressed me when I joined Peoples Temple in 1970 was its children. They were outgoing and open, eager and curious," wrote Donald Beck in 2013.[27] Beck knew many of the Peoples Temple children well, having served as the group's junior choir director and as a kindergarten teacher. Peoples Temple's move to Redwood Valley offered the community a fresh start to realize its vision of an interracial and self-sufficient socialist society. A core component of this utopian ideal was the welfare of children. Redwood Valley was a white-majority area that Jones once remarked would be more aptly named "Whitewood Valley," but the Peoples Temple settlement distinguished itself from the larger area by establishing what it saw as "the only Garden of Eden in America."[28] In this Eden, children of all races were educated in the Temple's Sunday School, an instructive period that, despite its name, tended to take place on Monday or Wednesday evenings and could include choir practice, music lessons, and assistance with homework.[29] Under Marceline Jones's direction, the Temple established nine senior citizen homes, six homes for foster children, and "Happy Acres," a forty-acre ranch for intellectually disabled children.[30]

In California, Jones built on his tradition of making church accessible and appealing to the youth.[31] With Father Jones's permission, the children were exempted from formal attendance at Sunday services and permitted to play outside, go horseback riding, or swim in the Temple's large indoor heated pool, a facility that was housed in the church building and took up half its footprint.[32] "Children of every race are invited to ride the ponies and swim in the indoor heated pool," advertised the Peoples Temple newsletter from October 1970.[33] The pool became a focal point of the Peoples Temple Redwood Valley complex, which opened on February 2, 1969, and served as

Figure 7.2. From the 1976 Pamphlet "Peoples Temple Christian Church, Jim Jones, Pastor." Image caption reads: "At the Redwood Valley Temple children swim in the indoor heated pool." *Source*: The Jonestown Institute, public domain.

a place for swimming, recreation, and baptisms.[34] "The young people liked the fact that Jim Jones had a swimming pool in the sanctuary in Redwood Valley," wrote Jynona M. Norwood, a Black pastor who lost many relatives at Jonestown. "People would peel their clothes off, put their bathing suits on, and jump in the pool right after morning worship."[35] At a time when Black adults and children continued to be barred from public pools and recreational facilities across the country, Peoples Temple's public promotion of its intergrated swimming pool in a segregated white rural area was an important way to signal its commitment to racial equality and firmly stake its position on another front of the culture war over racial integration.[36]

Religious Studies scholar Susan Ridgley has reminded researchers of child-centered studies that we "must always contend with the fact that children are simultaneously theoretical and actual beings, both current participants in religious life and placeholders for the future of communities."[37] Within Peoples Temple, this dynamic was transformed into social, spiritual, and economic capital. Children's welfare was routinely abstracted as the righteous cornerstone of Peoples Temple's interracial socialist vision for society and the attendant need for members' dedication. The vision for and experiences of children were upheld as testimony to Peoples Temple's integrity, and collectively the two functioned as moral signposts to undergird multiple functions: maintain members, attract new members, solicit donations, and justify the dedication of members as well as the actions of Peoples Temple leadership.

Beginning in Redwood Valley, children were increasingly the focus of media, both in publications authored by Peoples Temple and those in which Peoples Temple was referenced. Peoples Temple member Laura Johnston Kohl recalled that "pictures of Jim and his family—both primary and extended—were all around."[38] Photos of the family were included in contribution appeal letters and sold at church meetings. The community emphasis on interracial families and child welfare was further advertised throughout Peoples Temple's *The Living Word* magazine, the group's first serial publication, printed in 1970, which reads in part: "Following the example of our Pastor and his wife, Marceline, who have adopted and reared eight children of all races, our families have taken children into their hearts and homes as though they were their own. Many have opened up foster homes especially to meet the needs of these displaced young ones."[39] An editorial titled "Brotherhood is Our Religion" depicted Redwood Valley as a paradise: "From all corners of the country and even from many foreign lands, men, women, and children of all ages, races and social classes are coming to this Promised Land of Milk and Honey, this Noah's Ark in a time of storm."[40]

Figure 7.3. A 1972 photograph of Pastor Jim Jones and children used in promotional material to demonstrate Peoples Temple's commitment to racial diversity. *Source*: Courtesy of San Diego State University.

The editor of *The Living Word* was Garrett Lambrev, the Peoples Temple's first recruit in California and later a defector and vocal critic of the group. In 2013, Lambrev reflected on his participation in putting together *The Living Word* and derided the publication as "garbage" meant purely to seduce readers into giving funds to the church.[41] *The Living Word* included only one testimony by a young person—an article titled "God's Prophet Ran to Me" by twelve-year-old Mark Cordell. "If I hadn't been touched by the anointed hands of our Pastor, Jim Jones, I would be hopelessly crippled from the waist down," read Cordell's testimony. "Without him [Jones], I'd have to spend the rest of my life in a wheelchair, unable to run and play like other children." According to Lambrev, Mark Cordell's story was real,

"If you don't love children, you don't understand socialism" | 153

but the published version was carefully crafted by Lambrev and the rest of the editorial staff. Cordell's story may have been true, but his experience at Peoples Temple was not the idyllic version painted by the Peoples Temple magazine. Peter Wotherspoon, *The Living Word*'s assistant editor, was later charged with sexually abusing Mark Cordell. In a community predicated on

Figure 7.4. Temple member Mark Cordell, age twelve, raises a flag. The photograph was published alongside Cordell's testimony titled "God's Prophet Ran to Me!," which was included in *The Living Word, An Apostolic Monthly*, Peoples Temple's first serial publication published in 1972. *Source*: The Jonestown Institute, public domain.

the safety and well-being of children, physical and sexual abuse of Peoples Temple children was met with harsh physical punishment. The nature of the community's punishment of Wotherspoon was enough to prompt Lambrev to leave Peoples Temple for good.

Stephan Jones, in a 2018 interview with ABC about his life growing up in Peoples Temple and the ambiguities of his father's character, commented, "I lived in a community that was filled with every walk of life, every color in the rainbow, every level of education. For the most part, we lived in harmony most of the time, especially early on. It was not fake."[42] Life as a child or young person at Peoples Temple cannot be represented by any single voice, and the loss of so many youth at Jonestown forever erased hundreds of unique perspectives. Moreover, adult recollections of youth are not substitutions for child and youth perspectives and cannot be considered adequate stand-ins. Despite these limitations, recollections about Peoples Temple children and youth, and former members' experiences growing up in the community, can offer some glimpses into the environment the children and youth were raised in and experienced.

In "Remembrances of Temple Kindergarteners," Don Beck profiled five young members of Peoples Temple he taught in a Redwood Valley and Ukiah, California public school. The first was Martin Amos, who would later die in Guyana at the hands of his mother, Sharon Amos.[43] Beck recalled Martin as a "very independent, engaging and strong-willed kid. Never the shy type . . . almost always smart enough to make it happen." Stephanie Swaney was "shy and quiet . . . a very normal kid." Chris Buckley had an "awesome smile. Good humor. Loved to play: always eager to move around and help me and others do things . . . always learned quickly and worked well with others." Jimmy Moore was "a great kid, very eager to do things and help. Always good-natured. Loved responsibilities that let him move about." The last child profiled was Daren Werner Swinney. For Beck, Daren was "like many of our kids." He continued: "They [the children] needed more of our attention, consistently. Unfortunately we were often too busy to give the extra attention our kids needed. In many ways the activities we provided our kids, opened up much energy that we then couldn't seem to work with enough—this was one reason we wanted to build a community—a place—where we could do more things more effectively with our children."[44] The tension Beck points to between the community's vision for children and its practical limitations is underwritten with the grief surrounding the children's deaths in Jonestown.

"If you don't love children, you don't understand socialism" | 155

Figure 7.5. Don Beck (far right) poses with Peoples Temple children in his kindergarten class at Yokayo School in Ukiah, California. Second row: (fourth student) Stephanie Swaney; (last on left) Jimmy Moore. Back row: (eighth student from left): Chris Buckley. *Source*: The Jonestown Institute, Doxsee Phares Collection, public domain.

Children Are Not Dolls. They Are Our Future.

In November 1976, Julie Cordell held a three-year-old Black child up to the microphone in front of the Temple audience in San Francisco. The child sang the civil rights anthem "We Shall Overcome" in both English and Spanish. Children were active participants in Peoples Temple programs and church services, often to the chagrin of adult members who complained the children were too noisy or disruptive. A journal kept by Temple member and former college professor Edith Roller offers snapshots of children's presence and participation in Peoples Temple from 1975, when she joined at the age of sixty, until August 1978, just a few months before her death in Jonestown.[45] Among Roller's entries during the period were accounts of church meetings and Jones's sermons held in San Francisco. Services had been held in San Francisco since 1970, and in 1972 the group established a Temple on Geary Street. The building's original pews were replaced with chairs that could be easily moved to make room for dancing and Temple functions. Jones and Peoples Temple members became deeply immersed in San Francisco politics and protest movements. In turn, the community became widely known for their outreach to neighbors and the social services they organized, including a dining hall, daycare, diagnostic and outpatient clinic, physical therapy facility, drug rehabilitation program, and legal services, all offered at no cost.[46]

In 1976, visitors to the Geary Street temple observed the social dynamic of the Temple environment: "young and old, black and white—everyone interspersed. . . . Black children sat on the laps of white men or women, white teenagers sat next to elderly black people."[47] Children figured prom-

Figure 7.6. From a Peoples Temple pamphlet titled "Peoples Temple Christian Church, Jim Jones, Pastor," published in 1976. Caption reads: "Youngsters gather in the San Francisco Temple to learn about their history. Through the skillful guidance of trained counsellors [sic] the children find that study can be fun." *Source*: The Jonestown Institute, public domain.

inently in the church meetings, which were dual-purposed gatherings that served both spiritual and practical organizing needs for a community of around a thousand people. Children, even very young children, stood up to give testimonies. In large groups, they regularly sang songs, often in different languages, including "I Thank You, Jim," "I'm a Socialist," and "We Shall Not Be Moved."[48] Children were included in all variety of Temple business and announcements, from practical mentions about their need to continue pamphleteering and distributing Temple newspapers, to announcements about trips to Marineland, to commendations for good grades.[49] Their bad behavior was met with punishment during accountability sessions called "catharsis," where they were struck by a paddle in front of the entire community or assigned penance. Stealing, for example, was punished with having to raise money. Rudeness to seniors required service to older persons.[50]

Messages about proper conduct were communicated to members during services. On January 26, 1977, Marceline relayed guidance from Father, or Jim Jones, to the children: "Be good to your teachers. Be helpful and cooperative. Set an example of socialism. Treat each other kindly."[51] Adults were reminded to treat Temple children well, and those who didn't were publicly admonished. "Some of you play with children like stupid dolls," chastised Jones in December 1976. "Children are not dolls. They are our future."[52] Roller's notes on Jones's sermons include his regular undergirding of children's welfare. On September 29, 1976, Roller recorded, "Jim talked about the care of children." She summarized his sermon:

> We've inherited children who've been beaten, neglected. If we sacrifice our children we may as well cast ourselves into the sea. If you don't love children, you don't understand socialism. You are not in my spirit. Don't scream at them, but talk to them. There have to be rules but be sure that those rules have a foundation in love. Don't take out the hostility with which you were treated on them . . . Don't use corporal punishment of children without involvement of the office. Be inventive to find other means of discipline. Violence can't teach people to be non-violent.[53]

Threats to child welfare were presented as both internal and external. References to external threats facing children included lead poisoning, child labor, pollution, inferior schooling, physical abuse, and forced prostitution. "A child is being beaten every minute. Child abuse is the commonest crime," sermonized Jones.[54] He depicted America as a country with more racist oppression and child abuse than every other country combined.[55] Insufficient nutrition was similarly identified as a growing social scourge causing undue harm to children, one that Marceline chose to highlight in 1976. She discussed "The Unfinished Child," a public service documentary that had recently aired on ABC. The program sought to raise attention to the need for proper prenatal and infant nutrition to avoid developmental disabilities.[56] In response, Marceline called for the community's nurses to develop healthy menus for the communal homes where many of the young people lived. "Our young people will be physically prepared to replenish the earth," Marceline declared.[57]

Father Jim and Mother Marceline's ongoing directives to members to thoughtfully care for children were premised in the community's conception of the Temple as an extended family unit. This principle of a communal family stretching beyond racial and biological lines was reinforced by the extended kinship networks that knit many members together.[58] It was not uncommon for entire families to join the Temple en masse. Further cementing the extended familial bonds between Temple members was the relocation of individuals members from one Temple location to live with a family at another location, or the boarding of individual youth members or foster children with established families. As a result, single mothers, otherwise-isolated seniors, and children and youth without parents enjoyed the benefits of a robust and interconnected family dynamic.[59] This entrenchment of bonds across and beyond race and nuclear family lines was "the practical application of the principles Jim espoused," the socialist rainbow family of Peoples Temple that radiated outward from his own family at the center.[60] Within this layered breakdown of the traditional family unit, all children were the community's children. Their welfare was upheld as both a living testament of the Temple's principles and a beacon of the future society the Temple was building.

Now We Must Work to Save Our Children

Apocalypticism had been a constant theme in Jones's ministry from the beginning and steadily increased throughout Peoples Temple's development. Jones's sermons regularly inculcated members with a view of America as a fundamentally racist country on the verge of nuclear catastrophe. In the 1960s, Jones's convictions were reinforced by media coverage of urban riots that revealed the extent of police violence against Black Americans and the government's extensive surveillance of Black radicals such as the Black Panthers.[61] As early as 1972, Jones cited the King Alfred Plan, a set of fictional government documents then making the rounds of radical publications. The documents alleged that a fascist military dictatorship would soon take power in America, leading to the creation of concentration camps for Black people and the working class.[62] "The important thing now is survival. We'll have time later for travel, now we must work. We're facing genocide. Now we must work to save our children," Roller's journal recorded in 1976.[63]

As a Black-majority socialist movement, Peoples Temple members saw themselves among the government's primary targets in the pending fascist takeover. When Jordan Vilchez joined Peoples Temple at the age of twelve in the late 1960s, she was led to believe that "nuclear war was inevitable." A "perpetual climate of fear, doom and gloom" characterized Vilchez's years in Peoples Temple, a period that stretched until 1978, when she was twenty-one.[64] In 1973, news of the military coup that overthrew democratically elected socialist Chilean president Salvador Allende further bolstered Jones's belief in a budding global conspiracy to subvert socialism. Vilchez was taught that the same violent fate dealt to Allende and his family awaited the Peoples Temple family. In San Francisco, her blue choir dress from the Redwood Valley period was replaced with the black beret then characteristic of Black radicals, a look routinely complemented by revolutionary fist raising. Peoples Temple youth were primed for the imminent fascist attacks through regular vigilance and security drills. They were encouraged to relay important messages orally rather than risk their writing be intercepted.[65] Peoples Temple's camaraderie with the global struggle for revolutionary socialism was reinforced through screenings of footage from the Soviet Revolution of 1917, the Cuban Revolution of 1959, and films depicting threats to the left from right-wing nationalism. In addition, the youth were educated about socialist politics with reading lists that included Marx's *Das Kapital* and histories about turn-of-the-century labor activists Joe Hill and Elizabeth Gurley Flynn, a founder of the ACLU and leader of the Communist Party.[66]

Roller's journal entries corroborate Vilchez's recounting of the group's regular inculcation of socialist values among the youth and children. At Temple services, children as well as adults were encouraged to ask questions in front of the community. Roller recorded several instances of children asking the meaning of political terminology, such as capitalism, left-wing, and right-wing. During the question-and-answer period on January 16, 1977, children asked the following questions with the answers provided by Jones:

CHILD: How did Martin Luther King die?

ANSWER: Because he was socialist and started to tell how the poor black were exploited in Vietnam, he was shot down.

CHILD: What is [the] Third World?

ANSWER: It's us all black, brown, red and yellow people, and they're going to take over the whole world.

CHILD: Why do capitalists kill black people?

ANSWER: Not just black people, all people because they are selfish. They're mean.

Another exchange from the January 9, 1977 question-and-answer period reveals the threat the children and larger community believed they faced:

CHILD: Why do they want to kill [the] black liberation movement?

ANSWER: They know they owe us a debt. People avoid someone they owe. White America owes us 300 years of liberation. We make them feel guilty. They want us dead. We may go away but we'll be back. People of color are going to rule the whole world. They're afraid of black unity.[67]

The Opportunity Students

Among Peoples Temple's multifaceted approaches to subverting racism and poverty was an ongoing dedication to uplifting teens and young adults. Beginning in Redwood Valley and expanding to San Francisco and Los Angeles, Peoples Temple offered opportunities for teen education, free college and housing, drug rehabilitation programs, and job training. Jones's work to advance the youth earned him regular accolades from public officials and religious leaders and was cited regularly by the Temple to buttress the leader's social standing. A 1976 press release from Peoples Temple read in part, "For the first time in their lives, a multitude of young blacks live with a sense of utter pride and dignity, because Rev. Jones has fought to provide them the opportunity to realize their goals."[68]

In 1975, while in San Francisco, Jones enrolled 120 Peoples Temple youth at Opportunity II, a progressive high school founded on leftist values. The cohort of students were mostly Black, with some Asian, Native American, and white students. Among them were Jones's sons Stephan, Tim, and Jim Jr.[69] Two of the teachers recalled that the Peoples Temple students "carried themselves more like a family, sharing a closeness that reflected their lack of racism." They arrived at Opportunity II with a profound awareness of socialist and labor history, and their consciousness about racial inequality in America was routinely demonstrated in their art.[70] A poem by Willie Thomas, a Black teenager from Peoples Temple who attended the school, read in part:

> Young, old, poor and black
> Shot, burned, killed, beaten,
> For what reason?
> Our dark skin?
> Prejudice
> Please help
> They're laying down a little black child . . .
> Who killed that little boy?
> Somebody tell me
> Who killed him?[71]

When the youth cohort attended Opportunity II, Jones was a local political celebrity, and Peoples Temple was widely known in San Francisco for its high-profile activism and community services. In response, Cindy Cordell authored an article for the school's newspaper, *The Natural High Express*, which aimed to shed some light on Jones and Peoples Temple for her fellow classmates. She listed many of the activities the youth of Peoples Temple were then engaged with, including distributing the community's newspaper, visiting people in the hospital, aiding seniors, helping in the Temple kitchen, and cleaning the Temple's eleven buses often used for missionary travel.[72] "The youth of Peoples Temple also stay away from any unnecessary drugs and completely away from smoking and alcoholic beverages," Cordell noted.[73] The pride the cohort had in their Temple community can also be seen in the cover Marty Emmons, a Native American teen member of the Temple, drew for *In Small Dreams*, the school's poetry publication. The drawing shows Jones's face, looking very like Superman's, emerging from the center of a group of multiracial youth.[74] One by one over the course of 1977, Peoples Temple students unenrolled from Opportunity High to

Figure 7.7. Temple youth at a demonstration in Fresno, California, in 1976 in support of the "Fresno Four," a group of reporters who refused to reveal their sources. Among those pictured are Emmett Griffith, Tommy Beikman, Lew Jones, David Solomon, and Jocelyn Brown. *Source*: The Jonestown Institute, public domain.

move to Jonestown, the group's agricultural settlement in Guyana. They left behind a vacancy of spirit the school never recovered from, a void that only deepened when news about troubles in Jonestown started to reach San Francisco.[75]

Battlegrounds

Jones's regular citation of Peoples Temple as a safe haven for children and young people conflicted with several investigative journalist and defector accounts. In 1972, Episcopal priest, religion editor, and later conservative radio host Lester Kinsolving authored an eight-part exposé of Peoples Temple for the *San Francisco Examiner*. Kinsolving sought to reveal what he believed was Jones's false theology and the church's suspicious financing. Among four articles that went unpublished was "Sex, Socialism, and Child Torture with Rev. Jim Jones," which alleged that Jones had forced a child to eat his own vomit.[76] Kinsolving's report appeared concurrently with another exposé by *Indianapolis Star* reporter Carolyn Pickering. Peoples Temple responded that both series of articles were a form of harassment and deliberate attempts to discredit the good work of Peoples Temple.[77]

Far more damaging was an article published in *New West* magazine in 1977, which called for an official investigation of Jones and was based on interviews with former members. Among the many offenses referenced in the article was the Temple's routine corporal punishment. Elmer and Deanna Mertle reported that adults and children were regularly spanked up to one hundred times with a large paddle called "the board of education," after which the offender would have to say "Thank you, Father" to Jones. Their daughter, Linda Mertle, was reportedly struck seventy-five times when she was sixteen for hugging and kissing a female friend. According to her faither, Elmer Mertle, "she was beaten so severely, that the kids said her butt looked like hamburger."[78] The authors of the *New West* article alleged they endured repeated intimidation tactics from Peoples Temple to prevent the article from being published. Despite this, the article appeared in the magazine's August 1, 1977 edition. Even before its publication, the threat of negative media coverage had prompted a significant migration or "mass exodus" of Peoples Temple members to Guyana, a forced relocation interpreted by Temple members as further evidence of their persecution in America. "The power of right-wing media chased us miles across this country and over the rough seas," wrote Temple recording secretary B. Alethia Orsot. "They hounded, clamored, demanded, invaded, violated, discredited and destroyed us. They wouldn't leave us alone to heal and try to enjoy the happiness we had earned."[79]

To the Promised Land

On January 7, 1977, a child announced in front of the Temple that he wanted to go to the "promised land," the community's name for the agricultural settlement in Jonestown, Guyana. "That's a smart kid, what the black people need," responded Jones.[80] From 1972 to 1977, Peoples Temple had grown from a community of a couple hundred followers to several thousand spread over three California locations—Ukiah (and Redwood Valley), Los Angeles, and San Francisco.[81] Convincing Temple members to move to a new country thousands of miles away took work. "He [Jones] promised that our kids would never be prostitutes again, or never be hooked on drugs, and would never drop out of school," explained Jynona Norwood. "That's why my loved ones and relatives went to Jonestown. It was for the cause."[82] Jones told Norwood's aunt: "If you bring your children out of America, I will make your children great and they will have a place where they will not have to be in slavery to the white man any more. That was the reason his congregation stayed with him: they shared Dr. King's dream for a better life, for the paradise of equal rights."[83] As Norwood highlights, Jones leveraged child welfare to argue for Temple members' migration to Guyana. Jonestown survivor Laura Johnston Kohl corroborated this view: "When discussion about Guyana first came up, Jim spoke about constructing a Promised Land, a safe place for our children and for our community. His persuasive speeches and enthusiasm broke down even the fiercest opposition."[84] Those who moved to Jonestown were likened to refugees who were fleeing persecution. "Parents wanted their children to live in a just and healthy community, away from violence and drugs," Kohl added. "People wanted to participate in a rainbow family, an adoptive family, where all races and backgrounds were welcomed." Once they arrived in Jonestown, they could not easily leave.[85] The intricate and extended familial connections within Peoples Temple added to the difficulty of separation.

One of the people interviewed for the *New West* article was Grace Stoen, a former Peoples Temple leader turned ardent critic. Stoen was embroiled in a legal struggle to gain custody of her five-year-old son John Victor, aka John-John, whose care she had entrusted to Peoples Temple members. Stoen worked with her estranged husband, Timothy Stoen, also a former leader of Peoples Temple, to recover the child from Jonestown. Despite the Stoens' claims, Jones insisted John Victor was his biological son rather than Timothy's.[86] The Stoens' case was just one among several custody battles that became increasingly heated as more children and relatives relocated to the Promise Land. Concerns were amplified through the efforts of the Concerned Relatives, a group of parents, relatives, and former members of Peoples Temple who sought redress for custody battles and property disputes as well as access to relatives they believed were mistreated in Jonestown. The group petitioned US government officials and sought support in the court of public opinion to force Jones to release children and others living in Jonestown. A flyer distributed by the Concerned Relatives depicted Jonestown as a forced labor camp where adults and children were being held against

"If you don't love children, you don't understand socialism" | 165

Figure 7.8. A drawing included in a flyer distributed by the Concerned Relatives showing a child in the "Jonestown concentration camp." *Source*: The Jonestown Institute, public domain.

their will. Included in the flyer was a drawing of a child that appealed to readers from behind the bars of the "Jonestown concentration camp."[87]

Despite the Stoens' and Concerned Relatives' efforts, the US government was limited in its power to enforce custody claims in Guyana. According to Richard A. Dwyer, the deputy chief of mission at the American Embassy in

Guyana during the Jonestown period, the children under question were all either of legal age or had legal guardians present at Jonestown.[88] In a cruel twist of irony, the Stoens' custody battle, in combination with efforts by the Concerned Relatives to aid children, has been identified as one of the contributing factors that led to the mass murder and suicides that occurred in the wake of Congressman Leo Ryan's visit to Jonestown in November 1978. On this point, sociologist of religion John R. Hall has observed that "the opponents' own actions helped to precipitate a course of events that presumably led to the fulfillment of their own worst fears."[89] Custody battles and attempts by the Concerned Relatives to reclaim children through the Guyanese courts aggravated Jones's and Peoples Temple leadership's long-held conviction that the group was under siege from outside forces and that the safety of the community's children was compromised. On one of the "White Night" suicide drills in Guyana, Laura Johnston Kohl recalled, "Jim yelled that 'they' were coming for our children. He generalized that either the Guyanese Defense Force, or American soldiers, or someone, was going to come into Jonestown and get the kids, and the suggestion was that the invaders would snatch all the children, not just the nine living there without proper authorization."[90]

In September 1977, in what became known as the Six-Day Siege, the Stoens' attorney Jeffrey Haas successfully appealed to the Guyanese Supreme Court to issue a writ of habeas corpus to Jones regarding the legality of his custody claim of John Victor. Jonestown leaders interpreted the court order as a sign the community faced an imminent attack by the Guyana Defense Force and mounted an armed response, what Rebecca Moore has described as "a state of siege."[91] The Temple's fear was that if one child was taken, it would open the floodgates, and all of the Temple's children would be at risk. All members of Jonestown, including children, were armed with machetes, rakes, and farm implements and ordered to prepare for an attack. Jones attempted to leave Jonestown for Cuba on a boat with John Victor, but the Kaituma River was blocked.

During the siege, Angela Davis sent the following message to Jones: "I know you are in a very difficult situation right now and there is a conspiracy. A very profound conspiracy designed to destroy the contributions which you have made to our struggle. And this is why I must tell you that we feel that we are under attack as well."[92] The words lent credence to the Temple's growing conviction that the community was on the frontlines of a battle. Barbara Walker, a Black woman from Los Angeles who had moved to Jonestown in 1977, left behind a poetic account of the siege that reflects this sense of threat. Walker's poem reads in part:

> Gave you your country, and got a land of our own.
> We were freed from your shackles by our leader Jim Jones.
> When he gave us Jonestown, Guyana as our new-found home.
> It was his desire to give his people a chance to be happy, a chance to be free
> And to give our children the right to live free of the pain created by your capitalist society.
> This is ours, we are here to stay, we're committed to the socialist life, because it's the only way
> On my own land, proud and free. And nobody is going to take my freedom from me.
> I've come here to learn to love, share and build.
> And if I can't do this, I don't want to live![93]

Seven months after the siege, on April 11, 1978, the Concerned Relatives sent Jones their "Accusation of Human Rights Violations by Rev. James Warren Jones Against Our Children and Relatives at the Peoples Temple Jungle Encampment in Guyana, South America." The document included a "Summary of Violations," including Jones's refusal to allow family members to see their children at Peoples Temple, and his declaration "that it is better even to die than to be constantly harassed from one continent to the next," which threatened the lives of all members, but particularly those of the children.[94]

Former members and relatives have been adamant that within the debate over whether the night of November 18, 1978, was a mass suicide or a mass murder, there is no question that the infants and children were murdered. Jynona Norwood, who has stated they lost twenty-seven family members at Jonestown, explains: "They've tried to tell us it was suicide. But a three-week-old baby does not commit suicide. When an adult gives a child poison, that is not suicide."[95] Despite her profound loss and ongoing criticism of Jones, Norwood recalls the larger purpose of Peoples Temple with compassion: "The people of Peoples Temple were not selfish, crazy people. They were compassionate people who loved their children so much that they traveled to a strange land, carved a community out of the jungle with their own blood, sweat and tears, and did so in an effort to get their families away from a life of drugs, jail, discrimination, poverty and unhappiness."[96]

Conclusion

"They started with the babies," recalled Odell Rhodes.[97] Rhodes was one of fewer than a handful of surviving members to have witnessed the events of the night of November 18, 1978. A Black man, Rhodes credited Peoples Temple with saving him from a life of addiction. He was remembered as a mentor among Peoples Temple youth. Details of the mass murders and suicides he witnessed were reported in newspapers around the country. Among them were descriptions of children being force-fed poison. "It just got all out of order," recalled Rhodes. "Babies were screaming, children were screaming and there was mass confusion."[98]

In an undated memo found at Jonestown, Annie Moore, one of the community's nurses, wrote, "The main reason for suicide—to assure safety to the children."[99] Moore's conclusion reflected a larger Temple position, routinely impressed by Jones, that taking the lives of the children was superior to letting them be brainwashed, tortured, or murdered by fascist enemies. Moore's note reveals an internal struggle about the pending act of "revolutionary suicide," a recognition of the cruel irony that liberation and death could be so closely entwined. Rather than surrender John Victor, or any of the children, Jones and the leadership prepared the community for death. The decision, long rehearsed, was framed as an act of heroism akin to the Jews at Masada.[100] When the night came, only Christine Miller's voice

Figure 7.9. A photograph taken in Jonestown dated 1978 showing Pop Jackson, Lisa Rodriguez, and other children. *Source*: The Jonestown Institute, public domain.

countered Jones's call for "revolutionary suicide." She appealed to the group on account of the children. "But I look at all the babies and I think they deserve to live," argued Miller. Jones dismissed her reasoning and replied, "But don't they deserve much more? They deserve peace. . . . When they start parachuting out of the air, they'll shoot some of our innocent babies. Can you let them take your child?" A wave of shouting voices from the crowd erupted in response: "No! No! No!"[101]

Notes

1. I extend my sincere gratitude to Rebecca Moore for her thoughtful feedback on this chapter.

2. Precise membership numbers are difficult to ascertain due to the geographic scope of the community and differing assessments of who counted as members. Mary R. Sawyer has offered a range of around 2,000 to 3,000 active members for the period in San Francisco, 1971–1978. Mary R. Sawyer, "The Church in People's Temple," in *Peoples Temple and Black Religion in America*, ed. Rebecca Moore, Anthony B. Pinn, and Mary R. Sawyer (Bloomington: Indiana University Press, 2004), 169.

3. "How Many Children and Minors Died in Jonestown? What Were Their Ages?," The Jonestown Institute, September 29, 2013, https://jonestown.sdsu.edu/?page_id=35332.

4. Depending on the period and place of consideration, African Americans represented between 80% and 90% of Peoples Temple membership. Sawyer, "The Church in People's Temple," 169.

5. Hugh B. Urban, "Peoples Temple: Mass Murder-Suicide, the Media, and the 'Cult' Label," in *New Age, Neopagan, and New Religious Movements: Alternative Spirituality in Contemporary America*, ed. Hugh B. Urban (Oakland, CA: University of California Press, 2015), 245.

6. Lowell D. Streiker, "Reflections on the Human Freedom Center," in *The Need for a Second Look at Jonestown: Remembering Its People*, ed. Rebecca Moore and Fielding M. McGehee (Lewiston, NY: The Edwin Mellen Press: 1989), 161.

7. See Rebecca Moore, Anthony B. Pinn, and Mary R. Sawyer, eds., *Peoples Temple and Black Religion in America* (Bloomington: Indiana University Press, 2004); James Lance Taylor, "Bring Out The 'Black Dimensions' of Peoples Temple," The Jonestown Institute, https://jonestown.sdsu.edu/?page_id=29462; Sikivu Hutchinson, "Black Women and the Peoples Temple in Jonestown," Black Perspectives, January 31, 2017, https://www.aaihs.org/black-women-and-the-peoples-temple-in-jonestown; Sikivu Hutchinson, *White Nights Black Paradise: A Novel* (Los Angeles, CA: Infidel Books, 2015); Mary McCormick Maaga, "The Triple Erasure of Women in the Leadership of Peoples Temple," in *Hearing the Voices of Jonestown: Putting a Human Face on an American Tragedy* (Syracuse, NY: Syracuse University Press, 1998).

8. Sawyer, "The Church in People's Temple," 170.

9. "How Many Children and Minors Died in Jonestown? What Were Their Ages?," The Jonestown Institute, September 29, 2013, https://jonestown.sdsu.edu/?page_id=35332.

10. Don Lattin, a reporter for the *San Francisco Examiner* at the time of the tragedy, uncovered how some of the youth of Jonestown were sent there in lieu of juvenile hall through efforts made by Temple members working at county social service offices. Don Lattin, "Children of Jonestown and the Children of God," The Jonestown Institute, February 17, 2014, https://jonestown.sdsu.edu/?page_id=31412.

11. On the limited frameworks used to analyze children within NRMs, see Charlotte E. Hardman, "Children in New Religious Movements," in *The Oxford Handbook of New Religious Movements*, ed. James R. Lewis (Oxford: Oxford Handbooks, 2008).

12. Maaga, *Hearing the Voices of Jonestown*, 39.

13. Kenneth Wooden's 1981 *The Children of Jonestown* is perhaps the best example of a singular focus on child abuse within Peoples Temple.

14. Don S. Browning and Bonnie J. Miller-McLemore, eds., *Children and Childhood in American Religions* (Piscataway: Rutgers University Press, 2009), 12.

15. Browning and Miller-McLemore.

16. A large portion of the remembrances by former members and relatives as well as primary source material for this chapter is drawn from Alternative Considerations of Jonestown and Peoples Temple, an online archive of materials relating to Peoples Temple, sponsored by the Special Collections of Library and Information Access at San Diego State University. The collection is cited as The Jonestown Institute.

17. "Peoples Temple Newsletter, August 1970," The Jonestown Institute, https://jonestown.sdsu.edu/?page_id=14095.

18. Robert Spencer, "My Mother, Agnes Jones," https://jonestown.sdsu.edu/?page_id=61624.

19. "Korean Waifs' Adoption Called 'Lesson' in Religion," *Indianapolis News*, February 25, 1960.

20. "Can't Find Integrated Burial Place for Child," *Indianapolis Recorder*, May 16, 1959.

21. "Stephanie Jones," Find a Grave, https://www.findagrave.com/memorial/31289300/stephanie-jones.

22. Rebecca Moore, *Peoples Temple and Jonestown in the Twenty-First Century* (Cambridge: Cambridge University Press 2022), 12.

23. That same year, the Jones also adopted Timothy Glenn Tupper (often shortened to Tim or Timmy), whose birth mother, Rita Tupper, was a Temple member.

24. "Human Family," *The Indianapolis Recorder*, April 1, 1961.

25. Pat Williams Stewart, "White Liberal Suffers Abuse From 'Both Sides'; Still Struggles On," *The Indianapolis Recorder*, July 25, 1964.

26. Moore, *Peoples Temple and Jonestown*, 12.

27. Donald Beck, "Confessions of a Junior Choir Director," July 24, 2021, https://jonestown.sdsu.edu/?page_id=30782.

28. David Chidester, *Salvation and Suicide: Jim Jones, the Peoples Temple, and Jonestown* (Bloomington: Indiana University Press, 1991), 6.

29. Beck, "Confessions of a Junior Choir Director."

30. Moore, *Peoples Temple and Jonestown*, 48.

31. Jeff Guinn, *The Road to Jonestown: Jim Jones and Peoples Temple* (New York: Simon & Schuster, 2017), 83.

32. "Peoples Temple Christian Church, Jim Jones, Pastor," The George Moscone Collection, University of the Pacific Scholarly Commons, 1976, https://scholarlycommons.pacific.edu/mayor-moscone/3.

33. "Peoples Temple Newsletter, October 1970," The Jonestown Institute.

34. Lawrence Wright, "Orphans of Jonestown," *The New Yorker*, November 22, 1993, 68.

35. Jynona M. Norwood, "We Cannot Forget Our Own," in *The Need for a Second Look at Jonestown: Remembering Its People*, ed. Rebecca Moore and Fielding M. McGehee (Lewiston, NY: The Edwin Mellen Press: 1989), 175.

36. On the history of segregation and recreation, see Victoria Wolcott, *Race, Riots, and Roller Coasters: The Struggle Over Segregated Recreation in America* (Philadelphia: University of Pennsylvania Press, 2012).

37. Susan Ridgely, "Children and Religion," *Religion Compass* 6, no. 4 (2012): 239.

38. Laura Johnston Kohl, "Change and the Chameleon That Was Jim Jones," The Jonestown Institute, November 20, 2019, https://jonestown.sdsu.edu/?page_id=70623.

39. Garrett Lambrev, "Brotherhood Is Our Religion," in *The Living Word: An Apostolic Monthly* 1, no. 1 (July 1972): 33, The Jonestown Institute, https://jonestown.sdsu.edu/?page_id=14091.

40. Lambrev.

41. Garrett Lambrev, "*The Living Word* and Me: The Limits of Anarchism in Peoples Temple," The Jonestown Institute, June 17, 2018, https://jonestown.sdsu.edu/?page_id=32374.

42. Alexa Valiente, "40 Years after the Jonestown Massacre: Jim Jones' Surviving Sons on What They Think of Their Father, the Peoples Temple Today," September 28, 2018, ABC News, https://abcnews.go.com/US/40-years-jonestown-massacre-jim-jones-surviving-sons/story?id=57997006.

43. Joseph B. Treaster, "A Cult Mother Led Children to Death," *The New York Times*, December 5, 1978, 35.

44. Don Beck, "Remembrances of Temple Kindergarteners," July 24, 2021, https://jonestown.sdsu.edu/?page_id=29249.

45. It is possible Edith Roller kept a journal longer, but the pages have not been recovered.

46. Marshall Kilduff and Phil Tracy, "Inside Peoples Temple" *New West*, August 1, 1977, https://jonestown.sdsu.edu/?page_id=14025.

47. Judy Bebelaar and Ron Cabral, *And Then They Were Gone: Teenagers of Peoples Temple from High School to Jonestown* (Berkeley: Minuteman Press, 2018), 69.

48. Edith Roller, "Edith Roller Journals: January 1977," October 20, 2021, The Jonestown Institute, https://jonestown.sdsu.edu/?page_id=35686.

49. Edith Roller, "Edith Roller Journals: August 1976," February 24, 2022, The Jonestown Institute, https://jonestown.sdsu.edu/?page_id=35681.

50. Moore, *Peoples Temple and Jonestown in the Twenty-First Century*, 35.

51. Edith Roller, "Edith Roller Journals: January 1977," October 20, 2021, The Jonestown Institute, https://jonestown.sdsu.edu/?page_id=35686.

52. Edith Roller, "Edith Roller Journals: December 1976," December 26, 2021, The Jonestown Institute, https://jonestown.sdsu.edu/?page_id=35685.

53. Edith Roller, "Edith Roller Journals: September 1976," February 24, 2022, The Jonestown Institute, https://jonestown.sdsu.edu/?page_id=35682.

54. Edith Roller, "Edith Roller Journals: May 1976," December 30, 2020, The Jonestown Institute, https://jonestown.sdsu.edu/?page_id=35678.

55. Edith Roller, "Edith Roller Journals: November 1976," October 22, 2021, https://jonestown.sdsu.edu/?page_id=35684.

56. Les Brown, "TV: Formula Maker Paid for ABC Film on Infants," *The New York Times*, June 9, 1976, 56.

57. Edith Roller, "Edith Roller Journals: June 1976," transcribed by Don Beck, August 2009, The Jonestown Institute, https://jonestown.sdsu.edu/?page_id=35679.

58. For a detailed understanding of the expanded kinship connections between Peoples Temple members, see "The Family Trees of Jonestown," The Jonestown Institute, https://jonestown.sdsu.edu/?page_id=35705.

59. Milmon F. Harrison, "Jim Jones and Black Worship Traditions," in *Peoples Temple & Black Religion in America*, 128.

60. Laura Johnston Kohl, "Migration and Emigration," The Jonestown Institute, November 20, 2019, https://jonestown.sdsu.edu/?page_id=81226.

61. Merve Emre, "How a Fictional Racist Plot Made the Headlines and Revealed an American Truth," *The New Yorker*, December 31, 2017, https://www.newyorker.com/books/second-read/how-a-fictional-racist-plot-made-the-headlines-and-revealed-an-american-truth.

62. "Two Sermons," Q1059-2 Transcript, June 19, 1972, The Jonestown Institute, February 18, 2016, https://jonestown.sdsu.edu/?page_id=27332.

63. Edith Roller, "Edith Roller Journals: July 1976," December 30, 2020, The Jonestown Institute, https://jonestown.sdsu.edu/?page_id=35680.

64. Jordan Vilchez, "Insight and Compassion: Vestiges of Peoples Temple," March 4, 2014, https://jonestown.sdsu.edu/?page_id=33208.

65. Vilchez.

66. Vilchez.

67. Edith Roller, "Edith Roller Journals: January 1977."
68. "Public relations release (September 26, 1976)," "Social Ministry for Social Justice," California Historical Society, MS 3800, The Jonestown Institute, https://jonestown.sdsu.edu/?page_id=18711.
69. Bebelaar and Cabral, *And Then They Were Gone*, 35.
70. Bebelaar and Cabral, 39.
71. Bebelaar and Cabral, 51.
72. Bebelaar and Cabral, 115.
73. Bebelaar and Cabral, 117.
74. Bebelaar and Cabral, 45.
75. Bebelaar and Cabral, 139.
76. Rev. Lester Kinsolving, "Sex, Socialism, and Child Torture with Rev. Jim Jones," September 1972, The Jonestown Institute, https://jonestown.sdsu.edu/?page_id=14089.
77. "The Temple Response to Carolyn Pickering," The Jonestown Institute, December 31, 2019, https://jonestown.sdsu.edu/?page_id=18809.
78. Marshall Kilduff and Phil Tracy, "Inside Peoples Temple" *New West*, August 1, 1977.
79. Alethia Orsot, "Together We Stood, Divided We Fell," in *The Need for a Second Look at Jonestown: Remembering its People*, ed. Rebecca Moore and Fielding M. McGehee (Lewiston, NY: The Edwin Mellen Press: 1989), 103.
80. Edith Roller, "Edith Roller Journals: January 1977."
81. Tanya M. Hollis, "Peoples Temple and Housing Politics in San Francisco," in *Peoples Temple and Black Religion in America*, 96. Mary McCormick Maaga has demonstrated that there were three distinct groups within Peoples Temple: white and Black families from Indiana, younger white members from California, and urban Blacks who joined from San Francisco and Los Angeles. Maaga, *Hearing the Voices of Jonestown*, 75.
82. Norwood, "We Cannot Forget Our Own," 171.
83. Norwood.
84. Kohl, "Change and the Chameleon That Was Jim Jones."
85. Jennie Rothenberg Gritz, "Drinking the Kool-Aid: A Survivor Remembers Jim Jones," *The Atlantic*, November 18, 2011, https://www.theatlantic.com/national/archive/2011/11/drinking-the-kool-aid-a-survivor-remembers-jim-jones/248723/.
86. Moore, *Peoples Temple and Jonestown in the Twenty-First Century*, 40.
87. "Concerned Relatives Flyer," "This Nightmare Is Taking Place Right Now," The Jonestown Institute, https://jonestown.sdsu.edu/wp-content/uploads/2013/10/ConRelflyer.pdf.
88. Richard A. Dwyer, interviewed by Charles Stuart Kennedy, The Association for Diplomatic Studies and Training Foreign Affairs Oral History Project, July 12, 1990, 94, The Jonestown Institute, https://jonestown.sdsu.edu/wp-content/uploads/2020/12/Dwyer-Richard-A.toc_.pdf.

89. John R. Hall, Philip D. Schuyler, with Sylvaine Trinh, *Apocalypse Observed: Religious Movements and Violence in North America, Europe, and Japan* (London: Routledge, 2000), 42.

90. Laura Johnston Kohl, "Guyana 40 Years Later," The Jonestown Institute, November 20, 2019, https://jonestown.sdsu.edu/?page_id=81250.

91. Rebecca Moore, *Understanding Jonestown and Peoples Temple* (Westport, CT: Praeger Publishers, 2009), 76.

92. "Statement of Angela Davis to Jim Jones over Radio Phone-Patch," September 10, 1977, The Jonestown Institute, https://jonestown.sdsu.edu/?page_id=19027.

93. Barbara Walker, "The Front Line," December 1977, The Jonestown Institute, https://jonestown.sdsu.edu/?page_id=13071. Barbara Walker died on the night of November 18, 1978, with her three children.

94. "Accusation of Human Rights Violations by Rev. James Warren Jones Against Our Children and Relatives at the Peoples Temple Jungle Encampment in Guyana, South America," April 11, 1978, The Jonestown Institute, https://jonestown.sdsu.edu/?page_id=13081.

95. Professor of Psychology Katherine Hill has not been able to account for each member of the "Norwood 27," despite efforts. The number is a potential sign of the extended family networks characteristic of Peoples Temple, in which nonbiological relatives were routinely considered family. Katherine Hill, "In Search of the Norwood 27," The Jonestown Institute, https://jonestown.sdsu.edu/?page_id=40218; Norwood, "We Cannot Forget Our Own," 178.

96. Norwood, 178.

97. Charles A. Krause, "Survivor: 'They Started with the Babies,'" *The Washington Post*, November 21, 1978.

98. Charles A. Krause, "Gunmen Prevented Escapes," *Los Angeles Times*, November 21, 1978, 1.

99. Annie Moore, "Memo from Annie Moore," The Jonestown Institute, https://jonestown.sdsu.edu/?page_id=78448.

100. Guinn, *The Road to Jonestown*, 311.

101. "Q042 Transcript, by Fielding M. McGehee III," The Jonestown Institute, July 6, 2001, https://jonestown.sdsu.edu/?page_id=29079.

8

Kabbalah, Sex Magic, and the Trans-Utopia

Powerful Sexualities in the *Zohar* and
Moshe Cordovero's Writings

MARLA SEGOL

This chapter explores the utopian function of medieval and early modern kabbalistic sex magic rituals in the thirteenth- and fourteen-century *Sefer ha Zohar* (Book of Splendor) and in three works by the kabbalist Moshe Cordovero, who lived from 1522 to 1570 in Ottoman Palestine. These works narrate a divine creation process that begins with an androgynous deity who creates by means of differentiation. This differentiation is imagined through gendering, and these kabbalistic texts articulate rituals that utopianize this primal androgyny and work to restore it. It focuses on two interlinked rituals: domestically performed practices of sacred sexuality and those of *Gerushin* (exile, divorce) which are walking meditation rituals meant to sexually unite separated elements of the divine, performed while wandering through the countryside. Both of these are based in a kabbalistic cosmogony narrating creation by means of divine separation into ten gendered aspects or sefirot, which then create the universe by means of sexual reproduction. As a result of this separation, one of the sefirot, the feminine Shekhinah, is exiled and separated from her husband, Tiferet.[1] Her state of exile mirrors that of the Jewish practitioners of sex magic rituals, and so when they act for her, they also act for themselves.[2] Kabbalistic sex magic rituals are thus aimed at imitating and participating in an ongoing divine creation process to attain blessings and prophecy, but ultimately repairing the divine separation and ending human exile. In performing these rituals, practitioners reimagine their own genders and sexualities, cultivating and enacting a trans-androgyny by identifying with both male and female sefirot and erotically engaging with human and celestial partners. The rituals create a utopian space that centers the human body as the site and the agent of change, reimagining gender, sexuality, and corporeality as they seek to restore the primal androgyny, the state of God and human before creation was completed. This accords with Michel Foucault's understanding of the utopian body, arguing that all utopias are "born from the body itself," such that "the human body is the principal actor in all utopias."[3] Thus, sex magic rituals, born from the body, perform acts of regendering to engage in a sacred sexuality that acts on the human being, the cosmos, and the divine. This is in the end a trans theology, aimed at restoring the primal androgynous state of both human and divine.

This queering and transing is key to the utopian function of kabbalistic sex magic. As it is understood here, kabbalistic sex magic is ritualized sexuality meant to access divine power. It operationalizes kabbalistic myths based in interpretations of biblical narratives alluding to divine creation by means of sexual reproduction, which, though strange to us now, were quite common in Ancient Middle Eastern mythology. The Genesis narratives are important to these myths. Genesis 1:27 describes the first human beings as androgynous, like the divine before creation. It reads: "And God created the man (ha-Adam) in his own image, in the image of God he created him; male and female He created them."[4] The passage describes the creation of a singular, androgynous primordial man, "ha-Adam," which then becomes plural, male, and female. This is modeled on the gendering of the divine, first unified and androgynous, and then through the process of creation, separated and gendered. Genesis 1:28 follows with the commandment to "Be fruitful and multiply, replenish the earth, and subdue it; have dominion over the fish of the sea and the fowl of the air, and over every living thing that creeps on earth."[5] The narrative positions human procreation as an iteration of the divine creative process, allowing participation in divine creative power by reproduction, which in turn sustains the created world and grants power over it. This tale of androgyny, separation, reproduction, and participation imitates an implied narrative divine androgyny and separation. Genesis 2:23–24 narrates the separation and gendering of human beings, and it presents sexuality as mode of repair. Genesis 2:23 re-narrates creation as a process of separation: "The man said 'This is now bone of my bones, and flesh of my flesh, she shall be called woman, because she was taken out of man.' "[6] Genesis 2:24 imagines sex as remedy for that, reuniting male and female through sex as they become "one flesh," to restore the primal human androgyne of Genesis 1:27 and 2:23.

Feelings of erotic love and desire are also important to sex magic, and kabbalistic sources use the biblical *Song of Songs* as an affective model for the relations between human beings, between human and divine, and between the sefirot, or aspects of the divine.[7] Such expressions of desire open the work as the main character (nameless, but commonly called "the Shulamite Woman") exclaims: "Kiss me, make me drunk with your kisses!"[8] These lines often find their way into the mouths of male practitioners as they assume the role of the female lover. Kabbalistic literature builds on these texts as practitioners of sex magic re-gender themselves to restore human and divine to their primal, androgynous, undifferentiated state. Because transgendering is a crucial element of the rituals, it is helpful to think about this in terms of recent developments in trans theory that view it as a mode of movement rather than as a fixed state.[9] Modern trans theory often defines "trans" in a way that does not reify the gender categories that it moves across. Susan Stryker argues that transing is "a practice that takes place within, as well as across or between, gendered spaces."[10] This is to say that we are asked to consider it first, as not necessarily opposed to and exclusive of cis, and second, as a form of movement not necessarily attached to the gendered and sexed history of the body. Thus trans is not always a unidirectional journey from one biologically determined gender to another, but a state of being all by itself, a mode of movement between categories. So, too, these multiplicitous genderings and sexualities produce a trans-historicity, meant to establish new grounds for the making of history, and with it, new sorts of stories, generated and authorized in new ways.[11] The kabbalistic texts examined here repertoires of gendering and sexuality are central to the utopian efficacy of sex magic rituals, and with this we turn to them.

Zohar

Most scholars agree that kabbalah begins with the *Zohar*, a large literary compendium mainly composed by Moshe de Leon and his disciples in Castile between the years of 1280 and 1286, with its later strata dating to the fourteenth century. [12] It narrates a series of fictional, mystical conversations between the second-century Gallilean legal sage Shimon bar Yohai and his circle of students. The *Zohar* is distinguished from earlier Jewish mystical works by its articulation of a sefirotic cosmos that begins with a divine separation and an emanation into ten different gendered aspects, or sefirot. While they were indistinct within the divine unity before creation, in this process they acquire discrete, gendered identities with individual characteristics, familial roles, and sexual relationships. The passages examined here focus most intently on the relationship between the three sefirot of Tiferet, Yesod, and Shekhinah. Tiferet (Beauty) is a bigendered sefirah married to the feminine Shekhinah or Malchut (God's revealed presence), and they are connected by Yesod (foundation, penis). These three sefirot act as a channel for divine power to descend through the upper sefirot, and they also facilitate human interaction with the divine. Because Shekhinah is sometimes exiled from home and separated from Tiferet, the rituals aims to reunite them and in this to participate in the divine, access divine power, and transform human and divine alike. In this way, the myths that give meaning to sex magic are also those that underlie kabbalah.

Here we examine three passages from the *Zohar* that describe domestic sacred sexuality and walking meditation rituals meant to effect human and celestial sexual unions. These include *Zohar* 3 on the *Song of Songs*, *Zohar* 1:49b–51a on Genesis 1 and 2, and *Zohar Midrash ha Ne'elam* (*Hidden Interpretation*) on the *Song of Songs*.[13] These passages first articulate Zoharic models of divine gendering and sexuality, and second, they show how human participation in it, by means of transgendering and multiplicitous erotic relationships, is intended to change the cosmos and even the divine. This is a series of queerings and transings that allow for the telling of new and different sorts of stories, which in turn constitutes a trans-history. We begin with *Zohar* 3, on the *Song of Songs*, which rather succinctly describes and theorizes Zoharic sex magic. Zohar 1:49b–50a describes the walking meditation and its relation to domestic sacred sexuality, and with it, the process of ritually transing the body to engage in sexual relationships that generate new narratives. Finally, *Zohar Midrash haNe'elam* shows us what sorts of new stories are being told, as the writer reverses the biblical conception of human creation in the divine image to assert that divine creation is actually modeled on human reproduction. Together these passages provide instructions for transing the human body to engage in sex magic rituals that remedy cosmic binarity to restore the idealized primal androgyne.

Zohar 3 on the *Song of Songs* describes the theurgic power of sex magic. According to this passage, human union stimulates celestial union to brings blessings (and babies) to the community. In the process it articulates a repertoire of feelings, genderings, and sexualities that are key to its efficacy. This oft-quoted passage theorizes the relation between desire, transgendering, and theurgy in sex magic: "[W]hen a man cleaves to his mate and his desire is to receive her, he worships before the holy King and arouses another union, for the desire of the Holy One, blessed be He, is to cleave to the community of Israel."[14] At first its repertoire seems to consist of feelings of heterosexual desire and pleasure, central to the *Song of Songs*. However these feelings of desire are tied to an erotic orientation that is cut loose from an embodied gender. This is so because the participants assume a variety of gendered positions within this heterosexual model. While the authors imagine human sexual union, initiated by desire, to actuate a celestial one, its efficacy is dependent on role-play, as the singular male character takes the part of the plural, female assembly of Israel, begging her lover to lie with her:

> Concerning my bed I pleaded with him, that he might lie with me, and give me pleasure, and bless me with perfect delight; for we have learned that, as a result of the king's cohabitation with the Assembly of Israel, large numbers of the righteous come into their sacred inheritance, and a multitude of blessings are bestowed upon the world.[15]

This transgendering is necessary to access sacred power,[16] which bestows blessings on participants and on the cosmos as a whole. This begins to articulate the Zoharic model for sex magic, based in feelings of love, pleasure, and delight. These feelings are situated in a repertoire of mobile genderings as the characters move from singular male to plural female, and in an erotic multiplicity as ever more characters join in sexual union, dissolving the boundaries between human and divine. Together they bring "a multitude of blessings to the world." The passage then articulates the repertoire of feelings, genderings, and sexualities and their transformative, utopian affordances characteristic of Zoharic sex magic.

Zohar 1:49b–151a employs a similar repertoire of feelings, genderings, and sexualities for similarly transformative purposes. Also drawing on the language of the *Song of Songs*, it grants efficacy to feelings of love, desire, and delight. As in the above passage, it locates power in transgendering and multiplicitous sexuality. It describes a complex of three cumulative domestic and walking rituals of sacred sexuality, the first at home, the second conducted on the road by erotically engaging celestial powers, and the third again at home, which concludes with a multi-partnered performance as the traveler comes home to "delight his wife." These interconnected practices hinge on reimagining the categories of gender, sexuality, corporeality, humanness, and divinity as they layer a series of celestial sexual unions with embodied ones. This effects a union of all the divine forces invoked on the journey to culminate in prophetic trance. This prophecy, arising from embodied experience and flowing through the body, serves a utopian function, generating new interpretations of the sacred texts that undergird society in order to change it. This becomes the model for *gerushin* (ritualized voluntary exile) in sixteenth-century Cordoverian kabbalah, to be discussed below.

Zohar 1:49b opens by describing the walking ritual, which idealizes trans-androgyny achieved by the practice of sacred sexuality. The narrative begins as the main character, the second-century sage Rabbi Shimon bar Yochai, separates himself from his wife and wanders the Galillee with his companions to emulate the experience of the exiled Shekhinah, woefully separated from her celestial husband, Tiferet. The group is walking the Galillee together when they chance on another traveler who is "eager to hear some of those sublime words you speak every day."[17] The new companion, then, wishes to the hear the prophecy attained in the course of the journey. Shimon Bar Yochai sanctifies the journey and designates his insights as prophecy by quoting Genesis 13:3, the portion of the Torah that recounts Abraham's travels at the divine behest. 12:1 reads: "The LORD had said to Abram, "Go from your country, your people and your father's household to the land I will show you."[18] Genesis 13:3–4 narrates Abraham's travels, and the authors seize on the plural form of the word "journey." This text reads: "And he went on his journeys from the South even to Beth-El . . . unto the place of the altar."[19] According to the writers of the *Zohar*, the plural form of the word is used because it includes the Shekhinah. With her presence, Abraham achieves an apotropaic and prophetic state of androgyny, and following this model the practitioner cultivates two genders and two identities:

> Rabbi Shim'on opened, saying, "*He went on his journeys from the Negev as far as Bet-El* (Genesis 13:3). *He went on his journeys*. The verse should read: *his journey*. Why *his journeys*? Because there are two journeys: one, his; one, of *Shekhinah*. For every human being should manifest as male and female to fortify faith; then *Shekhinah* never separates from him.[20]

When husband and wife are not together, he is merely male, and thereby vulnerable. Thus without androgyny he is deficient, and the prophetic journeys are not possible.

To remedy the traveler's male gendering, the text instructs the reader to engage in a ritual of domestic sacred sexuality before leaving home. Its protective function is clear here, as it is conflated with prayer:

> Come and see: Whoever sets out on the road should offer his prayer to the blessed Holy One to draw upon himself *Shekhinah* of his Lord before he leaves, while still male and female. Once he has offered his prayer and *Shekhinah* rests upon him, he can leave, for *Shekhinah* has coupled with him so that he will be male and female: male and female in town, male and female in the countryside, as is written: *Righteousness goes before him, and he sets out on his way.* (Psalms 85:14)[21]

But let's examine the mechanics here: First, the traveler at home is gendered male and female, because of an implied union with his wife. Second, while still in this state, he is instructed to offer a prayer to a male aspect of divinity, Tiferet.[22] Third, this prayer allows the traveler to couple with Tiferet's wife, the feminine Shekhinah, who will help him maintain his androgyny away from home, which brings a state of righteousness that protects him. So when the traveler couples with his own wife, he unites the sefirot too, which makes the protection of sex portable as they all accompany him on the road.

The narrative comes full circle as the traveler's wife joins the multiplicitous union that accompanies her husband on the road, for he is commanded on his return to "delight" his wife with "the joy of coupling." The text requires this for several reasons: first, because she engendered, literally gave birth to, the coupling between her husband and the sefirot; and, second, omitting this earthly union would obstruct the celestial one. At the same time, both husband and wife take on fluid sexual and reproductive roles that initiate a prophetic trance:

> Upon entering his house he should delight the lady of his house, for she engendered that supernal coupling. As soon as he reaches her he should delight her anew, for two nuances. First, because the joy of this coupling is joy of *mitsvah*, and joy of *mitsvah* is

joy of *Shekhinah* . . .[23] Mystery of the matter: Supernal Mother appears with the male only when the house is arrayed, when male and female join.[24]

Here then, the Upper Mother (Binah) enters the house during sexual union. It is worth noting that in both Talmudic and kabbalistic literature, the word "house" often refers to the wife and her genitalia, which also applies here.[25] Accordingly, the proper array of the house designates the body of the wife, through whom the Supernal Mother enters sexually, bringing all the sefirot with her. This narrates the entrance of the upper mother into the lower, making this a multi-partnered and at times a same-gender union. The "arraying of the house" refers to a ritual meditation that attaches the couple to the celestial powers to make them a part of the divine body. The text instructs the reader as follows:

> There is a fire devouring fire, devouring and consuming it, for there is a fire fiercer than fire, they have established. But come and see: whoever desires to penetrate the wisdom of holy unification should contemplate the flame ascending from a glowing ember or a burning candle. For a flame ascends only when it is grasped by a coarse substance.[26]

The meditation directs practitioners to imagine the transformation of material actions to celestial ones. In this way, meditation joins their bodies to the divine one.

When the house, or the wife, is ritually "arrayed," Binah, the Upper Mother, blesses the couple, and the human male practitioner "nourishes" his wife. But, strangely, both characters do so using images usually associated with genders other than theirs. The text explains:

> She then pours blessings upon them. Similarly, Lower Mother appears with the male only when the house is arrayed, when the male approaches his female and they join as one. She then pours blessings upon them. So a man at home is adorned with two females, as above.[27] . . . Similarly below, when a male is married, *the desire of hills of eternity* verges toward him, and he is adorned with two females, one above and one below: the upper to pour blessings upon him, the lower to be nourished by him, unite with him.[28]

The vocabulary here also shows us, first, a multiplicitous sexuality in the form of a triplet rather than a couple, and, second, that husband and wife take on fluid sexual and reproductive roles. First, the lady of the house, in "engendering" the coupling on the road, here gives birth to sex. Second, the female sefirot, Binah and Shekhinah, "pour blessings." In these texts, the act of pouring is associated with ejaculation (*shofekh*—pours, ejaculates). And finally, as the upper feminine aspects ejaculate on him, his own semen turns to milk as he nourishes (*mazin*) the feminine elements.

This is, in the end, a source of revelation, for a scholar practices sex magic not only to reunite the sefirot, but also to authorize the body as a utopian space for the creation and sanctification of new sacred myths. Here the male operator, united with the two females, enters a prophetic trance to embody the concealed aspect of Torah (typically gendered female), which is then transformed within him and revealed through his own mouth. Rabbi Shim'on said,

> Similarly Torah stands between two houses, as is written: *for the two houses of Israel* (Isaiah 8:14), one concealed on high, the other more revealed. The concealed one on high is the *mighty voice*, as is written: *a mighty voice unceasing* (Deuteronomy 5:19). This voice is inward, inaudible, and unrevealed, as the larynx wells, whispering ה (*heh*), flowing incessantly, tenuous, internal, eternally unheard. From here emerges Torah, *voice of Jacob*, audible issuing from inaudible. Afterward speech merges in it, resounding from its potency. The voice of Jacob, Torah, is embraced by two females: this inner, inaudible one, and this outer one, audible.[29]

Sex magic rituals initiate a simultaneous union and a bifurcation; as the operator unites with the human and the celestial females, he is feminized as Torah. The feminized Torah is in turn split into audible and inaudible aspects, upper and lower mothers associated with concealed and revealed interpretations. As he enters a state of entrancement, the concealed interpretations enter his body, his larynx wells, and the inaudible (flowing incessantly, tenuous, internal, eternally unheard) becomes audible. His male gender is (partly) restored as he becomes the voice of Jacob, and yet he is embraced by two females, the three of them forming one multiply transed, inter-embodied unit that makes revelation possible.

We conclude our discussion of the Zohar with an analysis of *Midrash ha Ne'elam* on the *Song of Songs*. The text exemplifies a new sort of story, generated and authorized by the medieval Zoharic sex magic rituals described above. It places the human body at the center of the cosmogony, showing its power to make and remake the cosmos. To do so, it reverses the creation account in Genesis 1 by asserting that human beings are created in the divine image, even down to a description of divine ejaculation. It begins by asserting that "Everything is modeled after the human . . ." Implicit in this is a model of sympathetic magic that posits the human affecting its celestial likeness. The text then describes the divine creation as specifically modeled on human sexuality:

> Similarly, the blessed Holy One took snow from beneath His throne of Glory. The snow was warmed up in diverse ways, and then He cast it into the waters of the Female. It follows that a woman does not conceive until she discharges waters, and into those waters a man infuses snow—seed that congeals more readily than the woman's discharge, just like snow compared to water.[30]

Here then, it is not human sex that is modeled on that of the divine but the reverse, so that human sexuality is actually at the center of the cosmos, reversing the Genesis narratives so that human beings initiate the divine creation. In this, the utopian vision is, as Foucault argues, "born of the body itself," as the human being is indeed "the principal actor"[31] in making and changing the world. The texts we've examined so far do this by movement across space and gender categories. Thus we see that these texts model rituals that generate and sanctify new narratives and, along with them, new ritual practices. These repertoires of feelings, genderings, and sexualities together operate to trans: they trans people, cosmos, and God. They also transform religion, for sex magic occurs in a ritual space in which is it possible to innovate and authorize new myths, new modes of being, and even new rituals. In this way they articulate a trans theology that is rooted in a trans-historicity. This is to say that they idealize and attribute power to a primal androgyny that proliferates because of a change in the conditions in which myths and rituals were generated, and in the sorts of stories that people were allowed to tell. Later sources, such as the work of Moshe Cordovero, take this power into new territory, as he too uses these repertoires of feelings, genderings, and multiplicitous sexualities to develop new rituals in which the divine imitates the human.

Cordovero

Moshe Cordovero (1522–70) picks up where these texts leave off, closely reading the Zohar to develop its sex magic practices; expand its repertoires of feelings, genderings, and sexualities; and amplify its ritual creativity. Cordovero was a central figure in the mystical school of sixteenth-century Safed kabbalah in Ottoman Palestine. He spent much of his life working to synthesize divergent textual traditions in kabbalistic thought, but also, more importantly, to codify and to democratize kabbalistic practice.[32] To that end, he composed pedagogical, introductory kabbalistic works, which were aimed at the communal, messianic practice of kabbalah. This was a utopian vision based in the idea that creating a fully observant and devoted community, of the sort that would exist in the messianic period, would pre-enact, and thereby effect, the coming of the messiah. For Moshe Cordovero, sex magic was an important part of this belief system. We focus here on his writings that instruct in the study of the *Zohar* in Zoharic sex magic and its walking meditation practices. The first is the introductory kabbalistic work *Or Ne'erav* (A Pleasant Light), which instructs in kabbalistic study using terms that are similar to those used for sex magic. The second is *Tefillah Le Moshe* (Prayer of Moses), a commentary on the Jewish prayer book and an instructional manual for sex magic that understands prayer itself as form of sexual union. In this work he builds on *Zohar* 1:49b–50a to provide detailed instructions for sex magic rituals, strengthening the link between human sexuality, divine sexuality, and prayer. Many of his works develop the walking rituals of the *Zohar*, which here become *gerushin*, walking meditation rituals performed while wandering through the countryside and meant to sexually unite separated aspects of the divine, and for these we draw on a few texts but focus on *Or Yaqar* (Precious Light). *Or Yaqar* describes a model of *gerushin* (divorces or exiles) that expands the cosmological scope of the sex magic practices underpinning Zoharic walking meditation. For in this ritual the practitioner consciously imitates the exiled Shekhinah to impregnate himself with the spirit of a departed male saint to gain kabbalistic insight, which may in turn generate new ritual.

In the end, *gerushin* blurs boundaries between the categories of male and female, animate and inanimate, and living and dead, as the operators move between them. The *gerushin* ritual also facilitates a trans-historicity by creating a queer genealogy in which the practitioner goes reproductively backward into the past to impregnate himself with myth and ritual to be performed in the future. It links sex and death in the generation of a new, queered futurity. This trans-historicity is engendered by transing the body, and in this changing the way that stories are generated, authorized, and told. In all of these, beginning with *Or Ne'erav*, Cordovero expands the Zoharic repertoires of emotion, gendering, and sexualities to amplify their innovative, prophetic, and transformative affordances.

We begin with his *Or Ne'erav* (Pleasant Light, after 1542). This is an introduction to kabbalah, which is meant to justify its study, introduce the reader to its cosmology, and prescribe the attitudes and affective states required for learning. In this process, Cordovero develops Zoharic conceptions of the utopian, messianic functions of androgyny and sexual multiplicity. Expanding on the *Zohar, Or Ne'erav* connects prayer and sex to a concept of theurgic mystical study, which empowers the practitioner to effect sefirotic union.[33] The work begins by asserting this redemptive power of mystical study. The third chapter discusses ritual and emotional preparations for study that bear a strong resemblance to those for sex magic. The third and sixth chapters idealize androgyny, undoing gender to present it first as a precondition for study and later as a celestial model for the practitioner to emulate. We begin with the first chapter, which empowers human beings to effect the sexual union of the sefirot through prayer and study. Discussing *Shekinah* and *Tiferet*, it explains that reciting the *Shema* prayer eases the dryness of the male and female elements of the divine. The *Shema* is the Jewish declaration of faith, taken from Deuteronomy 6:4–9 and recited twice daily. The prayer opens with an assertion of divine unity and a commandment to love the divine: "Hear, O Israel: The LORD our God, the LORD is one. Love the LORD your God with all your heart and with all your soul and with all your strength."[34] When this prayer is interpreted in the context of the sefirotic cosmos, divine unity is understood as the sexual union of Shekhinah and Tiferet, the commandment to love is understood erotically, and the prayer, like sex magic, is accorded the power to accomplish this. Cordovero clearly understands it this way as he addresses the crisis of sefirotic "dryness," which can be mitigated by prayer: "At that time when he is dry and she is dry, sons cry out below in unification and say, *Hear, O Israel* (Deut. 6:4)."[35] Next it presents study as a more powerful version of the *Shema*, explaining that the student's

> [utterance] was called "prayer." Though he was occupied with the mystery of the unification and [related] matters, [nonetheless]

he is aided with regard to the affairs of the world "as though he had prayed all day."[36]

We see then that Cordovero frames the study of kabbalah as an intensified form of prayer that works not just to declare divine unity but also to effect it, acting "as though [the practitioner] had prayed all day."[37] In this way Cordovero asserts that the study of kabbalah, an amplified form of the *Shema* prayer, unifies the sefirot to end the divine crisis, alleviating sefirotic dryness, reuniting the divine, and even magically taking care of daily business.

Chapter 3 provides instructions for ritual preparation for study, which strongly resemble those required to practice sacred sexuality. Both mystical study and sex magic require ritual purification, androgyny through marriage, and the cultivation of intense and dichotomous affective states that break down the barriers of the self. Together these are meant to facilitate prophetic possession, which gains greater authority and sanctity as kabbalistic literature develops. The text specifies that kabbalistic study must be performed in a state of ritual purity by married men (though it seems worth noting here that there are several well-known women who studied kabbalah in 16th Century Safed).[38] Cordovero writes: "There is no doubt that it is improper for one to commence [the study of] this science if he has not married a woman and purified his thoughts . . ."[39] As in sex magic (described in the *Zohar* and in *Tefilla Le Moshe*), it should commence at the midnight hour or on Shabbat:

> The third [division] concerns the proper time for learning. It is certainly easy for a person to study throughout the day. However, the optimum time for gaining profound wisdom is the long night, from midnight on . . .[40]

Thus study takes place at the same time as sacred sexuality and requires similar ritual preparation.

Or Ne'erav develops a Zoharic emotional repertoire for sex magic that destabilizes the body and dissolves the boundaries of the self. Cordovero specifies the cultivation of "three virtues" required for study, and then adds a fourth:

> [In his study,] the student must combine fear and joy, as it is written, *rejoice with trembling* (Ps. 2.11). [He must] add modesty

> to these two virtues. The reason for the combination of these three virtues [is this]: He requires [the virtue of] fear lest he err and sin. Moreover, he is delving [in his studies] in the place of the flame of the fire of joy . . . Also, the Torah certainly depends upon [the virtue of] joy . . . Modesty is most important. [The student] should say, "Who am I? What is my life that I should pursue the mysteries of the divine Torah which the Holy One, blessed be He, has hidden from flesh and blood? . . . I almost believe that one must add to these three [qualities] regret for one's spoiled youth and for the various activities which constitute a divisive barrier [to esoteric knowledge].[41]

These virtues consist of conflicting emotions (fear and joy) and self-abnegation (modesty and regret). They are manifest in bodily trembling, disavowal of one's identity, and repudiation of one's history in "regretting one's spoiled youth." This is a means of undoing the self, and with it gender, to cultivate a receptivity similar to that required for sex magic.

Further developing the similarity between study and sex magic, and building on the transgendering repertoire of the *Zohar*, Cordovero describes the secrets of the (female) Torah as her genitalia. He argues that teaching the Torah's mysteries to the wicked makes her sexually vulnerable to demons. In the third chapter he warns that

> he who reveals mysteries [of the Torah] to the wicked, it is as if he revealed the genitals of the Torah for the sons of Lilith, the evil maidservant, mother of the wicked evil multitude.[42]

Here then, this is as though he has exposed the Torah's genitals to demons who may rape and impregnate her. At the same time, if he succeeds in gaining knowledge and teaching the right people, the scholar unifies the celestial couple in marriage. He also gets to join in himself, becoming

> . . . one of the righteous for whom much good is stored away for that [future] world. In that world] the innermost place of all of these is [reserved] for those who know the secret of their Master and know to cling to Him daily.[43]

In this way the scholar wields great power, for ill or for good, and in the end, achieves redemption through study that is understood as coitus, a cleaving or a *devekhut* with the divine. This is effected by the cultivation of destabilizing emotions and by a comprehensive gendering that suspends male and female together in a sexualized prophetic relation to the deity.

Tefilla Le Moshe

We turn now to Cordovero's *Tefilla Le Moshe* (probably after 1547),[44] analyzing its commentary on the *Shema (the Jewish declaration of faith)* and the instructions for sex magic that accompany it.[45] As group, they include ritual preparation, enaction, and meditation, with the second and third occurring together. Interestingly, these mirror both the *Zohar*'s instructions for sacred sexuality and Cordovero's instructions for study in the *Or Ne'erav*. We begin with the instructions for ritual preparation. Much as in preparing for study, Cordovero's sex magic instructions require corporeal and emotional ritual purification, to be performed at midnight. Physically, the practitioners must wash. Emotionally, the purification involves purgation of evil thoughts, repentance, and the cultivation of conflicting feelings of fear and joy, and modesty and delight, among others. The enaction phase occurs with a ritual meditation that narrates the act as a sefirotic unification, activated by imaginative re-genderings and a multiplicitous sexuality. In this way, the couple become one bigendered entity understood as the divine body, the *Shiur Qomah*. Its ultimate goal is messianic and utopian, as it restores the human and divine androgynes. His prayer book provides instructions for human beings to bring about the celestial union by means of an earthly one. We begin with instructions for ritual preparation:

> Here is its mystery and the meditation required with regard to it: firstly one will wash one's hands at midnight or during the hours that follow and will purify one's consciousness and void the spirit of all evil thought; one could also meditate on the repenting of one's faults and prolong one's prayer according to one's force. Then [the man] will gladden his wife with speech relating to the commandment [of sexual union], at the same time he will bring his awareness closer to the sacred. He will conduct his meditation to the best, according to his force. Then he will undertake to meditate on the secret of the embrace . . .[46]

The secret of the embrace here alludes to each of their embodiment of the sefirot, which they unify through sex. In this process, each human organ is mapped onto the organs of the *Shiur Qomah*, the body of God.

> On the subject of the meditation in the course of the [sexual] act, it should be known that the male comprises 248 organs . . . This is the case likewise of the secret of the female: she has 248 organs [. . .] When the male and the female below conjoin, they meditate on the liaison and the union of the Male and the Female on high: 248 [organs] joined to 248 [organs], as really the attachment of flesh to flesh. One will thus meditate on the secret of the superior union.[47]

In this way it specifies the dissolution of the individual body, organ by organ, by conjoining male and female bodies with those that ultimately comprise the body of God. Both partners individually and together comprise the whole sefirotic array:

> He will bear in mind that the secret of the head against the head [implies] that the first three sefirot which are in him [unite] with the first three sefirot which are in her: [Keter Hokhmah, Binah of the Male reunite with their homologue in the Female]. He will think that the arms, which are Hesed and Gevurah which are in him [unite with] Hesed and Gevurah [that is, the arms] which are in her. He [will then be aware] that body in body, that is to say, the six extremities [the six lower sefirot which are in him rejoin] the six extremities [which are in her], that the two thighs, i.e., Netzah and Hod, the penis, i.e., Yesod, [rejoin] the two thighs which are in her . . .[48]

In this way their bodies constitute the body of God, such that

> The male completes her and this member is half included in her and half included in him: male and female unite in such a manner that in the Shiur Qomah[49] which is in him there are ten [sefirot] and in that which is in her there are ten . . .[50]

In this way they are both made androgynous, embodying the entire sefirotic pleroma through sex, uniting them, and all together returning to a single primal androgyne. They are thus ungendered, undone, and melded with each other and the cosmos part by part, to become divine. In this way Cordovero builds on the text of the *Zohar* to expand the powers of its repertoires of feelings, genderings, and sexualities, working from the body to dissolve it, and as in the *Zohar Midrash ha Ne'elam* (*Hidden Interpretation*) on the *Song of Songs*, to act on the divine body with the human. Thus, this text enacts the myths that are generated and authorized in earlier ones.

Rituals of Exile and Spiritual Pregnancy

So too, Cordovero's works expand on the ritual structures of the *Zohar*. Several describe the performance of *gerushin* or voluntary exile, which was used to generate automatic speech understood as prophetic insights into sacred texts.[51] These insights occurred within the framework of a peripatetic dialogue between the companions, which developed and expanded those described in the *Zohar*. And they too generate new historicities, and with this new myths and rituals. In Zoharic texts such as *Zohar* 1:59b, the main character, Shimon bar Yochai, and his disciples wander the countryside speaking the wisdom of Torah. In the process, the group gains insights they might not otherwise have achieved. This occurred by means of *devekhut*, or cleaving, understood sexually as in Genesis 2:24, when Adam and Eve become "one flesh." This prophecy is often described as involuntary, for in one of his works Cordovero explains that "the lyre sounded of itself."[52] This means that though he actually spoke in his own voice, he did not consciously do so. *Devekhut* achieved by *gerushin* induced a prophetic trance by means of celestial sexual union, which yielded spontaneous insight into the Torah, spurring automatic speech as part of a communion trance, wherein the divine speaks through the practitioner.[53]

Gerushin could take other forms besides the walking meditation, and these forms expand the Zoharic repertoires of gendering and sexualities and even of historicities. In the descriptions contained in *Sefer Gerushin* (*Book of Exiles*) and *Or Yaqar* (*Precious Light*), it involved a sexualized prostration on the gravesites of departed saints, an eroticized interaction between a living man and a dead one, which resulted in *ibbur*, or spiritual pregnancy. *Or Yaqar* describes these rituals as follows:

> It has been the custom of some mystical practitioners to dig a pit above the head of a deceased [sage], whereupon they would pray amidst the crowd and *cleave* [their] soul to the soul [of the deceased sage] in great concentration. [. . .] And this is the secret of binding one soul with another—given only to he who is among the living in this world and is capable to bind his soul

> while still in its body with the soul of the [deceased] sage. This is done as he *pours* his soul into the grave of the sage, cleaves to it and arouses the sage's soul toward edification—whereas the soul [of the deceased] awakens the other souls in turn [. . .].[54]

This first part of the passage describes the process of cleaving, as the living practitioners bind their souls to those of the dead. They literally enter the earth that covers the corpse, digging a pit and prostrating themselves at his head. Then the practitioner pours his soul, implying that he ejaculates it into the earth. This "pouring" enacts the cleaving that leads to *ibbur* or impregnation.

Thus Cordovero's rituals of *Gerushin* result in a spiritual pregnancy that brings together prayer, sacred sexuality, and prophecy in the structures of a mobile trans-androgyny to generate new sacred myth and reimagine history. A scholar of Cordovero's work, Zohar Raviv, points out that whenever Cordovero discusses these practices he uses the same sexual vocabulary, describing their actions as "(*middabek*—attaches, cleaves), (*shofekh*—pours, ejaculates), (*modi'o / yadu'a / yedu'im*—notify, known, engage in intercourse), (*yifkod*—take note of, impregnate), and (*maẓa / moẓe'*—find, attach)—consistent with the biblical vocabulary for sex."[55] Thus the grave prostrations imitate sex, but again this sex occurs between several parties, on both sides of the grave, who have repeatedly re-gendered themselves. This happens as Cordovero and his entourage assume female roles to arouse deceased male sages to become impregnated by them. For Cordovero this was not remarkable; in *Pardes Rimonim* he states matter-of-factly that "There is no perplexity whatsoever concerning the impregnation of males in that manner.[56] So too, this impregnation queers ontological categories of life and death, as the living male sage becomes impregnated by the dead one. The fact that he finds no perplexity in what we might indeed find puzzling reveals a gap between medieval and modern perceptions of gendering and how it works, which for us now veers toward fixation in the body, but which for Cordovero and his circle, tended toward the relational. The same applies to categories of life and death. This trans-gendering, in the end a trans-history, is rooted in an androgynized body that itself remakes the cosmos.

Conclusions

In exploring medieval and early modern kabbalistic sex magic rituals, we have seen the power of feelings, genderings, and sexualities as a site of participation, power, and cosmic change. In examining the *Zohar*, we saw that its repertoires of feelings, genderings, and sexualities were interconnected, that they idealized a trans-androgyny, and that as whole they located in this androgyny the ability to participate in divine creative processes and even to influence them. Key to this trans-androgyny is the capacity to assume multiple sexual roles with both human and divine entities, so that the practitioner not only attained androgyny in sex magic, but was also able to inhabit many different sexual roles and relationships simultaneously. This is because practitioners saw gendering as a rupture and sexuality as a way to participate in the divine and to mend it. Zoharic sex magic transforms the process of making myth and communal history, as it authorizes narratives generated from the ritually reimagined body.

Cordovero expands the Zoharic repertoires of feelings, genderings, and sexualities to accord greater transformative power to the practitioners, so that it is possible to help or harm the Torah and the sefirot themselves—to nourish them (and God) or to subject them to sexual assault by demons. They have also extended imaginative transgendering to facilitate eroticized relations with the dead to include male impregnation with the children of other dead men, and in this, to authorize new, salvific historical and mythological narratives. This blurs the lines not only between male and female, but also between past and present and between living and dead, to queer the very structures of genealogy and history. Together this group of rituals uses the transed body to open the possibility of a utopian trans-historicity founded in an idealized and powerful androgyny.

Previous scholarship on kabbalistic androgyny has engaged its function up to a point. For example, some argue that the androgyny of kabbalah is ultimately a male one that absorbs the female.[57] It makes sense to say so, but to my mind this is possibly a consequence of the gap between our modern thinking about gender, which tends toward fixing it, making it stable, and medieval and early modern approaches, which narrate a process of moving through genderings and sexualities to move ourselves and even the cosmos somewhere else, somewhere quite out of them. In my interpretation, readings that fix gender get off the train one stop too early. For the text valorizes an androgyny that utterly undoes gender as a part of the messianic project. And the same applies to time. This is to say that for moderns, gender is often imagined to be located in the body and therefore stable, while for medieval and early modern kabbalists, it was positional and changed according to the situation, and even according to what the operator wanted to accomplish. In some ways this points to the continual contingency of gendering, and it shows that its power is embedded in the relations between celestial entities. And yet their gendering is also affected by human operators, so that the whole system and everything in it is continually in motion. In short, human and divine alike participate in a transness that, according to Susan Stryker, "assembles gender into contingent structures of association with other attributes of bodily being" and, I would add here, with cosmic being. These texts operate on an "awareness of contingency [of gender], and the suspension of assumptions" that asserts "the noninevitability of binarity."[58] These texts and their ritual practitioners are trans, and continually so. Together they instruct their readers in cultivating multiplicitous and destabilizing feelings, genderings, and sexualities that reimagine myth, history, and divinity. These kabbalistic texts locate transing as a source of power, and they find in it a primal utopian ideal. In this way these works, and the rituals they describe, open the possibility for a trans-theology that undoes gender, detaches it from the sexed history of bodies, and in the end undoes time. It includes all possibilities without stopping at any of them, and this is its definition of wholeness.

Notes

1. According to kabbalistic theology, she is exiled from her husband when the community sins, fails to fulfill the *mitzvot*, or Jewish legal commandments, and is reunited with him when they faithfully adhere to them.

2. Sharon Flatto, "The Doctrine of Exile in Kabbalah," in *The Oxford Handbook of the Jewish Diaspora* (Oxford: Oxford University Press, 2021), 73. She writes: "Longing to terminate exile has fueled the entire kabbalistic enterprise." See also Marla Segol, "Performing Exile in Safed School Kabbalah," *Magic, Ritual, and Witchcraft* 7, no. 2 (2012): 131–63.

3. Michel Foucault, "Utopian Body," in *Sensorium: Embodied Experience, Technology, and Contemporary Art* (Cambridge: MIT Press, 2006): 229–34, 231.

4. Adele Berlin and Marc Zvi Brettler, eds., *The Jewish Study Bible* (Oxford: Oxford University Press, 2014), 14.

5. Berlin and Brettler, *Jewish Study Bible*, 14.

6. Berlin and Brettler, *Jewish Study Bible*, 16.

7. This mythological structure is also a ritual one, for the texts were recited and even performed in a wide range of settings that added layers to their meanings.

8. Song of Songs 1:1, Ariel Bloch and Chana Bloch, *The Song of Songs: A New Translation with an Introduction and Commentary* (Berkeley: University of California Press, 1998), 43.

9. Kyla Wazana Tompkins, ed., *Keywords for Gender and Sexuality Studies*, vol. 13 (New York: New York University Press, 2021), 237.

10. Susan Stryker, Paisley Currah, and Lisa Jean Moore, "Introduction: Trans-, Trans, or Transgender?," *Women's Studies Quarterly* 36, no. 3/4 (2008): 13. Rafael Rachel Neis argues that "Along with this awareness of contingency, and the suspension of assumptions, is the non-inevitability of binary. In this way to trans is also to allow for the possibility of multiplicity beyond seemingly fixed binary sex or gender categories such as male/ female or man/woman. In other words, gender categories are historically and culturally provisional." Rafael Rachel Neis, *When a Human Gives Birth to a Raven* (Berkeley: University of California Press, 2023), 37.

11. For a wide ranging discussion of trans-historicities, see Bychowski, M. W., Howard Chiang, Jack Halberstam, Jacob Lau, Kathleen P. Long, Marcia Ochoa, C. Riley Snorton, Leah DeVun, and Zeb Tortorici. ""Trans* historicities" A Roundtable Discussion." *Transgender Studies Quarterly* 5, no. 4 (2018): 658–685.

12. For a thorough discussion of the dating of the Zohar, see Ronit Meroz, "Is the Taking of Damietta Alluded to in a Zoharic Story?," *Jewish Studies Quarterly* 20, no. 1 (2013): 33–60. Meroz argues that its earliest strata date to tenth-century Byzantium. See also Huss, Boaz, *The Zohar: Reception and Impact* (Liverpool, UK: Liverpool University Press, 2016), 67–111. See also Hartley Lachter, *Kabbalistic Revolution: Reimagining Judaism in Medieval Spain* (New Brunswick, NJ: Rutgers University Press, 2014), 12–13, 54.

13. *Zohar* 1 and 3 were likely composed in the same period, but assembled by their sixteenth-century Italian printers in the order of the biblical texts they comment on. As such, they can be studied in any order, while *Midrash ha Ne'elam* was composed in the fourteenth century and should be analyzed last.

14. Isaiah Tishby, *The Wisdom of the Zohar: Anthology of Texts* (Liverpool, UK: Liverpool University Press, 1989); *Zohar* III, 37b, 1357–60.

15. Tishby, *Wisdom Zohar* III 42a–b, 411–12.

16. Moshe Idel, "Sexual Metaphors and Praxis in the Kabbalah," in *Ultimate Intimacy* (Abingdon, UK: Routledge, 2018), 224.

17. Daniel Chanan Matt, *The Zohar*: Pritzker edition, *Sefer ha-Zohar* (Stanford University Press, 2004). Zohar 1:49b, 274.

18. Berlin and Brettler, *Jewish Study Bible*, 30.

19. Berlin and Brettler, *Jewish Study Bible*, 33.

20. Matt, *Zohar*, vol. 1, 1:49b, 278.

21. Matt, *Zohar*, vol. 1, 1:49b, 275.

22. While the practitioner is understood to travel with a full array of celestial forces, becoming plural and androgynous, the writers still refer to him using a singular male pronoun.

23. Matt, *Zohar*, vol. 1, 1:50a, 276.

24. Matt, *Zohar*, vol. 1, 1:50b, 278.

25. Tal Ilan, Tamara Or, Dorothea M. Salzer, Christiane Steuer, Irina Wandrey, Monika Brockhaus, Tanja Hidde et al., eds. *A Feminist Commentary on the*

Babylonian Talmud (Tubingen: Mohr Siebeck, 2007). "Bayit—"house" as euphemism for female genitalia . . . ," 80–81.

26. Matt, *Zohar*, vol. 1, 1:51a, 283.

27. Matt, *Zohar*, vol. 1, 1:50b, 278.

28. Matt, *Zohar*, vol. 1, 1:50b, 278.

29. Matt, *Zohar*, vol. 1, 1:50b, 279.

30. Joel Hecker, "The *Zohar*/Volume 11," in *The Zohar Pritzker edition, Sefer ha-Zohar* (Stanford: Stanford University Press, 2016). Midrash Ha Ne'elam Shir ah Shirim, 32.

31. Foucault, "Utopian Body," 229–234, 231.

32. J. H. Chajes calls R. Moshe Cordovero "the great systematizer of kabbalistic knowledge accumulated up to his time." Jeffrey Howard Chajes, "He Said She Said: Hearing the Voices of Pneumatic Early Modern Jewish Women," *Nashim: A Journal of Jewish Women's Studies & Gender Issues* 10 (2005): 99–125, 99.

33. Boaz Huss writes: "Cordovero regarded the Zohar not only as the principal source of kabbalistic knowledge, but also (through its descriptions of R. Shim'on bar Yohai and his companions) as a model for the proper religious conduct for himself and his circle. Furthermore, Cordovero (similar to other contemporary kabbalists) regarded the study of Zoharic literature as a primary religious duty that carried theurgic and messianic import." Huss, "The Kabbalah of Moshe Cordovero," *The Jewish Quarterly Review* 88, no. 3/4, 1998): 310–13, 311.

34. Michael David Coogan, Marc Zvi Brettler, Carol Ann Newsom, and Pheme Perkins, eds., *The New Oxford Annotated Bible with Apocrypha: New Revised Standard Version* (Oxford: Oxford University Press, 2010), 262.

35. Moses ben Jacob Cordovero and Ira Robinson, *Moses Cordovero's Introduction to Kabbalah: An Annotated Translation of His Or Ne'erav*, vol. 3 (Brooklyn, NY: KTAV Publishing House, 1994), 1:1.

36. Cordovero and Robinson, *Or Ne'erav*, 1:4.

37. The fifth- to seventh-century *Shiur Qomah* asserts that "he who recites this as a Mishnah, it is as though he prayed all day." The eleventh-century Iberian Bahya ibn Pakuda writes that "The trust in God will lead one to empty his mind from the distractions of the world, and to focus his heart to matters of service to God." Ibn Paquda, *Duties of the Heart*, trans. Menahem Mansoor (Liverpool, UK: Liverpool University Press, Littman Library of Jewish Civilization, 2004), 225. The second, twelfth-century layer of the *Bahir*, asserts the same thing. Verse 68 of the second layer of the Sefer Bahir (twelfth-century Hebrew, Ashkenaz) takes up similar wording: But whoever turns his heart from worldly affairs and delves into the Ma'aseh Merkavah is accepted before God as if he prayed all day. Aryeh Kaplan, ed., *The Bahir* (Lanham, MD: Jason Aronson, 1977), 24. Guilio Busi points this out in his translation of the Bahir: Giulio Busi and Guglielmo Raimondo Moncada, *The Book of Bahir: Flavius Mithridates' Latin Translation, the Hebrew Text, and an English Version*, vol. 2 (Torino: Nino Aragno, 2005), 16.

38. These women include Rachel Aberlin, Francesa Sarah, Sonadora, the Daughter of Raphael Anav, and many others who are either unnamed, or described by first name and occupation. All three of these named women were well respected in the community, and there is clear evidence that they took part in legal and kabbalistic study with men. For more information on these women practitioners of kabbalah, see Jeffrey Howard Chajes, "He Said She Said: Hearing the Voices of Pneumatic Early Modern Jewish Women," *Nashim: A Journal of Jewish Women's Studies & Gender Issues* 10 (2005): 99–125; Lawrence Fine, "New Approaches to the Study of Kabbalistic Life in 16th-Century Safed," *Jewish Mysticism and Kabbalah: New Insights and Scholarship* (2011): 91–111; Alexandra Cuffel, "Gendered Visions and Transformations of Women's Spirituality in Hayyim Vital's Sefer ha-Hezyonot," *Jewish Studies Quarterly* 19, no. 4 (2012): 339–84.

39. Cordovero and Robinson, *Or Ne'erav*, 3:1.
40. Cordovero and Robinson, *Or Ne'erav*, 3:1.
41. Cordovero and Robinson, *Or Ne'erav*, 3:2.
42. Cordovero and Robinson, *Or Ne'erav*, 3:4.
43. Cordovero and Robinson, *Or Ne'erav*, 4:2.
44. There is no scholarly consensus on the composition date, but its ideas seem consistent with other works completed in the late 1540s. The work first appeared in print as *Sefer tefilla le Mosha*, Premislany, 1892.
45. The *Shema* is the Jewish declaration of faith, recited twice daily by observant Jews, and known as the unification prayer because it begins with the exhortation "Hear O Israel, the Lord is One." Cordovero's instructions for sex magic conceptualize it as a form of prayer.
46. Moshe Cordovero, *Tefilla Le Moshe*, vol. 1, fol. 213a–b. Charles Mopsik, Yosef Avraham G'ikatilyah, Daniel Abrams, and Dani'el Abrams, trans., *Sex of the Soul: The Vicissitudes of Sexual Difference in Kabbalah*, vol. 15 (Solihull, UK: Cherub Press, 2005), 134.
47. Mopsik, *Sex of the Soul*, 134.
48. Mopsik et al., *Sex of the Soul*, 135.
49. This is the title of the fifth- to seventh-century Hebrew esoteric text that describes the divine body in detail, providing the names and measurements for each part. The text is narrated as an ascent to the heavens, and it describes a celestial prayer service in which the androgynous divine is engaged in coitus. The *Shiur Qomah*, as used here, refers to that coitus, so that sex magic performs that divine body and allows human participation in it.
50. Mopsik et al., *Sex of the Soul*, 135.
51. See J. Zwi Werblowsky, "Mystical and Magical Contemplation: The Kabbalists in Sixteenth-Century Safed, *History of Religions* 1, no. 1 (summer 1961): 9–36. See also Marla Segol, "Performing Exile in Safed School Kabbalah," *Magic, Ritual, and Witchcraft* 7, no. 2 (2012): 131–63, 147.

52. This phrase occurs frequently in sixteenth-century Safedian Kabbalah, appearing in Cordovero's *Sefer Gerushin, Hayyim Vital's Sefer Hezyonot* and Joseph Caro's *Maggid Mesharim*.

53. According to Gilbert Rouget, this is comparable to "Elisha's trance in the Bible, when he feels the hand of Jehovah upon him before he begins to prophesy (2 Kings 3: 10–15): he senses the presence of God upon or within him, but there is no question of identifying with Him or imitating Him." These examples are different because they occur by means of imitation of the divine, and they are meant to achieve participation. Thus, while the practitioners do retain a sense of personal identity, it occurs alongside an identification not just with the divine but its multiple aspects. See Gilbert Rouget, *Music And Trance: A Theory of the Relations Between Music and Possession* (Chicago: University of Chicago Press, 1985), 28.

54. *Or Yaqar*, vol. 3:164, Zohar Raviv, trans., "Fathoming the Heights, Ascending the Depths: Decoding the Dogma Within the Enigma: The Life, Works and Speculative Piety of Rabbi Moses Cordoeiro (Safed 1522–1570)," PhD diss., 2007, 374.

55. Raviv, "Fathoming," 374.

56. *Pardes Rimonim* 31:9, https://www.sefaria.org/Pardes_Rimonim.31.9?lang=bi.

57. Elliot Wolfson has written extensively on this topic. See Elliot R. Wolfson, *Circle in the Square: Studies in the Use of Gender in Kabbalistic Symbolism* (Albany: State University of New York Press, 2012); Elliot R. Wolfson, "Bifurcating the Androgyne and Engendering Sin: A Zoharic Reading of Gen 1–3," in *Hidden Truths from Eden: Esoteric Readings of Genesis 1–3* (Atlanta: Society of Biblical Literature, 2014): 87–119; Elliot R. Wolfson, *Through a Speculum That Shines: Vision and Imagination in Medieval Jewish Mysticism* (Princeton: Princeton University Press, 2020); Elliot R. Wolfson, *Language, Eros, Being: Kabbalistic Hermeneutics and Poetic Imagination* (New York: Fordham University Press, 2009); Elliot R. Wolfson, "Occultation of the Feminine and the Body of Secrecy in Medieval Kabbalah," in *Elliot R. Wolfson: Poetic Thinking* (Leiden, Netherlands: Brill, 2015), 35–68.

58. Susan Stryker, Paisley Currah, and Lisa Jean Moore, "Introduction: Trans-, Trans, or Transgender?," *Women's Studies Quarterly* 36, no. 3/4 (2008): 13.

Part 4

Toward a Utopian Pedagogy

9

Migrantopias

Teaching the Dystopian/Utopian Narratives of Migration through a Pedagogy of Hope

RICHARD REITSMA

This chapter explores the strategies I have developed to help students explore the issue of migration by employing film, narrative, interviews, simulations, and community-based service learning. I discuss the origins and development of the approach, my pedagogical praxis, and conclude with student outcomes. Although primarily focused on a course taught in Spanish, the pedagogy and structure are equally adapted to a version of the course I teach in English and can be adapted for other disciplines. Starting from the perspective that many students often have their own family narratives about migration (including something as simple as their own migration to campus) or their own preconceived notions of why people migrate, particularly to the United States, we examine the utopian narratives of such perspectives. This leads to an understanding of the pull factors of migration, which the course quickly complicates by exploring the devasting push factors and their source (too often US policy or US policy's impacts on political, economic, and security issues, including narcotrafficking).

The course continues to peel away the veneer of utopia in the context of migration to profoundly explore how utopian dreams of migration have changed over the decades and become much more dystopian realities. The course explores legal issues, virtual tours of the border, artwork, and interviews with those who accompany migrants at the border. One main project of the course is student interviews with migrants, including American-born citizens who have migrated from the United States to Latin America and Latin Americans who have migrated within Latin America, from a variety of gender, racial, socioeconomic, and sexual orientation experiences. These interviews show both the struggles but also the hopes of immigrants and help us work our way out of the slough of migrant dystopia toward more hopeful utopias. To that end, we also work with local agencies addressing migrant issues and accompany migrants detained in Buffalo Federal Detention Center in Batavia. Once we've plumbed the depths of the dystopia that is immigration for many, in stark contrast to the utopian mythologies we are accustomed to, we work our way back toward hope with a final project that asks students to synthesize what they have learned and craft an action plan toward ameliorating the experience for all involved.

For many people, the idea of utopia is tangible, real, and present in those who live middle-class lives in developed nations. Such is the reality for many of the students I teach, as it was for me in my youth (absent the anxieties of being unknowingly gay in a hostile environment, but that's a different story). Concomitantly, many see dystopia as everywhere else, both abroad and too often in the inner cities of the United States, spaces inhabited frequently by immigrants and Black and brown people. Such perceptions of utopia/dystopia are mythic, but also do a grave disservice both to those people inhabiting these dystopian spaces, often those fleeing to the United States in search of utopia, as well as to those who live in this perceived utopia. My work has been dedicated to dismantling these myths of utopia in order to work toward a world that is actually more just and equitable, not merely performative in justice and equity. This is challenging work because people are comfortable in their assumptions about inhabiting a sort of comparative utopia; nevertheless, this dismantling is also a necessary act springing from a pedagogy of love, to awaken within students a deeper awareness of the problems that exist in the world, and to guide them toward solutions through hope. This pedagogy has multiple facets, which I explore below.[1] Before I get there, however, I want to explore how I got to this place.

I am a third-generation US-born descendant of mostly Dutch immigrants whose ancestors would more than likely not be admitted to the country today: they spoke no English, were not persecuted (though they had some theological disagreements with the Dutch church), had no skills (the only skill listed on immigration papers from 1887 was house painter for a family of twelve including a mother-in-law), and were poor. My paternal grandmother was a maid before she married. Eventually she and my grandfather did well for themselves, and my family would be considered solidly lower middle-class today.

Around 1984, when I was about fifteen years old, I had my first interaction with migrant workers from Mexico on a blueberry farm in Michigan. Prior to that I had lived a very sheltered life. That summer day I arrived well after workers were already in the field. I was disoriented, hot, angry, and frustrated. Like everyone else, I was paid by the weight of the berries in my bucket, the weight noted in pencil on a ledger. The bosses sorted out twigs, leaves, or bad berries. I was a slow picker and apparently picked unripe berries, too many twigs, and other detritus, and consequently I earned meager wages. I understood nothing and randomly chose a row and a bush to pick, but I was soon yelled at in Spanish and probably other languages for picking off a bush in a row a migrant family was working. I barely lasted the day. I had the privilege to leave, and when I went back the next day it was raining, so no berries were picked; instead, I was shown the interior sorting and washing operations. I didn't go back, and it was a long time before I came around to liking blueberries again.

In 1986, a few years later, while an undergraduate, I went to Guadalajara, Mexico, for a short-term study abroad. Two weeks in I called my

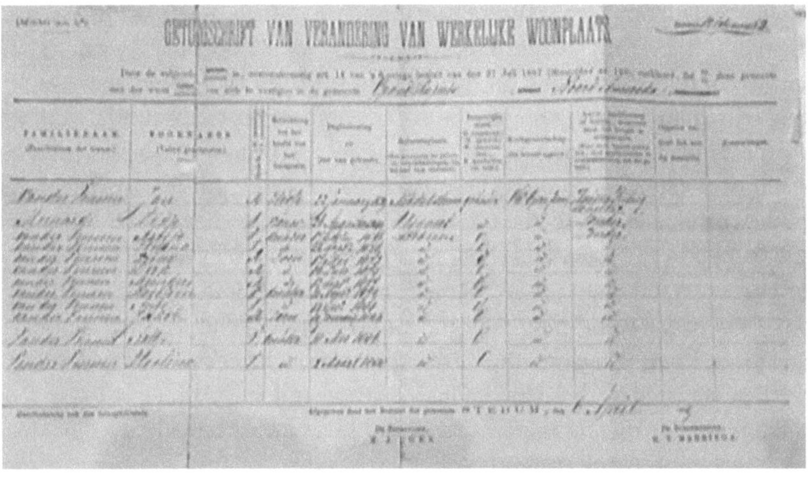
GETUIGSCHRIFT VAN VERANDERING VAN WERKELIJKE WOONPLAATS

Figure 9.1. Immigration papers of my great-grandparents. *Source*: Property of the author.

parents from the payphone on the corner to tell them I was staying. I had to find a job and an apartment, as they weren't going to support me. I hitchhiked around Mexico, including Michoacán, an area that sent a lot of migrant workers to the United States. I saw villages depleted of men, young and old; and I saw how *remesas*, money sent back to one's home country by migrant laborers, sustained the families left behind.

In the early 1990s, during graduate school, I worked with an agency where I coordinated the supply of teachers to migrant camps: we taught English, helped migrant workers earn a GED, and provided opportunities for them to earn a driver's license. This program, run through the county education department in conjunction with the Federal Migrant Education Program (MEP), focused on adult learners, though the primary outreach of MEP was for migrant children.[2] Every evening I would drive out to different farms throughout the week to check on the teachers, the students, and their progress. Not all farmers allowed us onto their property. Some farms only allowed males to work and live on the farm. Some allowed families or a few women. Most migrant workers on each farm were from the same towns in Mexico, frequently Michoacán, often related to each other in various ways, almost as if the whole town had picked up and moved to Michigan or was following the harvests up and down from Michigan to the Gulf States and returning to Mexico over winter. Generally speaking, the migrants lived in old trailer homes stuffed to the gills with people sleeping on any available surface and shared simple communal meals that reminded them of home, often cooked outdoors. They invariably shared their meals with me if I arrived at the farms during mealtime. They would do their lessons then, often well into the evening, in the dark. In the summer, the workday would generally follow the rhythm of the sunrise and sunset to maximize work in the fields planting, tending, and harvesting everything from below ground (onions, potatoes) to ground level (strawberries, zucchini, or asparagus) to bushes of blueberries to the apples, cherries, and peaches in the orchards. This sunup to sundown backbreaking labor was then followed by three hours of classes several days a week, though not everyone was equally invested.

I was in awe of these men and women and grateful for their kindness and for welcoming me into their lives, which, though backbreakingly difficult, were punctuated with levity, joking, sharing, and joy. Although I was too uninformed to understand why, and too unaware to actually ask, looking back, I think this is because they saw hope and possibility. The fact that the other teachers and I were there, working to help them make a better life in this country, affirmed for them the possibility of hope, that their belief in the American utopian dream was valid. This was, of course, all before the subsequent sea change in rhetoric and policy in the United States that has targeted—in increasingly barbaric ways—our immigrant brothers and sisters. Over time the migrant laborers or their children, who followed the crops and the seasons, often returning to Mexico for a part of the year, began to settle along the crop routes, becoming immigrants of mixed status. The place where I grew up integrated the migrant-cum-immigrant population: there are now TV and radio in Spanish, and I even recall the remarkable moment (to me, at the time in the early 1990s) when I saw Latinx youth dressed in traditional Dutch attire (including *klompens*—wooden clogs) dancing in the annual Tulip Festival celebrating the Dutch heritage of the region. Soon, however, my graduate studies, parenthood, and my own life took me to different places, and my work with immigrants faded into the background.

Nevertheless, immigration issues have never been entirely far from my mind: I am currently married to an immigrant (he is from Sicily), and my ex-wife is Cuban. It wasn't until I came to Buffalo, however, that a convergence of circumstances resulted in my renewed engagement with immigration in a more profound way, rekindling the embers that were lit all those years ago in the farms of Michigan.

Ten years ago, I moved to Buffalo for a tenure-track teaching job. Soon my research, teaching, and service began to coalesce into a renewed focus on migration, motivated by the peculiar realities of Buffalo that most people are generally unaware of. Buffalo is a border city, but this fact seems almost an afterthought, as it borders Canada, a country that speaks and acts similarly to the United States and barely seems foreign. Buffalo is also a refugee resettlement city that is experiencing an uneven renaissance because of its refugee and immigrant population. But there are other deeper complexities in Buffalo that have inspired me, of which locals seem blissfully unaware. Buffalo has a heavy ICE presence, lying within the 100 miles of extra-constitutional ICE authority. There is a federal detention facility forty-five minutes from downtown and an immigration/deportation court in the city. Despite this being a northern border, and thus a seemingly friendly border with Canada, the region is fraught with complexity, desperation, fear, and, too rarely, hope.

Although I teach Spanish language, literatures, and cultures, I have been able to employ migration as a central element in much of my teaching, primarily in my course on intermediate conversation and courses on Latinx in film and literature. The course on Latinx experiences was initially developed while I was at Johns Hopkins University, and I have been fortunate to teach variations of the Latinx course in Puebla, Mexico, and Warsaw, Poland, as well as Canisius. My approach to the topic and the teaching of borders and migrations in Spanish or English has of course evolved over time. My pedagogical approach is a mishmash of theories and experiences, from TPR (total physical response)[3] to HIL (high impact learning).[4] In addition, my pedagogy has been shaped by having led and interpreted for our campus ministry service trips abroad (to El Salvador and the US/Mexican border) and my own research in Latin America engaging with contemporary iterations of liberation theology. This is all further impacted by my decades-long engagement with Cuban *educación popular*[5]/popular education, a very utopian endeavor of popular education via communal learning and community engagement, and *concientización*,[6] raising or awakening one's— or a community's—consciousness, arising from Paolo Freire's work around pedagogy of the oppressed as expressed in the communal learning practices I have engaged with in Cuba. The pedagogy of *concientización* has at its core a utopian impulse. At the risk of oversimplifying it, the root idea is to create a context within which one can see and understand a problem and its roots, reflect on the causes of the problem, and engage in crafting solutions. My many years working in Cuba, and thus engaging with popular education and the mythic utopianism of the Revolution, reinforced for me the importance of communal learning and community engagement toward justice based on the needs or challenges within a given community. Concurrently, my years of work with pedagogically embedded service learning alongside my work on issues of justice in Latin America (women, race, LGBTQIA+, the poor) have provided a solid framework for helping students achieve a certain *concientización* around the issue of migration and the role of utopia/dystopia.

My approach to utopia/dystopia in this context of immigration studies is twofold. On the one hand, I research, teach, employ service learning, and organize events around the push/pull factors of immigration, namely the dystopian realities many are fleeing in an attempt to enter the perceived utopia of the United States (recognizing, of course, that there are degrees of dystopias).[7] It is worth noting that those who undertake the harrowing process of legal and extralegal migration do so out of desperation and a lack of hope, but with the belief that there may be a utopia and a place of hope on the other side. Such is their need to believe in a possibility that they knowingly will risk death rather than continue to endure in their dystopian realities back home. On the other hand, I'm also interested in guiding my students to understand that their own perceptions of their country, and

Buffalo specifically, are not the utopian idylls they imagine. Further, I want my students to understand that the immigration process is lengthy, costly, demoralizing, and fraught, and that it is not the mythic easy path to entry that family folklore may have them believe. The end goal of examining dystopias and dismantling myths of utopia is to have my students reflect on these matters so that they can take actions that may help us create a better world that assuages the dystopian experiences of so many and helps us craft a better, more just, and equitable world . . . a process toward a more utopian world, a world of hope.

My goal isn't simply to expose the challenging environments of countries of origin or the nightmares of detention, deportation, and the immigration process itself, but to find ways to see hope and to ameliorate the problems so that we can work toward a better world. This process of *concientización* or a raising of consciousness involves dismantling students' perceptions of the United States and the sense among many of my students that they live in a utopia, at least in relation to their perceptions of the rest of the world, that contrasts with a dystopia in which seemingly the vast majority of the rest of the world lives.

I employ migrant testimonies from partners at KBI/Kino Border Initiative[8] along with excerpts from one of my current research projects involving interviews with migrants who have been deported from the United States and find themselves restarting their lives in Mexico.[9] The stories of these deportees are diverse, but the majority of them found their lives in the United States to be difficult and not the utopia they expected. While some have managed to create new, affirming lives for themselves, and others, back in Mexico, created communities with other deportees, others continue to struggle through economic hardship and family separations. Helping students understand and empathize with the cost of deportation on both communities will, I hope, inspire us to change and to craft a society more on the arc toward our utopian idylls.

While exposing students to these narratives through testimonies, as well as through films, readings, graphic novels, and other narrative forms, I have crafted my pedagogy to incorporate carefully planned, community-based service-learning experiences to assist students in their nuanced evolution of understanding the immigration situation, challenges, and opportunities for change. To that end, I partner with JFMF/Justice for Migrant Families, crafting pedagogically embedded, high-impact service-learning experiences.[10] Based here in Buffalo, this organization of community volunteers came into existence about five years ago after an ICE raid on various Latinx-serviced restaurants in the city resulted in the arrest of twenty-five workers, throwing communities and families into chaos and galvanizing some segments of the city. Prior to COVID, students would go through a training and visit with and accompany migrants detained in the Batavia Federal Detention System and also support migrants in hearings at the courthouse. Though students initially found the idea of entering a detention facility daunting (it is a prison, after all), they found the experience deeply moving. In some fortunate instances, people they encountered in detention have been released and have visited our classes to share their experiences and their gratitude for the humanizing encounters of a single hour's visitation.

Since COVID has shut down visitation, we have switched to other means of support, including a pen-pal program, assisting JFMF in coordinating its food bank, and manning the phone line for detainees in Batavia to reach out for assistance, conversation, commissary, and other needs. These activities allow students to experience the challenging conditions of detention and the precarity of migrant life while also allowing the students to form meaningful relationships of support and to participate in community building. These activities actually accomplish the dismantling of previous notions of the utopian society many students think they live in while simultaneously encouraging them to look for ways to actually create something more utopian in response to the dystopia they encounter once they work through their rage and sadness.

One of the ways I help my students work through their rage, sadness, or frustration is to engage with those who are doing the good work of advocating for a more just society. My classes thus collaborate with actors on the ground who work alongside immigrants and other marginalized peoples in the United States, Mexico, and the rest of Latin America, such as KBI and JFMF. Speaking with people directly involved in the processes helps inspire students to see how we can create a better world.

As mentioned above, one of my most important partners is KBI/Kino Border Initiative, a binational Jesuit organization based in Dos Nogales, Arizona/Sonora. This organization focuses on providing accompaniment, food, respite, basic medical care, basic mental health care, resources, and temporary housing both for migrants attempting to cross into the United States as well as those who have been deported back across the border. In collaboration with our campus ministry, I have travelled with students to the border to witness and participate in their immersion programs. In addition to having speakers from KBI join Canisius in person or virtually, I recently crafted a hybrid study abroad/service learning/internship program for students to work at KBI (our first three students went in the summer of 2022). While this experience is quite challenging and too often heartbreaking, it is also transformative: students see the dystopia of what immigrants are fleeing and the dystopia of our immigration system. Witnessing such dystopia, however, encourages them to reassess their understanding of the United States and the utopian rhetoric we inherit and to work toward creating a more utopian society from a place of truth rather than mythological assumptions and inherent prejudices.

I arrange for lawyers who are graduates of our program, who work as advocates for immigrants, to speak to my classes so that students can appreciate the intricacies of a constantly changing, dehumanizing, costly, and frustrating immigration system. These conversations simultaneously raise consciousness while showing students an option to address the injustices they are exploring. Many students are often inspired by the trajectory of the work these students have engaged in and decide to go to law school, other graduate work, or a year of service that will help them find their place in advocating for a more authentically utopian and humane society.

Of course, immigration is not all a dystopian nightmare. Students also engage in a geocaching project exploring Latinx/Hispanic sites in Buffalo, often interviewing people involved with the sites. This helps contextualize more positive experiences of immigration and migration. While my focus is specifically Latinx/Hispanic, Buffalo is a city rich in immigrant histories, and many sites could be explored relative to a wide variety of immigrant communities both past and present.

Students also interview immigrants (primarily women, POC, and LGBTIQIA+) who have immigrated through the legal system successfully and now live in the United States or who immigrated from the United States to live in Latin America. This adds yet another nuanced dimension for students who often only think of immigration as occurring into the United States, not away from it, and further complicates their understanding of migration.

One of the signature experiential learning pieces developed with KBI and colleagues at Canisius has been the Immigration Simulation. I have conducted versions of this simulation in English and Spanish, in person, online, and hybrid, and have done this in the United States, Latin America, and Poland. This exercise, a sort of role-playing game, helps students experience, however briefly and artificially, the complicated, challenging choices immigrants face. All of the roles in the role-playing game are based on real people, and at the conclusion of the activity, students hear the outcomes of the real people whose lives they briefly assumed. After students have reflected on their relationship to power in the process, many are awed and humbled at how difficult the reality is, given their levels of frustration and anger in a role-playing game that lasts less than an hour. This experience, along with guided reflection, helps students appreciate the challenges of those populations they are engaging with; they develop a greater sense of empathy and support for immigrants. I incorporate a framework for this simulation that includes my own family's migration history, maps of migration over time, historical and current causes of migration, and historical and current legal policies, and finally conclude with what can be done now. Students are generally shocked at how few of the cases they explore actually are successful at entering the United States. Students are also tasked with taking a citizenship test, which most fail. This brief experience of walking in the shoes of an immigrant is frustrating for students; they are confused that their assumptions about the United States and the relative ease of migration are, in fact, myth. The reality is shocking to them, and many feel that the personal experience helps make it more "real."

My largest undertaking combining pedagogy, service, and research is the establishment and continuation of the Canisius University Borders & Migrations Initiative, which I founded in fall 2018 after being exhorted by colleagues at KBI to take action after witnessing the issues at the border. Events are hybrid, with both in-person and streaming options, and all events are housed on our website.[11] The initiative organizes approximately four events per semester that are free and open to the public on a wide range of topics related to the global issue of borders and migrations. These activities explore the dystopian realities of borders and migrations in a global context while also providing a framework to challenge people to think about positive responses that can carry us toward a place of hope, an utopian idyll. I want people to deconstruct their notions of utopia, confront dystopic realities, and then envision a more realistic approach toward utopia, as unreal and unattainable as that may be. It is important to show people not just how bad things are in a dystopian way, but also how to make things better, to give hope and comfort not just to the victims of perverted immigration realities, but also to those of us whose eyes have been opened. That is the start of a movement toward utopia.

The combination of these activities leads students to reflect on and confront mythologies of US exceptionalism so they can educate their peers and their families about the realities many people face, and they can chart a course of action to address these injustices in the creation of a more just and equitable world for all. Happily, this work has resulted in several honors theses on immigration and has repeatedly helped students focus their studies (and sometimes, dare I say, change their majors) with an eye toward working in the areas of migrant justice and support.

I want to conclude with a reflection shared with me by one of my students. This student is one of my research assistants and one of my brightest students. Her comments reflect those of many of my students:

> My phone bank experience taught me a lot of harsh realities in only two hours. One caller had been in prison in the United States for 22 years and had been awaiting deportation from Batavia for two years after that. The next caller asked me about my Dunkin Donuts order. His birthday is on Christmas, and he always got double the presents growing up: his favorite birthday present was a remote-control car. All of them missed their families. They wanted to hear about the snow in Buffalo. I signed them up for commissary money and penpals, an idea that each of them profusely thanked me for. The third caller had to leave after 15 minutes. "Alright, Emily"—he had misheard "Emma" and I didn't have the heart to correct him—"Thanks so much for your help. I've gotta run." His wording seemed somewhat inappropriate. Run to where? I waited for all of them to hang up first. It felt like the only piece of freedom I could offer. I told Richard the experience made me sad and frustrated. "Welcome to my life," he responded. "Now: write about it."
>
> "I'm too sad to write about it. I need to cry it out of my system first," I said.
>
> It was true—the experience deeply saddened me. I felt the pain of these broken men who missed glazed donuts and New York City and hugging their moms. (It's made me hug mine a little tighter, that's for sure.) But it also enraged me. Caller 2 has served his time and he just wants to go home to Trinidad. There is an entire world waiting for him. He's never had a cellphone. He's never been married. He doesn't know if his brother even knows where he is. I wanted to personally march down to whomever is in charge and demand I be allowed to personally aid in his journey home. I don't even know whom I'd talk to: I don't even know who's in charge. And I hate that they get to make money off of destroying the spirits of these already broken men. If I needed a reminder of my own good luck, privilege

or what it means to have compassion and love for others, this was it. I was also reminded that I am not powerless against a complicated, malignant system: to those callers, for those two hours, I was their connection to the world.

My pedagogy, research, and service intersect with my own personal history, which has given me the ability to craft space and context for the connections the student mentions above. Students benefit from the personal relationships developed through the community-based service learning in combination with statistics, dramatic narratives of film, trauma of testimonials, explanations of the legal and social realities, and virtual exploration of crossing the border and processing through immigration proceedings. Some students need numbers and statistics to understand the problem, while others prefer to approach the difficult topic of migration through narratives and emotional experiences. Balancing the aforementioned variety of approaches with direct human interaction, building relationships in some form, is an essential aspect of this pedagogy, so that the transformation, the *concientización* that occurs, is not merely a temporary awakening that fades away once the semester ends, but rather becomes a durable shift in their perspective.

Through a pedagogy of hope, I want to remind students that despite the overbearing sense of dystopia we may feel, there is always hope; we are not powerless. The malignancy of dystopia has a cure, and that cure is a sort of utopian hope arising from, and reacting to, difficult realities with an awakened consciousness engaged with truth and not mythology. This is the task students conclude the semester with: finding hope by creating an action plan. For some, the action plan is simply a resolve to confront their family member at the next family gathering. For others, this action plan means changing their major. Students learn that all actions, no matter how seemingly small, can have an impact and can transform the world around them in small intimate moments such as a phone conversation with someone they've never met in detention. This is the basis of hope, the perseverance of the human spirit against our worst nature.

Notes

1. See also Richard D. Reitsma, "Teaching Spanish Conversation Through the UAPs: A Pedagogy of Jesuit Values and Mission," *Jesuit Higher Education: A Journal* 11, no. 1 (2022), https://epublications.regis.edu/jhe/vol11/iss1/7.

2. This legislation, and what is allowed under it, has undergone numerous modifications, and I can only speak to my own experience of how it worked in the district I was in. See https://results.ed.gov/idr-manual/article/chapter-1-background-and-overview-of-the-migrant-education-program/organization-of-the-mep. See also Malin A. Heiderson and Edgar R. Leon, "Patterns and Trends in Michigan Migrant Education," JSRI Statistical Brief No. 8, Michigan State University, East Lansing, Julian Samora Research Institute, June 1996, https://files.eric.ed.gov/fulltext/ED401056.pdf. See also https://www.michigan.gov/mde/services/school-performance-supports/educational-supports/programs/title-i-part-c-migrant.

3. On TPR/Total Physical Response, see https://www.theteachertoolkit.com/index.php/tool/total-physical-response-tpr#:~:text=Total%20Physical%20Response%20(TPR)%20is,student%20inhibitions%20and%20lowers%20stress.

4. On HIL/High Impact Learning, see https://uwaterloo.ca/centre-for-teaching-excellence/support/integrative-learning/high-impact-practices-hips-or-engaged-learning-practices.

5. On popular education practices in Cuba, see https://ipsnoticias.net/2007/08/cuba-la-alternativa-de-la-educacion-popular/#:~:text=La%20educaci%C3%B3n%20popular%20se%20ha,con%20las%20estructuras%20del%20Estado. See also https://www.ecured.cu/Educaci%C3%B3n_popular.

6. Luis Chesney Lawrence, "La Concientización de Paulo Freire," *Rhec*, no. 11 (2008): 51–72.

7. These push/pull factors include grinding poverty (often resulting from neoliberal economic policies, debt structures, and economic neocolonialism, such as NAFTA), political corruption and/or instability, drug and gang violence (often financed directly or indirectly by US domestic policy), war, and climate change, to name a few. See, for example, National Immigration Forum, https://immigrationforum.org/article/push-or-pull-factors-what-drives-central-american-migrants-to-the-u-s/.

8. See KBI/Kino Border Initiative overviews, https://www.kinoborderinitiative.org/ See also subpage, https://www.kinoborderinitiative.org/category/migrant-stories/ for migrant stories. Newsletter page also highlights the ever-changing policies at the US border.

9. *Empezar de Cero: Historia de vida y experiencias en el retorno a México*, Sistema Jesuita Universitario, ITESO & Ibero, 2018.

10. https://www.justiceformigrantfamilies.org/.

11. https://blogs.canisius.edu/border/.

10

The Classroom as a Community of Learning
Confronting Utopia by Teaching Dystopia

Anita C. Butera

I am an immigrant, and my story, as told by others, is that of a faceless someone who left dystopia in search of utopia in the land of opportunities. My story, as told by myself, is that of a young woman who left the dystopia she knew to find a different one. My story is not unique because, from the point of view of immigrants, the history of immigration is mostly a story of personal defeats and losses. It is a story marked by the doubt that what was found is worth what was lost. More importantly, it is the story of every person who came to the United States either by choice or by violence. Yet it is a story that is systematically silenced because, if spoken, it will force us to confront the reality that our *Utopia is a place that does not exist.* Instead, it is a place where a carefully constructed narrative of exceptionalism is the most powerful justification for a still deeply racist and patriarchal country that was built on the genocide of First Nations, slavery, and the exploitation of immigrants, minorities, and women.

The United States prides itself on being a country of immigrants. This form of national identity is so ingrained in the collective consciousness that Americans seldom define themselves as just Americans. They are Americans and a percentage of something else. Americans, indeed, have a public identity as "American" that is expressed by unifying economic and political values, mostly capitalism and democracy, and a private identity as a "percentage of something else" that is defined by family history. However, family history is not defined by the personal stories of immigrants, but by the history of immigration as told by those in power. This so-called "official history" ties the personal identity of the individual to the acceptance of the story of themselves as told by the dominant group. In doing so, it legitimizes power by creating a form of authoritative utopia where personal stories of exploitation and defeat become collective memories of opportunities and success that, paradoxically, deprive individuals of their personal identity as told by themselves. The ultimate outcome of this form of dual identity is that a country built on genocide, slavery, and exploitation becomes the land of opportunity for all and a defender of democracy and freedom.[1]

Because the personal identities of Americans are based on a superimposed and utopian definition of self, teaching immigration and diversity is very challenging because students must confront the utopia on which their personal identity is based by questioning the official history. This can be achieved by teaching the personal stories of immigrants and minorities. In other words, utopia must be challenged by teaching dystopia as experienced by those living in the United States, especially immigrants and minorities. This requires the transformation of the classroom from a hierarchical setting into a community of learning. The Ignatius Pedagogical Paradigm ("IPP") and the work of bell hooks on transformative pedagogy provide the theoretical framework for turning the classroom into a community of learning where utopia can be challenged by teaching dystopia.

The IPP arose out of the spiritual exercises developed by St. Ignatius de Loyola, the founder of the Society of Jesus or Jesuits, in the sixteenth century. These exercises are based on a cyclical paradigm that connects experience, reflection, and action.[2] The spiritual exercises provide the framework for the creation of the IPP. Indeed, the IPP is based on the understanding that learning is cyclical and that praxis and theory exist in relation with each other.[3]

The IPP is based on five elements: context, experience, reflection, action, and evaluation. Specifically, the IPP demands that all learning be based on a specific context that is rooted in prior experiences so that reflection about present and past experiences can result in a transformative action reinforced by the evaluation of how experience has transformed the context and ourselves.[4] However, for the most part, these elements are interpreted and applied, first, within the context of the classroom and, second, within the community. In so doing, the implied danger of the IPP is that it does not directly address the role that the classroom has played in maintaining the status quo by re-creating and legitimizing dominant forms of knowledge and relations of power. bell hooks's work on transformative pedagogy addresses this limitation of the IPP.

The conventional understanding of education is achieving a predefined level of literacy and skills through the delivery of a specified curriculum within the context of a hierarchically organized classroom where the professor is in charge of delivering knowledge. The classroom is essential in reproducing mainstream knowledge and social relations of power because students are seen as more or less passive receptacles of given knowledge. To turn education into a transformative experience, this conventional understanding of education needs to be challenged and the hierarchical structure of the classroom needs to be dismantled.

To bell hooks, the ultimate purpose of education is to help students identify and challenge dominant relations of power.[5] Within this context, the classroom must be transformed into a collective structure where both the professor and the students seek knowledge. This, in turn, connects the classroom with the community because changing relations of power within the classroom challenges dominant relations of power outside the classroom. Indeed, a relevant contribution of bell hooks's work is the understanding that the classroom is not separated from the community, but is part of the community. Therefore, both the IPP and bell hooks connect theory and praxis because the ultimate purpose of education is to transform reality. However, bell hooks focuses on the classroom as a focal point of social change. The combination of the IPP and bell hooks's pedagogy allows me to turn the classroom into a community of learning where the professor and student engage with each other and the community in search of knowledge to promote changes. Approaching the classroom as a segment of the larger community and applying within the classroom the five steps of the IPP is essential when teaching immigration and diversity.

As discussed above, Americans have a national identity as Americans and as a percentage of something else. While the first is defined by unifying values, the latter is defined by the official history of immigration. Fundamental to the narrative is the belief that the United States is the *land of opportunities* where those willing to work hard can achieve upper-social class mobility. This narrative ignores the systematic exploitation of immigrants and minorities by silencing how immigration and minority status have historically served the need for cheap labor through the delivery of a compliant and easily exploitable labor force.[6] More importantly, this tale of the *land of opportunities* reinforces the embedded racism of the United

States because by presenting the country of origins as defining the identity of the individual, even when the ties with the sending country have been severed for generations, it has the ultimate outcomes to present race/ethnicity as historical and *deeper than skin*. By ignoring the socioeconomic milieu behind the history of different groups of immigrants and native minorities, this narrative places groups of immigrants against each other. Within this context, diversity becomes a showcase of colors rather than a means to understand the multifaceted complexity of humanity and human history. Most relevantly, this understanding of diversity never questions race or ethnicity and ignores the role of both in justifying exploitation.

For example, the largest influx of European immigrants came to the United States between 1880 to 1924, with the peak between 1900 and 1910, to fuel the unprecedented demand for cheap labor as a result of the industrialization of the northern United States and the inability of recently freed slaves to leave the South because of the Compromise of 1877 and the beginning of Jim Crow. Most of these immigrants lived under horrific conditions, in some cases even worse than those they left behind. By ignoring the stories of European immigrants, the official history reinforces racism because it separates the experience of the immigrants from that of the freed slaves and, more importantly, from the needs of the growing industrial economy. Furthermore, it ignores the common history of exploitation of different nationalities once they arrived in the United States. Finally, by tying the personal identity of European immigration to an ahistorical and everlasting definition of race and ethnicity as well as the narrative of the *land of opportunity*, it reinforces racism because it presents some groups, white Europeans, as inherently more able to succeed compared with others, such as brown Europeans and African Americans. Indeed, immigrants understand the value of whiteness as soon as they arrive in the United States, and different groups have fought to be considered white, even though they will never be considered as white as the original settlers. The ultimate outcome is to divide immigrant and minorities along racial and ethnic lines.[7] Therefore, silencing the stories of immigrants is essential to avoid an interracial/ethnic allegiance among different groups in the labor force because it ignores their common history of exploitation. In other words, it uses race and ethnicity as a proxy for social class and avoids the creation of a critical mass that can subvert relations of power by demanding large scale socioeconomic reforms.[8]

As discussed above, the IPP has five steps. The first step is *context*. This is commonly understood as the professor becoming familiar with the background, skills, and goals of the students as well as anything else they may deem important and conducive to the process of teaching. The second step is *experience*. This means the involvement of the whole person in the learning experience. Traditionally, this is interpreted as the professor guiding the students to use what they learned in the first step in order to differentiate what they understand in terms of facts, feelings, values, and intuitions. *Reflection* is the third step of the IPP. This is a formative step that shapes the consciousness of students and encourages them to take action. Usually, this steps has been interpreted as the professor formulating questions that help students to engage across a range of involvements that prepare students into taking action. The fourth step is *action*. This is the step that connects theory and praxis. Typically this step has been interpreted as faculty helping students to consider what they learned from the prior three steps and use this knowledge to promote changes in themselves and the community. The fifth and final step is *evaluation*. Usually this refers to a comprehensive assessment by the professor of students in terms of both academic achievement and personal growth.

Thus, the IPP emphasizes the connection between theory and praxis through a pedagogical paradigm based on an understanding of education as the ability to master academic skills as well as a process of personal growth whose ultimate purpose is to promote changes. Nonetheless, the learning experience of the IPP takes place in a classroom that is hierarchically organized, with the professor in charge of delivering knowledge. This hierarchical structure of the classroom tends to reciprocate mainstream relations of power because the professor is in charge of the educational experience and is not an equal participant in the learning process. As a result, praxis becomes informed by mainstream relations of power. To remedy this hierarchical structure and turn the classroom into a community of learning, the professor must become an equal participant in the learning process. This can be achieved by redefining the five steps of the IPP through the lens of the pedagogical work of bell hooks, especially her understanding that the classroom is a focal point of social change.

When the classroom becomes the focus of social change, the five steps of the IPP must be adjusted to define a learning experience where the professor is an equal participant and education is seen as a collective learning experience. Specifically, *context* must also include the background, skills, and goals of the professor. The outcome is to create a more equalitarian structure in the classroom where the professor is seen as a participant in the learning process. *Experience* must also include the cognitive and emotional involvement of the professor, and the process of learning must be guided by the backgrounds of the students as well as that of the professor. The purpose of this step is to create awareness of the content of education as well as the process of learning and the larger implications of both education and learning. The third step, *reflection*, must include the full participation of students in evaluating the context and the experience. This can include, among other tools, students participating in the creation of questions to evaluate the learning process and/or students engaging in periodic self- and peer evaluation. *Action* is the step that seeks a practical application of learning and, thus, connects theory to praxis. When this step is implemented in the context of the classroom as a community of learning, students must have a role in deciding the action both in terms of activities within the classroom and in connecting the classroom experience with the community. The final step, *evaluation*, cannot be just the realm of the professor, but must include the students evaluating the process of learning, especially in terms of how it can be enhanced and challenged as well as how learning can be used to challenge relations of power and promote changes in the community at large. While the classroom as a community of learning can be used to teach both scientific and humanistic subjects, it is particularly helpful when teaching immigration and diversity.

When teaching immigration and diversity, professors and students must confront and challenge the official history by rediscovering their personal history and identity. In other words, they must confront utopia by learning about dystopia. Dystopia can be taught through the use of personal stories. Personal stories give a human face to those who have been exploited and silenced by the official history. It gives humanity back to those who were deprived of it and gives us all the understanding that true diversity is to discover our common humanity and that we all experience injustice because we all live in a system that is inherently exploitative.[9] Accordingly, justice cannot be achieved without reforming/changing the system. Therefore, within the context of teaching immigration and diversity, personal stories make education a transformative experience because they force us to confront our personal identity and, in so doing, compel us to find ourselves in the other.

The use of personal stories cannot be effective without the professor breaking the power structure of the classroom. This is not an easy task because it requires that the professor gain authority by relinquishing power. An effective way to achieve this end is to make students aware of power relationships in the classroom. Once the students are made aware of the power structure of the classroom, the professor can share her or his background, skills, and goals with the students and seek their cooperation in the definition and periodical evaluation of the class.

To address and question the hierarchical structure of the classroom, I found it particularly effective to share with students my main cultural shock in being an international student in the United States. Usually on the first day of class, I explain to my students how, in other countries, there is no mandate that students report on their fellow students if they are found to be cheating. I then continue to have a discussion about the implication of that difference in terms of creating cohesiveness among students and how this will influence their relationship with coworkers later in life. After sharing this experience, I discuss what my goals are for the class, especially in terms of learning from the students as much as I hope they will learn from me and how we are "partners in crime in this adventure we call learning." After the power structure of the classroom has been addressed, personal stories can be used to challenge utopia by teaching dystopia.

Within the classroom as a community of learning, context and experience intermingle with each other because establishing the context forces both students and professor to confront their personal history as told by ourselves rather than others. Indeed, the collection and narration of personal stories establishes the context through experience. This is not an easy task because students must be willing to listen to the stories of others without preconceived ideas about race, ethnicity, gender, and immigration status. In other words, students and professors must be willing and able to look at their reality from the point of view of others. The role of the professor is essential in this step because he or she must create a nonthreatening and nonjudgmental environment where stories can be told and analyzed.

Being an immigrant and a woman, I bring to the classroom two strong identifiers of my personal story and use them to start a conversation about the personal stories of students. Indeed, I find it useful to start with my personal story because by showing my humanity I become *more equal* to the students. Second, as an attorney who represented migrant workers and minorities, I often discuss some of the cases I was involved in or the stories I witnessed. The use of speakers is also a successful tool to narrate personal stories. Nonetheless, the use of personal stories can still be tricky because it may encounter resistance from some students and professors, who may not be willing to share their personal experiences. In such cases, several tools can be used. One is the use of traditional pedagogical tools such as books, documentaries, and movies. However, with some remarkable exceptions, these tools reflect mainstream stereotypes about immigrants and minorities. A more helpful tool I have used is the story of legal cases defining race in the United States (included in appendix A) as well as the US census definition of race through the years.

I find the use of legal cases defining race in the United States particularly useful because it connects the definition of race to immigration via the 1790 Naturalization Act. This act limits citizenship to free "white" persons who have resided in the United States for at least two years and grants the US court system the power to define who is white and who is not. This gives students a powerful example of how race and ethnicity are social constructs enforced by the law that reflect relations of power as defined by the economic and political needs of society. Another tool is to ask students to personally collect stories of immigration and/or racial/ethnic experience from their family or community. Students have particularly enjoyed collecting stories from their parents, grandparent, and older relatives.

Because teaching immigration and diversity through the personal stories of immigrants and minorities should increase awareness of the role that race, ethnicity, and immigration status have in justifying exploitation, it is important that students compare and contrast different personal experiences to identify what they all have in common and what makes them unique. In particular, comparing and contrasting stories of immigration and discrimination is a helpful pedagogical tool because it provides a firsthand account of the dystopia many still live. It also forces students and professors to realize our common history of exploitation and the role that the utopia narrated by the official history has in defining our identity as *Americans*. I found discussion forums a very effective tool to facilitate this part of the learning experience. Discussion forums put students in charge of their learning experience while comparing their experience with that of their classmates. It is important that the professor also participate in these discussion forums by reading and answering the comments of all students.

Another useful pedagogical tool is to allow students to grade the work of their classmates. This enhances the learning experience by recognizing and challenging power relations within and outside the classroom. Thus, once power relations within the classroom have been challenged, the use of personal stories as a pedagogical tool allows us to define a learning experience that connects the personal identity of students and professors to larger social issues. Action is the next step.

Within the context of the classroom as a learning community, praxis and theory are intertwined by challenging the relations of power that exists within the traditional classroom. As discussed above, this form of learning experience also challenges relations of power in the community. Hence, action is not the step that connects theory and praxis; rather, it is a conscious act to change relations within both the classroom and the community. This step must be entirely directed by the students with the cooperation of the professor.

From a pedagogical standpoint, this can take several forms, from outreach outside campus to organizing an event on campus or establishing new classroom practices. Regardless of the type of action taken by the students, it is essential that the action be related to the issue identified during the prior steps. One effective pedagogical tool that was created by students was to organize a presentation of those who were killed during the civil rights movement by creating a fictional narrative of how they felt during the last moments of their lives. The students read their papers out loud during an in-class presentation that was open to the entire campus community. This was a very powerful experience because it gave humanity to those who lost their lives to challenge racism. Through the years, I found students to be incredibly creative in putting context, experience, and reflection into action.

Within the classroom as a community of learning, evaluation has an important role because it allows students and the professor to reflect on the entire learning experience. When using personal stories to teach immigration and diversity, evaluation must necessarily include a reflection on how the learning experience has shown the importance of personal stories to challenge the official history and how this has changed our perceptions of ourselves and others. This can be achieved through several tools. The one I found more effective was to ask students to discuss the limitations of the class and present suggestions for improvement while identifying the limitations of their action to challenge relations of power. Another effective tool was to ask students to write a short description of themselves at the beginning of the class and see how it changed by the end of the class. Regardless of the pedagogical tool, this step is essential because, by discussing the limitations of the learning experience in terms of "learning" and "challenging power," it creates a path for continued changes outside the classroom. Therefore, within the context of the classroom as a community of learning, personal stories can be successfully used to empower students and challenge relations of power. Hence, utopia can be challenged by teaching dystopia within the context of the classroom as a community of learning. Dystopia can be taught through the use of personal stories, giving voice to those silenced by the official history.

History is written by the winners, and the ultimate purpose of their account is to justify their victory and power by silencing the voices of those who lost. Within the context of US capitalism, the official history is based on a utopian narrative of benevolent exceptionalism that serves the ultimate purpose of justifying a system of exploitation that blames the exploited by presenting them as less human than the rest of us. This can be challenged by giving voice to the dystopia of immigrants and minorities. This use of personal stories has the ultimate purpose of making us aware of our common humanity by questioning the meaning of race, ethnicity, and immigrant status as well as other forms of discrimination. The classroom as a community of learning creates a suitable environment for the teaching of dystopia because it challenges relations of power within the classroom and empowers professors, students, and the community. Teaching dystopia to confront utopia makes education a transformative experience because it questions the relations of power on which our identity as *Americans* is based.

Appendix A

This lists some of the legal cases defining race in the United States. This is a dynamic list and it should be considered just a starting point to be used to spark a class discussion and students' interest in challenging the meaning of race and ethnicity. This list does not include cases defining gender, sexual preference, age, and disability status.

1771   *Somerset v. Stewart* held that slavery, although against Common Law, and Natural Law can be justified by positive law (colonial law).

1791   The Naturalization Act limited naturalization to immigrants who were "free white persons" of "good moral character." This gives courts the power to define who is white and who is not.

1783   *Commonwealth v. Jennison* made slavery illegal in Massachusetts.

1836   *Rachel, a Woman of Color, v. Walker* held that a slave taken to live in free territory is free; however, the case also declared that children take the status of the mother. This meant that children of female slaves were born into slavery regardless of their lineage.

1849   *Boston v. Roberts* upheld racial segregation in Boston Public Schools.

1850 The Fugitive Slave Act required that escaped slaves once captured be returned to their owner. It requires officials and citizens of non-slavery to cooperate.

1854 *People v. Hal* held that Chinese and Black people cannot testify against whites.

1857 *Dred Scott v. Stanford* held that Black people cannot be citizens even if they are free.

1858 In *Bailey v. Poindexter*, the Supreme Court of Virginia rules that John Poindexter's executor cannot legally fulfill Poindexter's intention to give his slaves the choice to be emancipated because slaves are not people. The Court held that Black people lack free will and cannot make decisions.

1861 The Civil War begins.

1862 Federal emancipation of slaves in the District of Columbia.

1863 The Emancipation Declaration takes effect.

1863 New York City Riots. Poor New Yorkers rebel against the draft that exempted rich whites (they could pay $300) and Blacks, who are blamed for the war. About 115 people, including twelve Blacks, died.

1864 Fugitive Slave Act repealed.

1865 Thirteenth Amendment to the US Constitution abolished slavery and involuntary servitude except as punishment for a crime. This loophole opens the door for the re-enslavement of young African Americans through the convict lease system.

1865 Act to Establish a Bureau for the Relief of Freedmen and Refugees.

1866 Civil Rights Act of 1866 guaranteed equal rights under the law for all people who lived within the jurisdiction of the United States.

1865 The Ku Klux Kan is funded. Originally it is a small social club in Poulanski, Tennessee. By 1870, it extended to almost every Southern state. The aim of the KKK is to reestablish white supremacy by waging a campaign of terror against primarily Blacks but also anyone who challenged white supremacy. An important strategy of the KKK was to target Black leaders elected to office and Black churches because they are symbols of the power of the African American community. The KKK also worked to elect officers who supported white supremacy.

1868　Fourteenth Amendment to the US Constitution grants citizenship to all people born or naturalized in the United States. It prohibits states from denying any person the equal protection of the law or depriving any person of life, liberty, or property without due process of law.

1870　Fifteenth Amendment to the US Constitution granted African American men the right to vote.

1870–71　Three Enforcement Acts gave the federal government substantial authority to prosecute those who violated the civil and political rights of African Americans, especially members of the KKK.

1872　*Slaughter House Cases* established the principle that the Fourteenth Amendment should be strictly constructed because it was meant to protect the rights of former slaves, and thus it applies *only* to those rights emerging from federal citizenship and not those that are incidental to state citizenship; among them is the "police power" of the States. This power cannot be restricted by federal jurisdiction. The Fourteenth Amendment is dead.

1872　*Blyew v. US* held that a young girl cannot testify against the "white" people who have brutally murdered her family. This is one of the most tragic case of a series of cases that severely restrict the right of Blacks to have equal protection of law or use the Court System for abuses suffered from whites.

1873　*Colfax Massacre*. The White League, a paramilitary group intent on securing white rule in Louisiana, clashed with Louisiana's almost all-Black state militia. The resulting death toll was staggering. Only three members of the White League died, but more than one hundred Black men were killed. Nearly half were murdered in cold blood after they had already surrendered. As of today there is no historic account of the number of Blacks murdered because the bodies were thrown in the Red river and mass graves were quickly created.

1875 *US v. Cruikshank* decided that the Civil Rights Act does not apply to acts of private racism and releases the culprits of the Colfax Massacre.

1876 *US v. Reed* ruled that judges of election who exclude Blacks cannot be punished.

1880 *Strawder v. W.VA* restricts criminal juries to white only.

1883 *Pace v. Alabama* decided that interracial couples can receive harsher punishment under the law. An interracial couple whose marriage was not recognized in Alabama and thus accused of fornication and cohabitation is punished more severely than same-race couples doing the same.

1896 *Plessy v. Ferguson* creates the doctrine of "separate but equal." The Fourteenth Amendment is de facto overruled by the Supreme Court. This case also stands for the principle that "your race is what the law and the group in power says it is." Mr. Plessy was only one-eighth African American and his complexion was very light, yet under Louisiana law he was considered African American.

1901 *Downes v. Bidwell* Held that the US Constitution does not apply to the island of Puerto Rico because the island is not part of the United States.

1922 *Ozawa v. US* held that Japanese are not white and thus cannot become naturalized citizens. Ozawa claimed that he was white because the color of his skin was white. He also claimed that race should not matter because he was an American at heart. Benedict Arnold was white but was not an American.

1923 *US v. Thind* case held that Caucasians are not always white. Thind argued that as an Indian he was an Aryan and, thus, a Caucasian. The Court replied, "the Aryan theory, as a racial basis, seems to be discredited by most, if not all, modern writers . . . the Caucasoid division of the human family is 'in point of fact the most debatable field in the whole range of anthropological studies . . . [the 1790 Immigration and Naturalization Act] understood "white people" in its popular, and not scientific sense." In other words, the Court decides that white is whom they say is white and any form of "scientific classification" is irrelevant.

1944   *Korematsu v. US* held the internment of Japanese-Americans to be legal. This case is still the law in the United States. Although criticized, it has not been overturned.

1954   *Brown v. Board of Education* held that "segregation is inherently unequal." The *Plessy v. Ferguson* case is overturned.

1964   *McLaughlin v. Florida* held that state law cannot prohibit cohabitation between two individuals of different race. It does not overturn state law prohibiting interracial marriage.

1967   *Loving v. Virginia* held that state laws prohibiting interracial marriage are against the US Constitution.

1968   *Jones v. Alfred H. Mayer Co.* prohibited private discrimination in the sale or rental of property.

1968   *Green et al. v. County School Board of New Kent County* reversed the decision of the Virginia Court of Appeals that supported separate schools for whites and Blacks.

1969   Executive Order 11478 required equal opportunity and affirmative action programs in all federal agencies (passed under the Nixon administration).

1972   The Equal Opportunity Act amended the Civil Rights Act of 1964 to apply to local, state, and federal governments and allow the Equal Employment Opportunity Commission to bring suits.

1973   *Keyes v. Denver School District* distinguished between de jure (sanctioned by law) and de facto (true in fact but not officially sanctioned) school segregation.

1973   *San Antonio Independent School District v. Rodriguez* held that there is no constitutional violation in unequal school funding and ruled that education is not a fundamental right.

1973   *Milliken v. Bradley* found that de jure segregation in one school district could not justify busing children to and from surrounding school districts.

1976   *Hills v. Gautreau* determined that Section 8 housing cannot be limited to specific urban areas.

1978 *Regents of the University of California v. Bakke* held that college admission standards giving preferential consideration to minority applicants are constitutional.

1986 *Batson v. Kentucky* held that the intentional exclusion of African Americans from a jury denies an African American defendant the equal protection of law.

2003 *Grutter v. Bollinger* held that the limited use of race in admission policies is constitutional.

2014 *Schuette v. Coalition to Defend Affirmative Action* held that a Michigan referendum banning affirmative action in admissions at publicly funded state colleges does not violate the Equal Protection Clause of the US Constitution.

2017 Executive Order 13769, also known as the Muslim Ban. President Trump suspended entry for individuals coming from Iran, Iraq, Libya, Somalia, Sudan, Syria, and Yemen. Order 13769 was challenged in the case *Darweesh v. Trump* filed in 2017. The case was settled out of court.

Notes

1. Anita C. Butera, "Assimilation, Pluralism and Multiculturalism: The Policy of Racial/Ethnic Identity in America," *Buffalo Human Rights Review* 7 (2001): 1–31.

2. Elisabeth Meier Tetlow, trans., *Ignatius, of Loyola, Saint, 1491–1556. The Spiritual Exercises of St. Ignatius Loyola* (Lanham, MD: University Press of America, 1987).

3. Christopher Chapple, *The Jesuit Tradition in Education and Missions: A 450-Year Perspective* (Scranton, PA: University of Scranton Press, 1933).

4. Rolando E. Bonachea, *Jesuit Higher Education: Essays on an American Tradition of Excellence* (Pittsburgh: Duquesne University Press, 1989) and G. W. Trau, ed., *A Jesuit Education Reader* (Chicago: Loyola Press, 2009).

5. bell hooks, *Teaching to Transgress: Education as the Practice of Freedom* (New York: Routledge Press, 1994); bell hooks, *Outlaw Culture: Resisting Representations* (New York: Routledge Press, 1994); bell hooks, *Teaching Community: A Pedagogy of Hope* (New York: Routledge Press, 2003); bell hooks, *Teaching Critical Thinking: Practical Wisdom* (New York: Routledge Press, 2010); and bell hooks, *Feminism Is for Everybody: Passionate Politics* (Cambridge, MA: South End Press, 2000).

6. Anita C. Butera and Secil Ertorer, "Restrictive Asylum Policies and Reflections in the Labor Market: The Cases of Italy and Turkey," in *Current Challenges*

in Migration Policy and Law, ed. E. Freitas-Castro and S. Maia-Tavares (London: Transnational Press, 2020).

7. Butera, "Assimilation, Pluralism and Multiculturalism."

8. Oliver Cox, *Caste, Class and Race: A Study in Social Dynamics* (New York: Modern Reader Paperback, 1948).

9. Paulo Freire, *Pedagogy of the Oppressed*, 30th anniversary ed. (New York: Continuum, 2000).

11

The Impossible Project
A Utopian Pedagogy for a Dystopian Moment

DALIA ANTONIA CARABALLO MULLER

> My concern is with the relation between this (as it seems to me) dead-end present and, on the one hand, the old utopian futures that inspired and for a long time sustained it and, on the other, an imagined idiom of future futures that might reanimate this present and even engender in it new and unexpected horizons of transformative possibility.
>
> —David Scott, Conscripts of Modernity

Tragic Time and the Collapse of Our Utopian Horizons

In his influential text *Conscripts of Modernity*, David Scott questions our insistence on framing our historical narratives in a Romantic mode, as this means that the stories we are telling are stories of overcoming, vindication, salvation, and redemption. They "depend upon a certain (utopian) horizon toward which the emancipationist history is imagined to be moving."[1] But what if, as Scott suggests, our utopian horizon has collapsed and "is now a superseded future, one of our futures past"?[2] Reinhart Koselleck theorized that the disjuncture of the modern age can be explained by the growing distance between the "space of experience" and the "horizon of expectation."[3] Drawing on and expanding Koselleck's formulation, David Scott applies this idea to any historical moment or shift when past futures fade and when the future that once seemed guaranteed by the present is now undermined by it. Living today in a world of our "futures past," in the ruined present that was the hoped-for future of our ancestors, requires us to set aside *their* longings and dreams and find our own. It is only once we do this that, Scott insists, that we will be able to reclaim the future.[4]

This is an exercise that Robin D. G. Kelley attempts at the end of his impassioned exploration of freedom dreaming in the Black tradition. After guiding the reader through more than a century of freedom dreaming practices, he summons us to an act of imagination, insisting that we must learn how to "dream ourselves out of this dark place," as our ancestors did.[5] But our dreams will not be the same as theirs. Our dreams of freedom will be of a different character, color, and texture. Writing his book *Freedom Dreams* in the context of debates over what to do with the site of the World Trade Center tragedy, Kelley ends the text with an act of radical imagining, one wherein he proposes the creation of an open, radical, and inclusive space of gathering, coming together, experiencing, and building forward collectively as a way to honor the memories of those lost and meet the horrors of war with love and resistance. Kelley's text, with its voyage through dreaming practices, reminds us that our ancestors of the African diaspora, no matter their ordeal, never stopped dreaming. As the first truly modern subjects, Toni Morrison insists, Afrodiasporans experienced (and continue to experience) conditions that would become synonymous with modernity—alienation, dislocation, and dehumanization.[6] But still they dreamed, and those dreams often cost life and limb. Our antecedents left us a legacy that endures; they taught us that even in the direst circumstances, we can always find our voices and we can use our imaginations. Kelley's text challenges us to learn from our ancestors, find our own voices, and refuse those people and systems that would take from us not just our freedom, our lifeways and our subsistence, but also our imaginations. Kelley enjoins us to take back the future.

In a similar fashion, Frederic Jameson calls upon us to "reclaim the future." Quoting Walter Benjamin, Jameson argues that our future is superseded through colonization. Our future has been hijacked. It is no longer an open horizon of new possibility, but rather a future that futures traders have already claimed, a future shaped by new forms of "actuarial colonization."[7] Our future will simply be[come] our unending present, a now and tomorrow determined by the unfolding of disaster capitalism. We are living the future-present of our assured socioecological destruction. Against these forces, Jameson urges us to reclaim the "future as disruption," as a force capable of taking back the imagination, the space of dreams, the space of collective force and possibility, in defense of the possibility of another world.[8]

Whether we live in the present ruins of our ancestors' future hopes or in an unending present colonized by our oppressors, we must break free. But how? Our greatest guides, I argue, are to be found among those who urge us deeper toward an honest reckoning with suffering, with pain, and with dislocation, assuring us that we can and will rise together from those depths because our people have done so before: Achille Mbembe begs us to recognize that we live in a world of death-causing rather than life-giving. To change this orientation, we must bring into being a new humanity.[9] Similarly, David Scott urges us to relinquish our romantic dreams of progress and embrace our fundamentally tragic condition. We must dream new dreams, born of tragedy though they may be.[10]

Similarly, Christina Sharpe invites us to "stay in the wake" of slavery and learn to think from there because only then will we be able to find a way of "inhabiting and rupturing the episteme" of human bondage and its afterlives.[11] Similarly, Edouard Glissant calls on us to return to the "womb abyss" of our dispossessed beginnings. In the womb abyss, fear becomes knowledge and new ways of knowing ourselves "as part and whole" are born. Collective suffering and disorientation birth new onto-epistemologies centered in Relation rather than filiation.[12] Similarly, Irvin Hunt argues that we must take up "non-progressivism" as a methodology and embrace "sustained incipience" as a way of being and bringing about change in our world. Eschewing a politics of both ends and means, he calls on us to learn from the Black cooperative tradition and to live radically "into the present" rather than for the future.[13] Similarly, Sylvia Wynter calls upon us to question all we know and how we know it, and invites us to abandon "Man" and unlearn his thought traditions. In the process, we will make way for submerged and disparaged modes of the human to take center stage and redefine humanity for all of us.[14]

What unites all of these thinkers, and many more not mentioned here, is that in this time of apathy, escapism, conspicuous consumption, and all-consuming digital life—a time in which it is easier for those of us with relative privilege to live on surfaces and evade deep dives for fear of what lies beneath—they invite us to submerge ourselves, to get real, to do the work. The work requires an honest interrogation of self, of self and society, of self-in-the-world. It requires that we build brave communities of practice capable of facing what lies in the murky depths. In the depths of our own consciousnesses and our collective consciousness, we will find not answers, but ways back to a breathable surface, and we will do this together.

These theorists all center some form of undoing or unlearning. The descent into the murky depths entails a process of unbecoming, which becomes central to moving into a different register and to opening the way to new futures, or to future possibilities reclaimed. These thinkers acknowledge that there is something fundamentally wrong not only with our ways of being-in-the-world, but with our ways of knowing ourselves in that world and knowing that world and the earth it inhabits as itself. Common to all is an invitation to refusal. They refuse progress as a value and an orientation. They refuse romance and its investment in history as progress. They refuse heteronormative patriarchy. They refuse death and death-dealing as a way of living. They refuse the refusal to engage with the history of slavery, colonialism, and its many persistent afterlives.

Finally, common to (nearly) all of these theorists is hope in the form of that breathable surface, those new visions, those new imaginings born of honest and earnest being together in committed unbecoming and unlearning. None provide a vision of what is to come, of what hope will bring. The act itself, the process of beginning and persevering in justice work, as Hunt puts it, or, as Jameson insists, the fact of having to think at the limits of the possible, allows us to begin to reclaim the future. "The Utopian form itself is the answer to the universal ideological conviction that no alternative is possible, that there is no alternative to the system," Jameson states. "But it asserts this by forcing us to think the break itself, and not by offering a more traditional picture of what things would be like after."[15] This idea of thinking "the break itself" is also what motivates Lola Olufemi, who, reflecting on the resistance traditions of Afrodiasporans in her text *Experiments in Imagining Otherwise*, begs her readers' patience and tests their resolve. Calling on them to follow, she writes: "If it seems I am holding on to nothing. I am. Hold on with me." For Olufemi, this is what the otherwise requires, a leap of faith into the unknown.

Our Education Systems

> The classroom remains the most radical space of possibility in the academy.
>
> —bell hooks, *Teaching to Transgress*

In reflecting on the pedagogical needs of our present moment, education theorist Henry Giroux insists that "we need to think otherwise as a condition for acting otherwise."[16] Like Olufemi, Giroux finds the concept of "the otherwise" useful for articulating the necessity of refusal, the work of undoing, and the centrality of thought-work in processes of productive unraveling. For to think and act otherwise is to think and act other than, or outside of, what is normalized. Giroux and many critical pedagogy theorists and thinkers have noted the ways in which our education systems uphold the broadly oppressive forces in our society, rather than inviting us to think through and against systems.

Noting the "deep grammar of violence" that permeates our society and our institutions of learning, Giroux laments how our schools and universities prize the preparation of highly competitive, individualized, skills-bearing, and market-ready subjects rather than critical thinkers prepared to question why the world is the way it is and how it came to be that way.[17] Our education systems, he argues, are fundamentally callous and uncaring. Students are treated as customers and clients, while institutions are held hostage to market-driven modes of accountability with disciplines and programs rewarded so long as they contribute to profitability. Prevalent in our current moment is a form of "neoliberal pedagogy" that stifles critical thought, reduces citizens to consumers, and defines certain marginalized populations as disposable. As Craig Steven Wilder has noted, the academy's complicity with bondage, oppression, and disposability is nothing new. Never passive beneficiaries, the US academy "stood beside church and state as a third pillar of a civilization built on bondage."[18] Institutions of higher learning were never conceptualized as inclusive or necessarily democratic spaces—a legacy that they continue to carry today. The threat to critical modes of education and democracy, Giroux argues, has never been greater than in the current historical moment, especially with the rise of right-populist movements and governments across the globe.[19]

Stefano Harney and Fred Moten agree that the university, as *Universitas*, replicates relations of power and domination and upholds our current unequal, extractive, and uncaring Man-made "universe." Giroux's "market ready subjects" are Harney and Moten's "professionals." Indeed, the latter insist that so-called critical education and critical thinking are employed in the service of an increasingly professional and professionalized education. "Professional education has become a critical education," they insist. In other words, critical thought is developed not to challenge or undo oppressive systems, but to uphold them, and, with them, the status quo. Giroux would not disagree. When he references the power of "critical pedagogies" to oppose "neoliberal pedagogies," he is thinking well beyond "critical thinking" and toward forms of continuous, open-ended, and justice-centered critical engagement and the creation of collective knowledge. Giroux defines pedagogy as "an ongoing individual and collective struggle over knowledge, desire, values, social relations, and, most important, modes of political agency."[20] Thus, critical pedagogy is a thoughtful, analytical, and disruptive "ongoing individual and collective struggle" and not a skill to be gained. In other words, to be guided by critical pedagogical practice in your classroom as an educator is to commit to much more than teaching your students to think critically. For Giroux, critical pedagogy alone is not apt to respond to the needs of our desperate times. A rigorous critique of domination and how it manifests institutionally can leave us feeling desperate. Thus, Giroux insists that we center hope. "[H]ope goes beyond acknowledging how power works as a mechanism of domination and offers up a vocabulary in which it becomes possible to imagine power working in the interest of justice, equality and freedom."[21]

This space of the imagination, of what is or becomes imaginable, is central to education as a practice of freedom, to quote Paulo Freire and later bell hooks.[22] For Harney and Moten, hope lies in the "undercommons of enlightenment," that is "the maroon community in the basement of the university," where the disparaged labor of the university takes refuge.[23] This is where true critical work is done. To the professionalized and market-driven concept of education, which he calls the "banking method," Paulo Freire opposes a "problem-posing education—which accepts neither a 'well-behaved present' nor a predetermined future." Such an education "roots itself in the dynamic present and becomes revolutionary." "Problem-posing education," he insists, does not and cannot serve the interests of the oppressor.[24] No oppressive order could permit the oppressed to begin to question: why? Indeed, the question *why?* is what Giroux centers in his hopeful critical pedagogy and what Harney and Moten insist animates the undercommons. Describing problem-posing education as "revolutionary futurity," Freire calls it "prophetic."[25]

Harney and Moten, too, invoke the "prophetic" organization of the undercommons, which becomes the place of hope within our institutions.[26] These sentiments can be found in bell hooks's writing as well. "Education is always a vocation rooted in hopefulness," she writes.[27] We teach because we believe in the possibility of learning and we believe that learning can lead to new ways of knowing. For hooks, hope is rooted not just in the act of teaching, but also in the call to build communities of, around, and through learning. These learning communities become the locus of "prophetic imagination." Citing Mary Grey, hooks writes that prophetic dreaming is an imaginary that is fully public, built by and for communities that share a "commitment to fuller visions of well-being."[28] Lorgia García Peña also finds building community to be the most effective form of resistance within an academy centered on cultivating and rewarding individual success.[29] Forging communities of care, support, and commitment to justice is a central and key strategy for countering oppression.

What we need, then, are spaces and methods of learning that value critical praxis, build communities of care, center justice, and cultivate bravery. We need education that, to quote Giroux, brings back "thoughtful reasoning, empathy, collective resistance, and the compassionate imagination."[30] The challenge, then, for theorists and practitioners alike is how to go about this work in our spaces of learning. How do we reach the murky depths, and how do we convince our students to take the plunge with us? How can we ensure the realization of bell hooks's affirmation that "the classroom remains the most radical space of possibility in the academy"?[31]

Thinking at the Limits of the Possible: A Call to Action

> My position is impossible, a colonialist-by-product of empire, with decolonizing desires. I am, and maybe you are too, a produced colonialist. I am also a by-product of colonization. As a colonialist scrap, I desire against the assemblage that made me.
>
> —la paperson, *A Third University Is Possible*

Descending into the murky waters where we will find hope with and for our students requires a significant commitment on the part of the educator. We must recognize that there is no assurance of what we will find once we make that descent, which constitutes a downward "leap" of faith very much at odds with our preparation as educators. Theorist and radical educator la paperson signals the unique difficulty of doing disruptive work within the academy for those of us who are already marginalized. Indeed, we are in the impossible position of being a "colonialist-by-product" that desires "against the assemblage" that makes us. However, this impossibility motivates la paperson, who recognizes that embracing impossibility requires that we theorize contingently. Our theorizations are contingent on the apparatuses of control that inform and surround us. Rather than a compromised position, however, this commitment to contingency is a way of refusing to establish any "ultimate position" on any one thing, and, as such, it opens space for many theorizations to be developed, especially by those that have been and, continue to be most marginalized.[32]

la paperson's focus on contingency reflects the value that Jameson placed on "thinking the utopian break" itself, as well as Kelley's investment in freedom dreaming, Giroux and Olufemi's embrace of "thinking otherwise," and Harney and Moten's faith in the undercommons of enlightenment. At a certain level, each of these theorists [insists] that we confront the impossible, that we recognize to varying degrees that our lives themselves are impossible. For some of us that has been a long-term condition, and for others it will assuredly be a future one.

In my pedagogical thinking and practice, I use the critical reflections of the many theorists acknowledged here as inspiration and guidance for my articulation of a new pedagogical praxis appropriate for addressing this historical moment. Weaving their insights together, I propose a new way of learning in and beyond our classrooms, one that centers failure and uncertainty, champions collective resilience and community, and demands that we conceptualize education as justice work. This praxis is called the Impossible Project.[33] The Impossible Project is not a model or a method. It is not a tonic that can be bottled. It is a generative and dynamic praxis that can become the totality of a learning experience or can be woven into an existing experience.

The Impossible Project draws together many intellectual threads but is most firmly rooted in the theoretical and epistemological traditions of the African Diaspora, traditions that have always been Afrofuturist. The impossible is that which cannot be conceptualized, that for which our descriptive categories are insufficient. Black theorists have described Black people as living impossible lives, while Black historians have noted how radical and resistant Black histories have often been rendered unthinkable and therefore impossible.[34] Erasing "others," has, after all, long been a tool of power. By struggling for freedom and justice and refusing erasure as a matter of daily practice, however, Back people and other racially oppressed peoples have rejected the knowledge/power systems that render them impossible and have consistently thought at the limits of the "possible" to envision an alternate future in which we exist free of racism and discrimination. This continuous (historical and contemporary) work against our own impossibilization is the foundation of the Impossible Project. From it emerges a new way to conceptualize teaching and learning, one that has the power to equip students with far more than expanded knowledge and critical thinking abilities.

Kodwo Eshun defines Afrofuturism as "a program for recovering the histories of counter-futures," adding that it was "created in a century hostile to Afrodiasporic projection and as a space within which the critical work of manufacturing tools capable of intervention within the current political dispensation may be undertaken."[35] Achille Mbembe adds that "Afrofuturism rejects outright the humanist postulate, in so far as humanism can constitute itself only by relegating some other subject or entity (living or inert) to the mechanical status of an object or accident.[36] Afrodiasporans, reduced to objects in the slave trade, represent humanity's other. The legacies of that multilayered dispossession live on today in slavery's "afterlives."[37] Thus, Afrofuturists center the recovery of "counter-futures" made impossible by Western humanism. For Eshun, it is within these practices of recovery and invention that useful tools may be forged for reshaping our present and our future. The Impossible Project invites learners to unlearn lessons, think new thoughts, and forge new tools in the interest of bringing about a just and sustainable future for all. Among the Afrofuturist practices that inform the Impossible Project are collective engagement with/recognition of suffering, an act of refusal and another of undoing/unlearning, an act of creation or invention, and an act of untethering (an act of flight/fugitivity). The Impossible Project as a pedagogical praxis uses these elements/experiences/commitments as the foundation of its core principles.

TRUE COLLABORATION AS AN ACT OF REFUSAL AND
ANOTHER OF UNDOING/UNLEARNING

In his now hallowed text *Poetics of Relation*, Edouard Glissant urges his readers to undertake hard and painful work. His interpretation of the generative space of wake work that Sharpe outlines is what he calls the "womb abyss" in the context of slavery and the slave ship. For Glissant, the belly of the slave ship brought death and also new knowledge. Forcibly deracinated and enslaved Africans built new forms of kinship and relation in and through the devastation of enslavement and passage to the new world. For Glissant, Afrodiasporans are the custodians of new epistemological insights born out of tragedy. This new epistemology could be our salvation, according to Glissant. What he calls "Relation" is a way of knowing yourself in the world differently or "otherwise" from dominant modes. Those who embrace Relation know themselves as "part and whole in an unknown that does not terrify."[38] The "unknown" or the "impossible" is no longer terrifying when we embrace Relation as our central mode of being.

Glissant describes the places where Relation is lived intentionally as "common places." Common place are spaces for those who listen to "the cry of the world" and feel compelled to answer it. Far from laboratories where solutions are found or concocted, Glissant's common place is a space of community-building, reflection, and imagination. To create common places in our classrooms would be to center collective work and invite students into Relation, to invite them to understand their identities as "extended through a relationship with the other."[39] Even though these common places "will be of absolutely no use against the concrete oppressions that stun the world," Glissant affirms, "[they] are nevertheless capable of changing the imagination of human communities: it is through the imagination that we will ultimately conquer these derelictions that attack us, just as it already helps us, by shifting our sensibilities, to fight them."[40]

Thus, spaces that center Relation and nurture true collaboration are necessarily transformative spaces. The idea that students working together in groups might generate profound transformation will be odd to those most familiar with the dynamics of high school– or college-level "group work." Traditional group work is outcomes focused. The purpose of the group is to complete an assignment. The assumption is that if all group members add their strengths to the endeavor, the work will get done and will be potentially better for having been carried out collectively. The whole, one hopes, will be greater than the sum of its parts. However, student groups are generally aggregates of individuals uneasily sharing space. Students rarely look forward to group work and rarely have faith that the group product will be superior to what they might have produced as individuals. Rather, they see working in the group as an inconvenience, a class exercise to be gotten over with. The idea that the collective work might be transformative exceeds the expectations of both teachers and students. At best, group work is sold to students (and teachers) as a necessary skill for competing in today's economy. Think here of the emphasis on the high functionality and innovation generally associated with "diverse teams." In contrast to this model, true collaboration sets its sights on transformation. Where group work is additive, true collaboration is transformative. The goal is for each member of the collective to be changed by the experience of working together and for the collective creative work of the group to exceed what any one member could have conceptualized. This is what Glissant means when he alerts us to the potential we have for changing the "imaginary of human communities." Cultivating Relation and creating common places opens the way not only for a change in what we can imagine, but in how we go about imagining as well.

Collective Unlearning as Collective Engagement with/Recognition of Suffering and Oppression

Our education systems are squarely centered on cultivating student resilience on an individual level. Students who have the opportunity to take full advantage of our systems learn to be competitive with themself and others. They learn to handle complex or challenging projects for which, or because of which, they win competitions/grants/fellowships and internships. These "successful" students often receive accolades from professors as well as high grades. The problem, of course, is that some students benefit disproportionately from this system while others struggle unfairly. Students from already marginalized or disadvantaged populations have a much harder time achieving "success" compared with those for whom the system was made and works. In addition to reifying existing inequalities, our education systems, focused as they are exclusively on individual student excellence and resilience, also do a disservice to traditionally advantaged students. I would argue that if our goal is to bring forth "education as a practice of freedom" that supports the furtherance of social and planetary justice, then all of our students need to learn how to live, work, and think (or unthink) together more than they need to learn how to compete and win. As we contemplate the many "Man"-made challenges besieging our world and planet, as we sit with the "tragedy" of our reality, taking up David Scott's invitation, we can become further alienated and apathetic, as well as delusional and disconnected. Becoming ever more isolated and competitive in our thinking and disposition will not prepare us to face the challenges of our day.

Indeed, what we need to cultivate is the capacity to embrace critical and radical unlearning with and among our students and fellow educators. Unlike individual resilience, radical collective unlearning, which centers community, promotes collective resilience. Facing or taking on the impossible within ourselves and in the world around us is psychically disorienting and dispiriting. But together we can find the strength and hope through honest engagement, rigorous exploration, and open dialogue. This work requires a high degree of bravery, a tolerance for discomfort, and a commitment to care that is unusual in our schools and academies. Thus, the role of the educator becomes one of holding space for big and difficult emotions, challenging reorientations, necessary unlearning, and bold new collective visions. No learner need be alone in this terrifying world we inhabit. We need to build hope together.

Calling on us to do brave, collective, and imaginative racial justice work, Christina Sharpe invites us to engage in what she terms "wake work." The wake represents a vigil for the dead, the wake of the slave ship, turbulence in flight, and awakening. In its multiple and varied significances, wake work, which is necessarily painful work, allows us to find new ways of "living in the afterlives of slavery" because we are choosing to confront rather than evade those afterlives. Sharpe posits wake work as "a mode of inhabiting and rupturing" these afterlives "with our known lived and un/imaginable lives." As such, Sharpe insists that by engaging in this work of inhabiting and rupturing, we can "imagine otherwise what we now know in the wake of slavery."[41] Like Olufemi and Giroux, the "otherwise" becomes a central concept for Sharpe, who recognizes its power to move us beyond our present state of knowing/being and toward a new horizon. Learning to think "otherwise" requires us to learn how to unthink and unlearn as well. To withstand the necessarily dislocating and destabilizing effects of unlearning, we need to build brave learning collectives in and beyond our classrooms.

Critical Imagining as an Act of Creation or Invention and as Untethering

In *Teaching to Transgress: Education as the Practice of Freedom*, bell hooks insists that there is a need for passion in the classroom and that opening space where learning and knowledge creation can be ecstatic is essential for the cultivation of what she calls the "critical imagination."[42] For hooks, who draws heavily on Paulo Freire's critical pedagogy, the building of open and engaged communities of learners within and beyond the classroom is foundational. Rather than creating safe spaces for students to experience discomfort without risk, she concentrates on cultivating brave and communally held spaces of respect and engagement where uncomfortable learning can be not only withstood, but also embraced.[43]

The space for imagination in our classrooms, critical or otherwise, is dwindling fast. We need to bring it back. Critical imagining is born in the space opened by Relation and in the brave common places where we face the impossible together. Critical imagining is not critical thinking. It cannot be reduced to analytical reading, writing, or speaking. Critical imagining joins Glissant's call to the imagination with the critical rigor and resilience needed to stay in Sharpe's "wake" and in Jameson's "utopian break." The act of "thinking from there," as Sharpe says, opens the way to the otherwise, availing us ways of "re/seeing, re/inhabiting and re/imagining the world."[44] Concentrating on "the break itself" rather than the utopian horizon constitutes for Jameson a necessary "meditation on the impossible." This mediation is capable of producing "a rattling of the bars and an intense spiritual concentration and preparation for another stage which has not yet arrived."[45]

With our intense emphasis on critical thinking in higher education, we have abandoned the imagination, which we see as belonging to the realm of the arts alone. Students, well trained by us, will rarely conceptualize their musical, poetic, literary, and other creative pursuits as having much in common with their hard-nosed medical studies, sociological analyses, programming languages, or historical explorations. In fields other than the arts, the imagination finds no place and seems an unhelpful distraction. But what if a new imaginary could lead us to do and think our scientific and analytical work differently? What if changing our "imaginary" is the first step to conquering these "derelictions that attack us," as Glissant holds?[46]

Sylvia Wynter certainly thinks so. Drawing on rigorous study across multiple fields, Wynter develops a keen understanding of the human condition. Her work begins with a rigorous interrogation of how and when our present and (scientifically centered, biological, and neo-Darwinist) dominant epistemologies were formed and why and how they no longer serve us. According to Wynter, humans have come to be represented as purely biological organisms in European thought. This mode has "overrepresented" itself, becoming dominant the world over and creating little space for other conceptualizations of the human. Furthermore, this conception of the human and his relationship to non-humans and to our shared planet is fundamentally destructive. Wynter proclaims the need for us to end this mode of the human. In contrast to the dominant epistemology, Wynter recognizes humans as both bios and logos (biological organisms and storytellers) and explores how we create our world (including our biological understanding) through words. Rejecting any form of biological determinism without denying biology, Wynter insists that the time has come for the ushering in of new (and perhaps the revaluing of existing and disparaged) onto-epistemologies. Wynter calls for a profound change in our imaginary, one she believes will help us begin to heal our world. By promoting critical imaging done by students collectively in true collaboration and in the service of justice, the

Impossible Project opens space for new imaginaries, enabling students to learn to think at the limits of the possible, as Wynter and other theorists urge.[47]

The four pillars of the Impossible Project spell the acronym BEND: Build true collaboration, Enact collective unlearning, Nurture critical imagining, and Discover purpose in and through justice work. The fourth pillar of the Impossible Project represents its loftiest aspiration and is meant to be the culmination of the first three. Having built true collaboration, we can create communities brave enough to embrace the hard work of unlearning oppression. Having opened ourselves to unlearning together, we become capable of releasing the critical imagination and engaging in freedom dreaming. Through collective freedom dreaming, we discover and affirm our commitment to making justice work a part of our everyday lives. That which BENDs does not break easily. Our suppleness is our strength.

The Impossible Project: Catalogue

> The Impossible attracts me . . . because everything possible has been done and the world didn't change.
>
> —Interview, *Sun Ra*

> The impossible is the least that one can demand . . .
>
> —James Baldwin, *The Fire Next Time*

The catalogue below illustrates my belief in James Baldwin's and Sun Ra's words. If the possible has been tried and has failed, let's try the impossible because that is "the least one can demand." Each of the projects below have been impossible, yet they have been undertaken and have produced new visions for our collective future. The short descriptions below offer the reader a sense of the scope of each project. All projects have been designed and run over the last five years and have been co-created by faculty and students at the University at Buffalo, SUNY.

Making Computing Anti-Racist (History and Computer Science and Engineering)

A team of faculty from the Departments of History and Computer Science and Engineering collaborated with a cross-disciplinary group of undergraduate student research assistants to create an anti-racist curriculum for an introductory computer science course. Impossible Project: Making Computing Anti-Racist is a two-week module embedded in a larger course. During week 1, students develop an understanding of the racist outcomes caused by algorithmic bias in one of two case studies: criminal justice or health care. The second week of the module is dedicated to "solutions finding," wherein students are asked to build on their critical understanding of the problem of algorithmic bias to come up with ideas for how to put an end to it. In the process, students harness their collective critical imagination to come up with a vision for a world in which computing is anti-racist. This Impossible Project is in its second year.

Ending White Supremacy Online (History and Computer Science and Engineering)

A team of faculty from the Departments of History and Computer Science and Engineering are building an Impossible Project that will span and link their separately delivered classes. The faculty in these different departments will offer courses at the same level and on the same day/time. Students from both classes will come together in cross-disciplinary groups to tackle the problem of white supremacist radicalization online. This project will extend over twelve weeks of the semester and involve rigorous study of the history of white supremacy and modes of resistance to it. Students will also receive fundamental education in machine learning systems. The student groups will harness their critical and cross-disciplinary imaginations to come up with proposals for combating white supremacy online. They will present their ideas to a public audience in Buffalo, where our city has recently been devastated by white supremacist violence. The Center for Information Integrity will sponsor the public finale and fund the continuation of student research on this project through the summer of 2023.

Forging the Afro-Future (History)

Delivered in a first-year history seminar titled "Afro-Futures' Past," Impossible Project: Forge the Afro-Future invited students to explore Afrofuturism in depth while becoming familiar with the work of a local Afrofuturist organization that supports youth development on Buffalo's East Side.[48] Following Tobias c. van Veen, students in this class came to understand that Afrofuturism is "as much a recovery project seeking to resurrect and reinvent the stolen legacies of the past as it is a radical dreaming of an emancipated future."[49] Students were thus challenged to engage with hemispheric Black history and resistance through an Afrofuturism lens and then create educative projects and activities that could be used by the local community organization to support the resurrection and reinvention of stolen legacies and apply these to the act of Freedom Dreaming. This project was developed over twelve weeks. Students presented their Afrofuturist activities to the leaders of the community organization, who offered critical feedback. Our grading rubric for the project was created in consultation with the community educators we were working with.

ENDING INEQUALITY (HISTORY AND MANAGEMENT)

The Impossible Project: Ending Inequality has been offered to master's-level students in the University of Buffalo School of Management for three years. Hailing from no fewer than five countries and attending class in multiple time zones online, students in this project draw on the UN Sustainable Development Goals to frame their work toward "Ending Inequality." Students study the problem of inequality within a specific area of focus in different country contexts, after which they come together to create one presentation that pulls together and synthesizes their ideas to form a perspective that is at once global, national, regional, and local. The class findings are presented to the public in an online forum. This project is delivered over sixteen to twenty weeks.

ACHIEVING LINGUISTIC JUSTICE (HISTORY AND ENGLISH)

Impossible Project: Linguistic Justice is co-created by faculty in the Departments of History and English with the collaboration of the Center for Excellence in Writing. Students in English 105, an introductory course, are invited to build true collaboration in the service of envisioning a world in which language will be truly liberatory for all and no longer a tool of domination. Students become familiar with each other's language stories while they read and learn about the relationship between language and power within the context of colonization. Equipped with a greater personal and sociohistorical understanding of language, students create proposals for linguistic justice in our present and future. This project is delivered across twelve weeks. Students present their work at the Center for Excellence in Writing to a public audience.

CRAFTING UTOPIA (HISTORY AND EDUCATION)

Crafting Utopia is delivered to students in middle school. The project endeavors to create Glissantian "commonplace" in a digital gaming platform called Minecraft. Students are invited into an intentionally modified digital gaming landscape where together they create an ideal world where human and non-human creatures thrive. Both the terraforming of the game and the creation of the curriculum is undertaken through the lens of Caribbean critical theory as well as environmental theory. Our goal is to build Relation among the students and support their capacity to work together to imagine a just, inclusive, and sustainable future. Crafting Utopia is an eight-week course at the end of which students present their work publicly. The last session of this course is held in person, and students are asked to manually build a material portal to their digital world and physically walk through the door to a new reality.

DECOLONIZING ARTS INSTITUTIONS (HISTORY AND ARTS MANAGEMENT)

Impossible Project: Decolonizing Arts Institutions was run as a collaboration between faculty in history and arts management. The project challenged students studying to become museum administrators to confront the colonialist origins and legacies of arts institutions, especially in Europe and the United States. After studying the problematic history of arts institutions, students worked together to propose ways of decolonizing these institutions. What emerged were fundamental reimaginings of what arts institutions could become. This Impossible Project was delivered over two weeks as part of a larger program on decolonization in the arts.

REIMAGINING "BLACKNESS" AND "LATINIDAD" IN K-12 EDUCATION: AFROLATINIDADES (HISTORY)

The project "Reimagining 'Blackness and 'Latinidad'" was developed in a core history class dedicated to the study of modern Latin American history. Students studied major topics in modern Latin American history while also participating in a project that invited them to apply their learning to the reimagining of K-12 curricula for Black History and Hispanic History Month in US public schools. Working directly with two middle-school teachers, students in this course created social studies class activities from an Afro-Latin American and Afro-Latinx perspective. Expanding notions of Blackness common within an African American history–focused Black History Month curriculum and challenging the erasure of Blackness that is frequently a feature of "Hispanic" History Month curricula, students were empowered to reimagine the limits of the possible within K-12 teaching.

Notes

1. Scott, *Conscripts of Modernity: The Tragedy of Colonial Enlightenment* (Durham, NC: Duke University Press, 2004), 8.
2. Scott, *Conscripts of Modernity*, 210.
3. Reinhart Koselleck, *Futures Past: On the Semantics of Historical Time* (New York: Columbia University Press, 2004), 255.
4. Scott, *Conscripts of Modernity*, 44.
5. Robin D. G. Kelley, *Freedom Dreams* (New York: Beacon Press, 2018), 196.
6. Paul Gilroy, "Living Memory: A Meeting with Toni Morrison," in Gilroy, *Small Acts: Thoughts on the Politics of Black Cultures* (London: Serpent's Tail, 1994).
7. Frederic Jameson, *Archaeologies of the Future: The Desire Called Utopia and Other Science Fictions* (London: Verso, 2004), 228.
8. Jameson, *Archaeologies of the Future*, 231.
9. Achille Mbembe, *Necropolitics* (Durham: Duke University Press, 2019).
10. Scott, *Conscripts of Modernity*.
11. Christina Sharpe, *In the Wake: On Blackness and Being* (Durham: Duke University Press, 2016), 18.
12. Edouard Glissant, *Poetics of Relation* (Ann Arbor: University of Michigan Press, 1997).
13. Irvin Hunt, *Dreaming the Present: Time, Aesthetics, and the Black Cooperative Movement* (Chapel Hill: University of North Carolina Press, 2022).
14. Katherine McKittrick, *Sylvia Wynter: On Being Human as Praxis* (Durham: Duke University Press, 2015).
15. Jameson, *Archaeologies of the Future*, 228.
16. Henry Giroux, *On Critical Pedagogy* (London: Bloomsbury Academic, 2020), 8.
17. Giroux, *On Critical Pedagogy*, 197.
18. Craig Steven Wilder, *Ebony and Ivy: Race, Slavery, and the Troubled History of America's Universities* (New York: Bloomsbury Publishing, 2013), 11.
19. Giroux, *On Critical Pedagogy*, 7.
20. Giroux, *On Critical Pedagogy*, 4.
21. Giroux, *On Critical Pedagogy*, 3.

22. Paulo Freire, *Pedagogy of the Oppressed* (New York: Continuum, 2000); bell hooks, *Teaching to Transgress: Education as a Practice of Freedom* (New York: Routledge, 1994).

23. Stefano Harney and David Moten, *The Undercommons: Fugitive Planning and Black Study* (Wivenhoe, UK: Minor Compositions, 2013), 26.

24. Freire, *Pedagogy of the Oppressed*, 64–65.

25. Freire, *Pedagogy of the Oppressed*, 65.

26. Harney and Moten, *The Undercommons*, 28.

27. bell hooks, *Teaching Community: A Pedagogy of Hope* (New York: Routledge, 2003), xv.

28. hooks, *Teaching to Transgress*, 196.

29. Lorgia Garcia Peña, *Community as Rebellion: A Syllabus for Surviving Academia as a Woman of Color* (Chicago: Haymarket Books, 2022), 25.

30. Giroux, *On Critical Pedagogy*, 197.

31. hooks, *Teaching to Transgress*, 12.

32. hooks, *Teaching to Transgress*, 12.

33. https://www.daliamuller.com/impossible-project.

34. These works include but are not limited to Saidiya Hartman, *Lose Our Mother: A Journey Along the Atlantic Slave Route* (New York: Farrar, Straus and Giroux, 2007); Christina Sharpe, *In the Wake: On Blackness and Being* (Durham: Duke University Press, 2016); Zakiyyah Iman Jackson, *Becoming Human: Matter and Meaning in an Anti-Black World* (New York: New York University Press, 2020); Marissa Fuentes, *Dispossessed Lives: Enslaved Women, Violence and the Archive* (Philadelphia: University of Pennsylvania Press, 2016); Michel-Rolph Trouillot, *Silencing the Past: Power and the Production of* History (Boston: Beacon Press, 1995); John Murillo III, *Impossible Stories: On the Space and Time of Black Destructive Creation* (Columbus: Ohio State University Press, 2021); Kara Keeling, *Queer Times, Black Futures* (New York: New York University Press, 2019); Frank B. Wilderson III, *Afropessimism* (New York: Liveright Publishing Company, 2021).

35. Eshun Kodwo, "Further Considerations on Afrofuturism," *CR: The New Centennial Review* 3, no. 2 (summer 2003): 301.

36. Achille Mbembe, *Necropolitics* (Durham: Duke University Press, 2019), 163.

37. Hartman, *Lose Our Mother*, 6.

38. Glissant, *Poetics of Relation* (Ann Arbor, MI: Michigan University Press, 1997), 9.

39. Glissant, *Poetics of Relation*, 11.

40. Edouard Glissant, *Treatise on the Whole World* (Liverpool: Liverpool University Press, 2020), 9.

41. Christina Sharpe, *In the Wake*, 18.

42. hooks, *Teaching to Transgress*, 195.

43. hooks, *Teaching to Transgress*, 40.

44. Sharpe, *In the Wake*, 22.

45. Jameson, *Archaeologies of the Future*, 232–33.
46. Glissant, *Treatise on the Whole World*, 9.
47. McKittrick, *Sylvia Wynter*, 9–89.
48. The Galactic Tribe, https://www.thegalactictribe.org/our-team.
49. Tobias c. van. Veen, "Black Star Lines: Ontopolitics of Exodus, Afrofuturist Hip-Hop, and the RZA-rrection of Bobby Digital," in *Boogiedown Predictions: Hip-Hop, Time and Afrofuturism*, ed. Roy Christopher (London: Strange Attractor Press, 2022), 290.

Contributors

Anita Butera is an assistant professor in the Department of Criminal Justice, Sociology, and Environmental Studies at Canisius College. She earned a JD from the University at Buffalo and a PhD in sociology from American University. In addition to her substantial legal work, Butera has published peer-reviewed articles in numerous journals, including *American Studies, Proteus, Buffalo Human Rights Review*, and the *Consumer Bankruptcy Journal*.

Francis J. Butler earned his BA in history from Siena College and his MEd from the University of Notre Dame. He teaches eighth-grade students US history in Connecticut and has a deep passion for a wide range of historical topics, especially Reconstruction. Currently he is pursuing an MA in American history through the Gilder Lehrman Institute of American History's MA Program at Gettysburg College.

Katelyn M. Campbell is an independent scholar whose work centers the role of land and property relationships in 1970s feminisms through the lenses of gender and sovereignty. She earned her PhD in American studies with distinction from the University of North Carolina at Chapel Hill in 2023. Campbell's research has been supported by the Margaret Storrs Grierson Fellowship from Smith College Special Collections, the Harry S. Truman Scholarship, and the Critical Ethnic Studies Collective at UNC-Chapel Hill. She currently lives and works on the traditional lands of the Cherokee and Shawnee in southern West Virginia.

Jennifer Hull Dorsey is a professor of history and the founding director of Siena College's McCormick Center for the Study of the American Revolution. She is a specialist on labor, race, and religion in the early American republic.

She is the author of *Hirelings: African American Workers and Free Labor in Early Maryland* (Cornell University Press, 2011) and co-editor with Spencer W. McBride, PhD, of *New York's Burned-over District: A Documentary History* (Cornell University Press, 2023). She was also the project director for two National Endowment for the Humanities–funded Landmarks of American History and Culture Workshops for School Teachers on the history of the Burned-over District (2013 and 2016).

Secil E. Ertorer is an associate professor in the Department of Sociology, Sociology, Criminal Justice, and Environmental Studies at Canisius College, Buffalo, New York. She received her PhD in sociology, specializing in migration and ethnic relations, from the University of Western Ontario, Canada. She has fifteen years of experience teaching sociology and honors courses in Canadian and American higher education. Dr. Ertorer's research interests are in the areas of racial/ethnic relations, international migration, refugee studies, integration, and identity. She has conducted fieldwork in England, Canada, the United States, and Turkey interviewing Kurdish, Karen, Burmese, and Syrian refugees and representatives of humanitarian agencies. She has published on asylum seeking, resettlement, and integration experiences of refugees and economic immigrants and the effects of these processes on identity. Her current research project examines AAPI racism in the United States during the COVID-19 pandemic. She is working on a book project on xenophobia based on this research.

Dalia Antonia Caraballo Muller is an associate professor of Latin American and Caribbean history at the University at Buffalo and the founder of the Impossible Project. Dr. Caraballo Muller dedicates herself to the twin (and intertwined) passions of historical research in her field and educational program development for social and planetary good. The through line that connects her historical work with her work in education is the concept of "impossibility." She is currently researching African and Afro-descended intellectuals in early twentieth-century Cuba who thought at the limits of the possible as they staked claims to rights, dignity, and equality in a world that denied their full humanity. In the classroom, Dr. Caraballo Muller invites her students to stretch their minds and think at the limits of the possible to dream up new futures for our ailing world and planet. Muller is the author of *Cuban Émigrés and Independence in the Nineteenth-Century Gulf World* (University of North Carolina Press, 2017) and a fellow of the SUNY Hispanic Leadership Institute.

Contributors | 253

Alix L. Olson is an assistant professor of women's, gender, and sexuality studies at Emory University, Oxford College (Atlanta, Georgia). She is an associate editor of the journal *New Political Science*. Her forthcoming books are *The End(s) of Resistance: Making and Unmaking Democracy* (Columbia University Press); the edited volume *Art, Activism and Contemporary Political Theory* (State University of New York Press); and *Feminist Redemption, Neoliberal Apocalypse* (Bloomsbury Publishing). Olson's scholarly essays have appeared in numerous edited collections and journals including *Contemporary Political Theory*, *New Political Science*, and *Wagadu*. Olson is also a widely published spoken word artist and the editor of *Word Warriors: 35 Women Leaders in the Spoken Word Revolution* (Seal Press, 2007).

Alexandra Leah Prince is a historian of American religions and an assistant professor of religion in the Religious Studies Department at Skidmore College. Their teaching and research focuses on the cultural history of minority American and Indigenous religions and the social study of insanity from a mad studies perspective. Currently they are completing their first book project, which explores how bio-psychiatric interpretations of religion came to dominate popular understandings of new religious movements over the long nineteenth century.

Richard Reitsma's research and teaching focus on gender, sexuality, race, and (im)migration. Dr. Reitsma teaches Spanish, Latin American studies, and honors at Canisius College and has taught graduate courses at Universidad IberoAmericana Puebla and the American Studies Center at the University of Warsaw. Dr. Reitsma directs study abroad programs in Cuba and Mexico. Current projects include an examination of Buffalo industry and slavery in Cuba and another on LGBTQIA+ issues in Cuba. He is the founding director of the Borders & Migrations Initiative and the Latinx and LGBTQ Speakers Series. Dr. Reitsma was recently appointed faculty associate dean of inclusion and engagement.

Marla Segol is a professor and the director of undergraduate studies in the Department of Global Gender and Sexuality Studies at the University at Buffalo. She earned her PhD in comparative literature at Rutgers University New Brunswick in 2001, with a dissertation on religious conversion and cosmopolitanism. Since then she has worked in the fields of Kabbalah, Jewish magic, modern esotericism, queer theory, and the history of the body and sexuality. Her most recent book, *Kabbalah and Sex Magic: A Mythical-Ritual*

Genealogy, discusses the history of the components that make up contemporary sex magic ritual as they appear in Jewish esoteric texts. Other books include *Word and Image in Medieval Kabbalah: The Texts, Commentaries and Diagrams of the "Sefer Yetsirah"* (Palgrave, 2012); *Sexuality, Sociality, and Cosmology in Medieval Literary Texts* (co-edited with Jennifer Brown, Palgrave, 2013); and *Religious Conversion in Medieval Romance* (Lambert, 2011). Recent awards include the Humanities Institute Fellowship and two research grants from the Gender Institute at the University at Buffalo. Professor Segol has published articles on magic and astrology, American Kabbalah, contemporary self-help literature, medicine and mysticism, and medieval cosmopolitanism. Her upcoming projects include applications of weird, queer, and trans theory in the study of medieval and early modern Kabbalah, magic, and esoteric literature.

Dan Shanahan is an assistant professor of entrepreneurship at Daemen University, where he recently helped launch the Leadership and Entrepreneurship in the Arts program. Mr. Shanahan is co-founder and executive artistic director of Torn Space Theater (2000), a company specializing in contemporary and site-based performance. He has directed more than forty works for both the stage and nontraditional performance spaces and has written or co-written more than fifteen original productions. He is currently focused on how cultural initiatives are supportive of neighborhood revitalization. The *Atlantic* referred to his work "as a powerful example of the artist's role in reactivating and imagining new public spaces." His work has been written about nationally in *PAJ: A Journal of Performance and Art* and *Chance* magazine, and his site-based work with Torn Space represented the United States at the Prague Quadrennial in 2019 and in the internationally curated exhibition "Acts of Assembly" as part of the Prague Quadrennial 2023.

Victoria W. Wolcott is a professor of history and the director of the Gender Institute at the University at Buffalo, State University of New York. She has published three books: *Remaking Respectability: African American Women in Interwar Detroit* (University of North Carolina Press, 2001); *Race, Riots, and Roller Coasters: The Struggle Over Segregated Recreation in America* (University of Pennsylvania Press, 2012); and *Living in the Future: Utopianism and the Long Civic Rights Movement* (University of Chicago Press, 2022). In addition, she has published articles in the *Journal of American History, Journal of African American History, Radical History Review,* and *Journal of Women's History* among others. She is currently working on a microhistory of a radical Black pacifist titled *The Embodied Resistance of Eroseanna Robinson: Athleticism and Activism in the Cold War Era*. Wolcott has also published pieces for popular audiences in the *Washington Post*, *New York Daily News*, and *The Conversation*, among others.

Alex Zamalin is the director of the African American Studies Program and an associate professor of political science at the University of Detroit Mercy. He is the author of numerous books, including *Against Civility: The Hidden Racism in Our Obsession with Civility* (Beacon Press, 2021), *Black Utopia: The History of an Idea from Black Nationalism to Afrofuturism* (Columbia University Press, 2019), *Antiracism: An Introduction* (New York University Press, 2017), *Struggle on Their Minds: The Political Thought of African American Resistance* (Columbia University Press, 2017), and *African American Political Thought and American Culture: The Nation's Struggle for Racial Justice* (Springer, 2015). In addition, he is the co-editor of *American Political Thought: An Alternative View* (Routledge, 2017). Zamalin's essays and reviews have appeared in various edited book collections and in peer-reviewed journals such as *New Political Science*, *Contemporary Political Theory*, *Political Theory*, and *Women's Studies Quarterly*.

Index

"Accusation of Human Rights Violations by Rev. James Warren Jones Against Our Children and Relatives at the Peoples Temple Jungle Encampment in Guyana, South America," 167
Acorn. See *Parable of the Sower* (Butler)
action, IPP, 219–20
Afrodiasporans, 232, 234, 239
Afrofuturism, 238–39, 245–46
After Utopia (Shklar), 4
Ahmed, Sara, 70
Alabama Sharecroppers Union (ASU), 53
Alabaster. See *Fifth Season, The* (Jemisin)
Allende, Salvador, 159
Allison, Dorothy, 76–77
Always Something Farm, 111
AME Zion Church, 19
"America Is Having a Moral Convulsion" (Brooks), 100–101, 115
American Anti-Slavery Society, 19
American Colonization Society, 19
American Grain Elevator, 107
American Malting Corporation, 107
American Missionary Association, 23, 34n42

American political thought. See political thought, utopia in
American Warehouse, 107, 113
Amos, Martin, 154
Amos, Sharon, 154
Annares. See *Dispossessed: An Ambiguous Utopia, The* (Le Guin)
apocalyptism, 158–60
archaeological impulse, 70
Arendt, Hannah, 109
Artaud, Antonin, 110–11
Ascent of Woman, The (Borgese), 131
Asian Americans, 95
Atkinson, Ti-Grace, 77–78
Atlanta Compromise Speech, 44–45
August 7th Survival Community, 77–79

Banks, Charles, 45
Baraka, Amiri, 56
Barker, Ella, 48
Baudrillard, Jean, 114
Beck, Donald, 149, 154–55
Becoming Utopian (Moylan), 5
Bell, Daniel, 4
Bellamy, Edward, 2
BEND. See Impossible Project: pillars of
Benjamin, Walter, 232
Berlant, Lauren, 135
Biden, Joe, 105

Big Mama Rag, 72, 73, 75
Black expectations. *See* interracial utopia, expectations for
Black feminism, 70
Black hearted, phrase, 15–17
Black No More (Schuyler), 124–25
Black Owenites, 44–46, 48, 52, 54–55
Black Power (Wright), 123–24
Black utopian thought, 122–30
  couching Afro-utopianism within Afro-pessimism, 128–30
  decentering meaning of freedom, 123–24
  envisioning horizon for radical transformation, 125–26
  fantasy of purity, 124–25
  hyper-empathy, 127
  transformative utopia in emancipatory action, 126–28
  uprising against white supremacy, 122–23
Blake (Delany), 122–23
Blake, Henry. See *Blake* (Delany)
Bloch, Ernst, 135–36
Bloss, William C., 17, 21
blueprint utopia, 2, 4–5
Boggs, Carl, 3
boxers, performance, 113–15
Boyd, Blanch, 71
Boyer, Jean Pierre, 41
Brave New World (Huxey), 3
Breines, Wini, 3
Broken Earth, series (Jemisin), 128–30
Brooks, David, 100–101, 115
Brooks, Owen, 54
Brookwood Labor College, 48
Brown v. Board of Education, 53
Brown, John, 16, 46
Brown, Rita Mae, 67, 71, 72
Browning, Don S., 146
Buckley, Chris, 154

Buffalo Cooperative Economic Society, 49, 54
Buffalo Food Equity Network and Cooperation, 38
Bunch, Charlotte, 72, 77
Burbridge, Stephen G., 24
Burma, refugees from, 92–93
Burroughs, Nannie Helen, 49
Butler, Francis J., 5
Butler, Octavia, 5, 126–28, 130

Califia Community, 80–82
Campbell, Katelyn M., 6
Canada
  immigrants in, 94–95
  refugees in, 92–93
Carnegie, Andrew, 45
catalogue, Impossible Project, 244–50
Cell 16, group, 72
Chambers-Letson, Joshua, 137
Chesler, Phyllis, 72
Chickasaw Indians, 40
childhood, defining, 145–46
children, Peoples Temple, 143–46
  apocalypticism and, 158–60
  forming rainbow family, 146–49
  investigations, 162–63
  Noah's Ark comparison, 149–54
  teen education, 160–62
  "Unfinished Child, The," 158
  upholding welfare, 155–58
Christian perfection, 18–19
Civil War, 23, 43
Cohen, Judy, 71
collective unlearning, 241–42
Collins, John, 22
"Comet, The" (DuBois), 125–26
community of learning, classroom as, 221–24
Community Organizing Project, 55
Concerned Relatives, 164–67. *See also* Peoples Temple

concientización, pedagogy, 8, 206–7, 212
conditional refugees, 94
Congress of African Peoples (CAP), 56
Congress of Industrial Organizations (CIO), 48
Congressional Confiscation Acts, 34n38
Conscripts of Modernity (Scott), 231
context, IPP, 218–19
Convention of the Colored Inhabitants of the State of New York, 20
Cooperation Jackson, 55
cooperation, defining, 47
cooperative commonwealth, building, 47–52
Cooperative Industries, 49
Cooperative League of the USA, 49
cooperatives (Black)
  commonwealth and, 47–52
  decline and renewal, 53–57
  Mound Bayou as symbol, 44–46
  Owenite dreams, 38–44
  post-shooting mobilization, 37–38
  rural Owenites, 52–53
Cordell, Cindy, 161
Cordell, Julie, 155
Cordell, Mark, 152–54
Cordovero, Moshe, 185–91
Corwin, Lynn, 71
counter-sites, 101
COVID-19, 56, 95, 208
cow, performance, 111
Crafting Utopia, Impossible Project, 247
Crandall, Prudence, 17
Crapo, Henry J., 21, 22
creation, critical imagining as act of, 242–44
creative placemaking, supporting public ritual through, 104–8
critical imagining, 242–44

critical thinking, 235–36, 239, 242–43
Crowin, Jan, 71
cruel optimism, 128–30
Cruising Utopia, 137
Cruising Utopia: The Then and There of Queer Futurity (Muñoz), 135
Cuban Revolution, 159

Daly, Mary, 71, 72, 79
Das Kapital (Marx), 159
Das Orgien Mysterien Theater (The Orgiastic Mystery Theater), 110–11
Davis Bend, plantation, 42–44, 46, 47
Davis, Jefferson, 39
Davis, Joseph, 4, 39, 41, 47
Davis, Joshua Clark, 56
Davis, Laurence, 5
Declaration of Independence, 25
Decolonizing Arts Institutions, Impossible Project, 247
Delaney, Samuel, 136–37
Delany, Martin, 122–23
Delta Cooperative, 53
Democracy in America (Tocqueville), 101
Democratic Socialists of America, 56
Department of Housing and Urban Development, US, 55
devekhut, 188, 191
Dietrich, Mary Lou, 83
Disciples of Christ, 146
Dispossessed: An Ambiguous Utopia, The (Le Guin), 131–32
Dorsey, Jennier Hull, 5
Douglass, Frederick, 16, 17, 22, 35n47, 45
DuBois, W. E. B., 45, 47–48, 125–26
Dusk to Dawn (DuBois), 48
Dwyer, Richard A., 165
dystopia, teaching
  classroom as community of learning, 221–24

cultural shock, 221
diversity, 218
Ignatius Pedagogical Paradigm, 216–20
land of opportunities narrative, 217–18
legal cases defining race, 224–29
national identity, 215018
personal identities, 215–16
teaching immigration and diversity, 220
use of personal stories, 220–21

Earthseed. See *Parable of the Sower* (Butler)
Echols, Alice, 72
"Economic Cooperation Among Negro Americans," study, 47–48
Eddy, Sherwood, 53
Edelman, Lee, 134
education
 conventional understanding of, 217
 pedagogy of hope, 201–13
 teaching dystopia, 215–30
 ultimate purpose of, 217
education system, Impossible Project and, 234–37
Electric Light and Oil, 112
Emancipation Proclamation, 24, 34
Emergency Skin (Jemison), 1
Emmons, Marty, 161
End of Ideology, The (Bell), 4
Ending Inequality, Impossible Project, 246
Ending White Supremacy Online, Impossible Project, 245
Ends and Means: An Inquiry Into the Nature of Ideals (Huxley), 3
Engels, Friedrich, 2
Erie Canal, 18
erotic love and desire, 177
Ertorer, Secil E., 6

Eshun, Kodwo, 239
Essun. See *Fifth Season, The* (Jemisin)
evaluation, IPP, 219–20
experience, IPP, 219–20
Experiments in Imagining Otherwise (Olufemi), 234

Faggin, Lucy, 21
Farm Security Administration (FSA), 53–54
Father Divine, 50–52, 144
Feeling Backward (Love), 68–69
Female Man, The (Russ), 131
feminism
 building and breaking Sagaris, 74–79
 portals, 69–71
 Sagaris and, 67–69
 two rivers converging at Sagaris, 71–74
Feminist utopian thought, 130–34
 indeterminate future and, 131
 inspecting power relations, 133–34
 reclaiming temporal/spatial landscapes, 130–31
 subverting utopia-as-dynamic, 131–33
Fifteenth Amendment (US Constitution), 16, 26, 29, 226
Fifth Season, The (Jemisin), 128–30
Firestone, Shulamith, 70
Flynn, Elizabeth Gurley, 159
Forge the Afro-Future, Impossible Project, 245–46
Foucault, Michel, 101–4
Fourier, Charles, 39
Fowler, Linda, 73, 76
Freedom Dream (Kelley), 232
freedom dreams, 38
Freedom Farm Cooperative, 54–55, 69
Freehill-May, Lynn, 106
Freeman, Elizabeth, 68
Freire, Paulo, 242

Furies, 72

Gadwa, Anne, 105
Garrison, William Lloyd, 22–23
Genesis, narrative, 176–80, 184, 191
Genius of Universal Emancipation, 41
Gerushin (exile, divorce), 175, 180, 185, 191–92
Gilman, Charlotte Perkins, 124
Giroux, Henry, 235–38, 242
Glissant, Edouard, 233, 239–43, 247
Goddard College, 73
Gradual Emancipation Act, 17
grain elevators, 107–8, 110
Grant, Ulysses S., 43
Great Depression, 48, 51
Great Refusal, The (Breines), 3
Green, Beriah, 17
grounded utopia, 5
Gumbs, Alexis Pauline, 69–71

Halberstam, Judith, 134
Hamer, Fannie Lou, 54
Hamlin, Hannibal, 23, 33n32
Harney, Stefano, 134, 235–26
Harper, Frances Ellen Watkins, 43
Hess, George, 17
heterotopia, ritual and performance in, 102–4
high impact learning (HIL), 206
Highlander Institute, 81–82
Hill, Joe, 159
Hood, Aurellius P., 45–46
hooks, bell, 217, 242
Hope, John, II, 50
hope, pedagogy of, 201–13
horizon (utopian), collapse of, 231–34
Houston, Houston Do You Read (Tiptree), 131
Human Rights Campaign, 135
Human Rights Commission, Indianapolis, 149

Hunt, Irvin, 233
Hutchinson, Sikivu, 144
Huxley, Aldous, 3
hyper-empathy, 127

Ignatius Pedagogical Paradigm (IPP), 216–20
impossibility, 137–38
Impossibility Now! (Spade), 137
Impossible Project
   Afrofuturism and, 238–39
   background for, 231–38
   call to action, 237–38
   catalogue, 244–50
   collapse of utopian horizon, 231–34
   collective unlearning, 241–42
   critical imagining, 242–44
   education systems and, 234–37
   pillars of, 239–44
   roots in African Diaspora, 238–39
   true collaboration, 239–41
In Small Dreams, 161
Indianapolis Recorder, The, 147–48
Indianapolis Star, 163
Institute for Policy Studies, 82
International Assemblies of God, 146
International Refugee Convention, 90
interracial utopia, expectations for, 15–17
Island (Huxley), 3

James, Thomas, 5–6, 15–17
   abbreviated account of life in slavery, 17–18
   attending National Convention of Colored Men, 27–30
   as beneficiary/agent of Christian evangelism, 19
   during Civil War, 23
   desegregating Eastern Massachusetts railroad lines, 22–23
   direction-action campaigns of, 21–23

James, Thomas *(continued)*
 finding like-minded allies, 21–22
 recalling July 4, 1865, ceremony, 24–25
 securing freedom for Lucy Faggin, 21–22
 settling in Rochester, 18–19
 as target of assault, 24
 white allies of, 25–26
 witnessing abolitionist movement development, 19–21
Jameson, Frederic, 130, 134, 232–34
Jemison, N. K., 1, 128–30
Jim Crow, challenging, 146–49
Joan, Jackie St., 75
Joint Special Committee, 23
Jones, James Warren, Jr., 147–49
Jones, Jim, 143–44, 146, 150–52, 156–57, 163, 167
Jones, Lew Eric (Eun Ok Kyung), 147
Jones, Marceline, 146–49, 157–58, 158
Jones, Stephan, 154
Jones, Stephanie (Kun Eun Soon), 147
Jones, Suzanne (Pac Chi Oak), 147
Jonestown, Guyana, Peoples Temple, 163–67
Justice for Migrant Families (JFMF), 207–8

kabbalistic sex magic. *See* sex magic, kabbalistic
Karenga, Maulana, 56
Kelley, Robin D. G., 232, 238
Kelly, Kevin, 99
Kelly, Thomas, 26
Kilgore, Kathryn, 71
Kimball, Asa, 17
King Alfred Plan, 159
Kino Border Initiative (KBI), 207–8
Kinsolving, Lester, 162

Knight, Joel, 22
Kohl, Laura Johnston, 164, 166
Kolkhozy, 54
Koselleck, Reinhart, 231–32

Lambrev, Garrett, 152
land of opportunities, narrative, 217–18
Le Guin, Ursula, 130–34
legal cases, defining race, 224–229
Leon, Moshe de, 177
Lesbian Tide, The, 73
Levitas, Ruth, 4
Lewis, John, 55
Liberator, The, traveler's directory in, 23
Liberty Party, 21
Life of Rev. Thomas James, by Himself (James), 16
Life of Thomas James, by Himself, 30
Linguistic Justice, Impossible Project, 246
Living Word, The, magazine
 "Brotherhood is Our Religion," 151
 "God's Prophet Ran to Me," 152–54
Looking Backward (Bellamy), 2
Lost Cause, 30
Love, Heather, 68–69
Loyola, Ignatius de, 216
Lucas, Sandy, 71
Ludlam, Henry, 21–22
Lumumba, Chokwe, 55

Maaga, Mary McCormick, 144
machines, performance, 112
Making Computing Anti-Racist, Impossible Project, 244–45
Marginal Bodies, Trans Utopias (Nirta), 137–38
Markusen, Ann, 105
Marquis de Lafayette, 41–42
Marx, Karl, 2
Massachusetts Constitution, 23

Mattapoisett. See *Woman on the Edge of Time* (Piercy)
Mbembe, Achille, 233
McAllister, Ada, 71
McClellan, George B., 27
McKissick, Floyd B., 55–56
Meola, Melissa, 102
Mertle, Deanna, 163
Mertle, Elmer, 163
Mertle, Linda, 163
migration
   Canadian immigrants, 94–95
   COVID-19 and, 95
   dystopia and, 90, 93, 96
   motivating, 89–90
   refugees and, 90–96
migration, teaching narratives of, 201–2
   Canisius College Borders & Migrations Initiative, 210
   concientización pedagogy, 206
   exposing students to narratives, 206–8
   geochaching project, 209
   interviewing immigrants, 209
   partnering with KBI, 208–10
   pedagogical approach, 205–6
   personal story, 202–5
   reflections, 210–13
millenarianism, 18–19
Miller-McLemore, Bonnie J., 146
Miller, Christine, 168–69
Mississippi Association of Cooperatives, 55
Mississippi Constitutional Convention, 45
Mississippi Freedom Labor Union (MFLU), 54
Montgomery, Ben, 43–44
Montgomery, Isaiah, 47
Moore, Annie, 168
Moore, Jimmy, 154

Moore, Rebecca, 144
Moore, Thomas, 2, 89, 99, 122
Morris, Thomas D., 32n25
Morrison, Toni, 232
Moten, Fred, 235–36, 238
Mound Bayou, 44–46, 47
Moylan, Tom, 5
Ms. Magazine, 74, 80
multicultural and welcoming, phrase, 95–96
Muñoz, Esteban, 69
Muñoz, Jose, 135–37
Murphy, Marilyn, 75–76, 80–81
Muste, A. J., 3
"My Own Utopia" (Borgese), 131
Myers, Jane, 71
Myers, Samuel Lloyd, 37–38, 47, 50

Nashoba, plantation, 40
National Black Feminist Organization, 80
National Convention of Colored Men, 27–3
National Endowment for the Arts (NEA), 105
national identity, 215–18
National Liberty Party, 21
Natural High Express, The, 161
Naturalization Act (1790), 222
Nazi Germany, 54, 121
negative affect, 134
Negro Convention, 34n46
Negro Cooperative Guild, 48
Nell, William C., 22
Nelson, E. E., 49
neoliberal pedagogy, 235
New Bedford AME Zion Church, 21
New Deal Programs, 54
New Harmony Gazette, 40
New Harmony, community, 39–41
New Left, 3–4
New Thought, 50

New West, magazine, 163
New York State Anti-Slavery Society, 20
New York State Constitution, 20, 46
New York State Convention of Colored Citizens, 20
New York Times, 52, 79
New Yorker, 70
Nirta, Catarina, 137–38
Nitsch, Hermann, 110–11
Noah's Ark, comparisons to, 149–54
"Non-Euclidean View of California as a Cold Place to Be, A" (Le Guin), 131
North Bolivar County Farm Cooperative, 54
Northampton Association of Education and Industry, 46
Norwood, Jynona M., 151, 167
Nyerere, Julius K., 56
Nyong'o, Tavia, 137

Olamina, Lauren. See *Parable of the Sower* (Butler)
Olson, Alix, 7
Olufemi, Lola, 234–35, 242
Opportunity II, 160–62
oppression, recognition of, 241–42
Or Ne'erav (A Pleasant Light), 186–89
Or Yaqar (Precious Light), 185, 191
Owen, Robert Dale, 2, 6, 37–38, 40–41
  applying ideas of, 38–44
  cooperative commonwealth and, 47–52
  reflecting leadership style of, 44–46
  resurgence of vision of, 56–57
Owenism
  application of ideas, 38–44
  Mound Bayou and, 44–46

Palmer, John M., 24–25
paperson, la, 237–38
Parable of the Sower (Butler), 5, 126–28
Pardes Rimonim (Cordovero), 192
Paris Review, The, 129–30
Parkot, Michael, 111
Passumpsic River. See Sagaris
Peace Mission, 50
Peace Mission Movement, 144
pedagogy, defining, 236
Pellegrini, Ann, 137
Peoples Temple, 143–46
  apocalyptism and, 158–60
  children in, 143–46
  comparing to Noah's Ark, 149–54
  investigations into, 162–63
  Jonestown, Guyana, settlement, 163–67
  magazine of, 151–54
  November 18, 1978, events, 167–69
  Opportunity II, 160–62
  rainbow family modeling, 146–49
  "Unfinished Child, The," 158
  upholding welfare in, 155–58
Perot Malt House, 108
personal identity, 215–16
Peters, Joan, 71, 72, 77
Phillips, Wendall, 22
Pickering, Carolyn, 163
Piss Christ, 105
Pittsburgh Courier, 48
"Plan for the Gradual Abolition of Slavery in the United States without Danger of Loss to the Citizens of the South," 40
Plato, 89
Poetics of Relation (Glissant), 239
political thought, utopia in
  Black utopia, 122–30
  counter-fairy tales, 138–39
  feminist utopia, 130–134
  queer/trans utopia, 134–38
  skepticism, 121–22

portals, 69–71
Prince, Alexandra Leah, 7–8
Promised Land, 51–52, 54
protopia, 99–100
Providence Cooperative Farms, 53–54
public place (as real place), 100–102
public ritual, 6–7
　people in space, 108–15
　protopia and, 99–100
　real place, 100–102
　ritual and performance in heterotopia, 102–4
　supporting through creative placemaking, 104–8

Queer Phenomenology (Ahmed), 70
queer/trans utopian thought, 134–38
　critiquing time, 135–36
　cross-class intimacy, 136–37
　embracing negativity, 137
　great refusal, 135–36
　impossibility, 137–38
　negative affect, 134
Quest, 82–83

Ra, Sun, 125–26
race, legal cases defining, 224–29
Radical Abolition Party, 21
Radical Abolitionist Party, 27
Radicalesbians, 72
railroad lines, desegregating, 22–23
rainbow family, forming, 146–49
Ramos, Connie. See *Woman on the Edge of Time* (Piercy)
Randolph, P. B., 27–28
Raviv, Zohar, 192
Raymond, Janice, 71
real place, public place as, 100–102
Reconstruction, 6, 29, 35n47, 45
Reddix, Jacob L., 49
Redwood Valley. See Peoples Temple
reflection, IPP, 219–20

Refugee Convention (1951), 93
refugees
　from Burma, 92–93
　defined, 90
　from Syria, 93–94
　Turkey and, 90–91
　from Ukraine, 94
refusal, true collaboration as act of, 239–41
Regional Economic Development Strategic Plan, 106
"Reimagining 'Blackness and 'Latinidad,'" Impossible Project, 247–48
Reitsma, Richard, 8
Relation, cultivating, 239–41
"Remembrances of Temple Kindergarteners," article, 154
Republic (Plato), 89
Republic of New Afrika, 55
Rhodes, Odell, 167–69
Richardson, James, 41
Ridgley, Susan, 151
Rochdale Society of Equitable Pioneers, 47
Rock, John S., 28
Roe v. Wade, 68
Roller, Edith, 155, 157, 159–60
Roosevelt, Theodore, 39
Rosenwald, Julius, 45
Ruggles, David, 22, 46
rural cooperative, 48, 51–52
Rush, Christopher, 19
Ryan, Leo, 166

Sagaris, 6, 67–68, 71–80
　August 7th Survival Community and, 77–79
　building and breaking, 74–79
　Califia and, 80–82
　coverage of, 75
　Dorothy Allison time at, 76–77

Sagaris *(continued)*
  funding, 73–74
  learning at, 75
  leaving, 79–83
  listening back to, 83–84
  Marilyn Murphy journey to, 75–77
  organizers of, 72
  overview of, 67–69
  participants at, 74–76
  portals and, 69–71
  Redstockings report and, 74
  Sagaris II, 80
  sessions of, 77–78
  and structure of university as locus for learning, 72–73
  two rivers converging at, 71–74
  years leading up to, 72
Saint-Simon, Henri de, 39
San Francisco Examiner, 162–63
Sargent, Lyman Tower, 38
Schlesinger, Arthur, Jr., 4
Schulman, Alix Kate, 78
Schuyler, George, 48, 124–25
Scott, David, 231–33
Sefer Gerushin (Book of Exiles), 191
Sefer ha Zohar (Book of Splendor), 175
sefirot, 175–78, 181–83, 186–90, 193
Segol, Marla, 8
Serrano, Andres, 105
Seward, William H., 23, 33n32
sex magic, kabbalistic
  expanding on ritual structures, 185–91
  feelings, 177
  interlinked rituals, 175–76
  myth operationalization, 176–77
  spiritual pregnancy, 191–94
  Zohar as beginning kabbalah, 177–84
"Sex, Socialism, and Child Torture with Rev. Jim Jones," 163

Shaker Villages, 19
Shanahan, Daniel, 6–7
Sharpe, Christina, 233, 239, 242, 243
Shekhinah, 175, 178, 180–86. See also *Zohar* (Leon)
Shema (the Jewish declaration of faith), 186–89, 197n45
Sherman, Susan, 78
Shevek. See *Dispossessed: An Ambiguous Utopia, The* (Le Guin)
Shiur Qomah, 189–90, 197n49
Shklar, Judith N., 4, 122
Shulman, Alix Kates, 83
Silo City, 7, 103–9, 112–14
Sisterhood is Powerful, 73
Six-Day Siege. See Peoples Temple: Jonestown, Guyana, settlement
"'68, or Something" (Berlant), 135
skepticism, 121–22
Smith, Gerrit, 16, 20, 46
Smith, James McCune, 16
Smith, Rick, 106–7, 108
social dreaming, 1, 6, 8–9, 38, 130
social unionism, 48, 56
Song of Songs. See *Zohar* (Leon): theorizing sex magic in
Southern Tenant Farmers Union (STFU), 53–54
Soviet Revolution, 159
Soviet Union, 4, 54
space, people in, 108–11
  boxer performance, 113–15
  cow performance, 111
  machine performance sequence, 112
Spade, Dean, 137
spiritual pregnancy (*ibbur*), 191–94
Stauffer, John, 16
Steinem, Gloria, 67–68, 72, 74
Stevens, Thaddeus, 23
Stewart, Alvan, 17
Stillness. See *Fifth Season, The* (Jemisin)

Index | 267

Stimpson, Catharine, 72
Stoen, Grace, 164
Stoen, Timothy, 164
Streiker, Lowell D., 144
Strongman, SaraEllen, 70
structures, expanding on, 185–91
Stryker, Susan, 194
suffering, recognition of, 241–42
Swaney, Stephanie, 154
Swinney, Daren Werner, 154
Syria, refugees from, 93–94

Taylor, James Lance, 144
Taylor, Jesse, 49
Teaching to Transgress: Education as the Practice of Freedom (hooks), 242
Tefillah Le Moshe (Prayer of Moses), 189–91
The Feminists, group, 72
Theatre of Cruelty, 110
Thirteenth Amendment (US Constitution), 27, 32n38
Thomas, Willie, 161
Tiferet, 175, 178, 180–81, 186. See also *Zohar* (Leon)
Time magazine, 144
time, critiquing, 135–36
Tocqueville, Alexis de, 101
Torah, 180, 183, 188, 191, 193
Torn Space Theater
    activating potential, 107
    creative placemaking, 104–8
    economics and, 104–5
    funding, 105–6
    grain elevators of, 107–8
    inrastrcutres of, 106–7
    people in space, 108–15
    protopia, 99–100
    as real place, 100–102
    ritual and performance in heterotopia, 102–4
total physical response (TPR), 206

Tougaloo, Mississippi, 69
tragic time, 231–34
trans theory, 177
Trans-sexual Empire, The (Raymond), 71
Trash (Allison), 76
"Trouble with Owning a Grain Elevator, The," 106
true collaboration, 239–41
Truth, Sojourner, 46
Turkey, refugees from, 90–91
"Two Rivers" (Gumbs), 69–71

Ujamaa, 56
Ukraine, refugees from, 94
Ulster County, New York, rural cooperative in, 51–52
undoing, true collaboration as act of, 239–41
United States, 2, 4, 8, 247
    Black Owenites and, 39–40, 47, 49, 56
    classroom as community of learning, 215–18, 221–22
    legal cases defining race in, 224–29
    narratives of migration and, 201–11
    Peoples Temple and, 144, 147
    political thought in, 123, 126
    racial utopia and, 16, 18, 25, 27–28
    Sagaris in, 68, 74, 95
    Torn Space Theater in, 99, 102, 105
Universitas, 235
University of Buffalo, SUNY. See catalogue, Impossible Project
university, radical feminist structure, 72–73
untethering, critical imagining as act of, 242–44
Up From Slavery, 44
urban cooperative, 51, 54
Urras. See *Dispossessed: An Ambiguous Utopia, The* (Le Guin)

utopia, 1–2
  American political thought, 121–41
  Black expectations for, 15–35
  blueprint utopia, 2, 4–5
  confronting by teaching dystopia, 215–30
  and cooperatives, 3
  cooperators (Black), 37–65
  deploying concept of, 2
  and desire to prevent violence, 2–3
  grounded utopias, 5
  Impossible Project and, 231–50
  kabbalistic sex magic, 175–98
  migration and, 201–13
  migration as pursuit of, 89–96
  Peoples Temple, 143–74
  public ritual and, 99–117
  Sagaris, 67–86
Utopia (More), 122
utopia-as-dynamic, subverting, 131–33
utopian socialism, 2–3, 39, 56, 124

velvet revolution, 2
Victor, John, 164, 166
Views of Society and Manners in America, 40
Vilchez, Jordan, 159
Vital Center, The (Schlesinger), 4

Wade, Benjamin, 23
Walker, Barbara, 166
walking, ritual form, 179–83
Wanderground, The (Gearhaert), 131
Washington, Alethea, 49
Washington, Booker T., 39, 45, 48, 50
Watkins, Jim, 106, 108
Webb, Marilyn, 71, 78
welfare, upholding, 155–58
Wilde, Samuel Sumner, 21
Wilder, Craig Steven, 235
Woman on the Edge of Time (Piercy), 131, 133–34
Women's Action Alliance, 74
Wonderful Eventful Life of Rev. Thomas James, by Himself, 30
World Social Forum, 2
world wars, 4, 49, 54
Wotherspoon, Peter, 153–54
Wright, Frances "Fanny," 4, 39–42
Wright, Richard, 123
Wynter, Sylvia, 233, 243

Yesod. See *Zohar* (Leon)
Yohai, Shiman bar. See *Zohar* (Leon)
Young Negroes' Cooperative League (YNCL), 48

Zamalin, Alex, 7
Zohar (Leon)
  modeling divine creation on human reproduction, 183–84
  narrative of, 177–78
  theorizing sex magic in, 178–79
  walking rituals in, 179–83
Zohar Midrash ha Ne'elam (Hidden Interpretation), 178, 183–84, 191

www.ingramcontent.com/pod-product-compliance
Lightning Source LLC
Chambersburg PA
CBHW030530230426
43665CB00010B/837